Wiring the Workgroup:
With Lotus Notes 4.0

Richard H. Baker

McGraw-Hill

New York   San Francisco   Washington, D.C.   Auckland   Bogotá
Caracas   Lisbon   London   Madrid   Mexico City   Milan
Montreal   New Delhi   San Juan   Singapore
Sydney   Tokyo   Toronto

Library of Congress Cataloging-in-Publication Data

Baker, Richard H.
 Wiring the workgroup : with Lotus notes 4.0 / Richard H.
Baker.
  p.   cm. — (McGraw-Hill series on computer communications)
 Includes index.
 ISBN 0-07-005725-7 (pbk.)
 1. Work groups—Data processing. 2. Groupware. 3. Lotus Notes.
I. Title. II. Series.
HD66.2.B35   1996
658.4'036'02855369—dc20   96-3084
                                                            CIP

McGraw-Hill

A Division of The McGraw·Hill Companies

1 2 3 4 5 6 7 8 9 0   DOC/DOC   9 0 1 0 9 8 7 6

ISBN 0-07-005725-7

The sponsoring editor for this book was Steve Elliot, the editing supervisor was Bernard Onken, and the production supervisor was Pamela Pelton. It was set in Century Schoolbook by Ron Painter of McGraw-Hill's Professional Book Group composition unit.

Printed and bound by R. R. Donnelley & Sons Co.

McGraw-Hill books are available at special quantity discounts to use as premiums and sales promotions, or for use in corporate training programs. For more information, please write to the Director of Special Sales, McGraw-Hill, 11 West 19th Street, New York, NY 10011. Or contact your local bookstore.

This book is printed on recycled, acid-free paper containing a minimum of 50% recycled de-inked fiber.

Wiring the Workgroup:
With Lotus Notes 4.0

McGraw-Hill Series on Computer Communications (Selected Titles)

Contents

Preface

The first automobiles were simple devices, even more primitive than some of the horse-drawn vehicles they were intended to replace. The idea was simply to get from place to place. Few people, if any, envisioned the dramatic social and economic revolution the inventors' early contraptions would create.

Electronic mail has had the same kind of history, but it's happened a whole lot quicker. The original idea was to use computer technology to send messages from one place to another. But people picked up this technology and ran with it. In fact, they ran like Forrest Gump. They found new ways to tie people together and to share information between them. If knowledge is power, access to information is access to power. E-mail has evolved into *workgroup technology*. As it does so, it is helping to build a nation of empowered employees. No longer just ordinary employees or—worse—"end users," they are now workgroup members, able to bring all their ideas and energy to the greater service of their organizations.

This process of natural evolution has brought us to Lotus Notes. Notes is both the prototype and the leading example of the class of software called *groupware*. It combines some familiar themes like e-mail and database management into a product that lets groups share their information and ideas. Workgroup members have new power to do their jobs because they have new kinds of access to information. In fact, this thought is so scary that some tradition-minded managers have actually said they are frightened of what Notes might do to their highly structured organizations. To others, Notes is the ideal vehicle to take us into an ideal world.

Time out for a reality check. The computer will never affect so many of us in so many ways as the automobile, though it may come close. By the same token, the workgroup component of computer technology, by itself, will not revolutionize the way we do business.

Notes does not exist in a vacuum, either. It is not alone in creating flatter, more flexible, organizational forms. These are happening in any event. For many years now, movements like quality circles and self-directed workgroups have been reshaping the way we work together. Some of these movements have been fads; some have shown substance. All have been a part of a gradual process of changing the traditional top-down business organization to flexible workgroups of empowered employees. Information is the source of that power, and workgroup technology is a major source of information. As such, it is a major part of the larger process.

This is yet another problem. Despite a lot of talk about empowering employees, many employees do not want to be empowered. They don't want to help direct their own work teams. They prefer the reassurance of specific tasks, assigned by someone else. Those who resist empowerment will also naturally resist empowering technology. Other employees, knowing full well that information is power, will resist sharing their information. Then, there are the ever-present forces of resistance to change. Dealing with these combined forces will almost certainly be a greater challenge than dealing with even the complex technology of communication.

Nevertheless, Notes is a big part of a big change in the way we do business. Those who capitalize on it can build lean, well-informed workgroups that can respond better and faster to nearly any challenge. Those who don't will be left behind. There is no third option.

This book is written for managers, technical or otherwise, who want to capitalize on workgroup technology. Like a Mississippi River pilot, a typical reader must complete a long voyage through waters that are both muddy and strewn with snags.

The trip is rewarding, though, and this book will give you detailed navigational advice. It will help you identify not only the dangers but also the opportunities. It places a special emphasis on the all-important human concerns as well. With the right combination of people and technology, you can help your workgroup members gain the power to help themselves help the entire organization.

Richard H. Baker

Acknowledgments

Some of the artwork in this book is from Lotus SmartPics for Windows. ©1991 Lotus Development Corporation.

Getting to Know Notes 4

There was a joke making the rounds of the Internet for a while:

Question: "Why would IBM pay $3.3 billion for Lotus?"

Answer: "Can you say replication 3.3 billion times?"

It's no secret that when IBM made its expensive acquisition, Notes was the product it was after. Never duplicated—but often replicated—Notes is a pioneering product that combines:

- E-mail
- A document-oriented database system
- Group discussion facilities
- The ability to replicate databases, sending copies to local workstations, remote work sites, and wherever else they might be needed

Designed to help people think

- Notes combines:
  - Electronic mail
  - A database
  - Group discussion
  - Replication

The basis of Notes's popularity is not any or all of these features but the way they can work together to help people work together. Start with a database that is more concerned with managing text than with pigeonholing data into rows and columns. Set it up so folks can contribute their ideas and comments. Make it easy by letting them use e-mail to share their ideas and responses. Then, to strengthen an already potent mixture, add the power of replication. This lets people take their work home, so to speak, instead of having to rely on connecting with a central resource.

As yet, no product—even those known to be on drawing boards—approaches Notes's ability to help people think. The nearest competitor, Microsoft Exchange, is primarily an e-mail product. Novell's Groupwise is in a similar situation. This does not mean they are not strong competitors. Exchange is projected as a top seller in part because it has the M word at the front of its name and in part because not everyone needs the full power of Notes. Notably too, when Novell decided to rid itself of its Word Perfect division, it served notice that it would hang onto Groupwise.

Notes and its competing products have been described as a way to "get information out of your brain and make it accessible to everyone else." Everyone's mind holds information. A groupware product gives people the means to share their thinking.

The Notes Workspace

Notes has two main components—e-mail and database management—and uncounted numbers of possible add-ons and variations. The secret of effectively using Notes, though, is to make all these pieces work together.

The Notes equivalent to Mission Control is the Workspace (Fig. 1.1). The Workspace is divided into several pages, each with its own tab like a file folder. Each workspace page can contain related icons; each icon represents a Notes database.

The workspace display includes:

- A bar of SmartIcons

- The tabbed pages that contain the database icons

- The Replicator, a special tabbed page that allows users to manage the replication process

- A status bar at the bottom of the screen

The SmartIcons display

SmartIcons are buttons that perform prescribed actions when you click on them. For example, one SmartIcon italicizes selected text. For many tasks, it's faster to click SmartIcons than to pull down menus or recall and type keyboard shortcuts.

Notes includes:

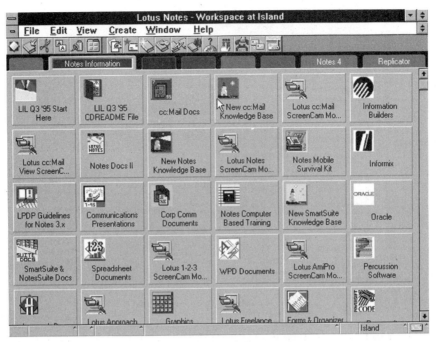

Figure 1.1 Database icons are arranged on workspace pages.

- More than 150 predefined SmartIcons, including icons for most Notes menu commands
- More than a dozen custom SmartIcons to which you can assign your own macros
- Several predefined SmartIcons sets, useful for specific tasks such as editing a document

You can also create and save your own sets of SmartIcons.

SmartIcons work with all the databases in your workspace. Notes displays SmartIcons in a bar that can appear across the top of the workspace under the menus, or in other positions you can select. SmartIcons are displayed in groups, or sets.

You can set Notes to change which icons are displayed depending on what you're doing at the time. For example, when you're editing a document, Notes can automatically display SmartIcons that you can use for editing (Fig. 1.2).

You can find out what any icon does by moving the cursor over the icon and waiting a moment. Notes displays an explanation of the icon. (Note: to use this feature, you must first turn it on.)

Tabbed pages

You can organize sets of related database icons on different tabbed pages, and give each tab a descriptive name. The last tab belongs to the Replicator,

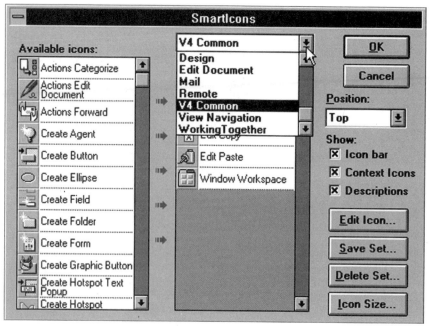

Figure 1.2 This screen manages the SmartIcon display.

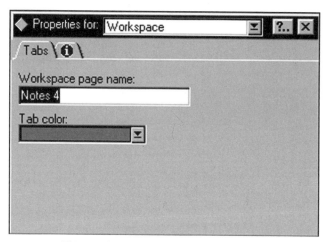

Figure 1.3 This window manages the names and other characteristics of database pages.

which allows you to manage replication while working away from the office. You cannot rename the Replicator tab.

Nevertheless, you can:

- Enter a name for or change the name of any tab (Fig. 1.3).
- Add and remove tabbed pages

■ Switch between tabbed pages

Suppose you work with three types of databases: your mail databases, databases related to sales issues, and databases related to human resources issues. You could enter the names Mail, Sales, and HR on different workspace tabs and move databases of each type to the appropriate workspace pages.

You can have as many as 32 workspace pages, not counting the Replicator page. If you add a page to the workspace, though, you alter the file that manages the desktop. You can no longer use that file with previous versions of Notes.

The status bar

The *status bar* is the area along the bottom of your Notes workspace. If you are using Windows 95, with its task bar at the bottom of the screen, the status bar appears above the task bar.

Using the status bar, you can:

■ See whether Notes is using the network (look for a lightning bolt)

■ Change the typeface, size, or paragraph style of selected text

■ Examine a list of recent messages displayed by Notes

■ Check your level of access to the open database

■ Display your current location and switch between locations such as your office and your home

■ Use a pop-up menu to perform common mail tasks such as creating a message or scanning for unread mail

Reading the menus

The Notes menu bar has seven main items. Six are there all the time; the seventh is a context-oriented menu that changes with the work in progress. Table 1.1 lists the standard menus and their functions.

The context menus include:

■ Text

■ Table

■ Attachment

■ Section

■ Link

■ Picture

Using Notes Databases

A Notes database generally contains information about a single area of interest, such as a new product discussion, a set of industry news items, or all the

TABLE 1.1.   Notes Menus Provide These Functions

Use this menu...	To...
File	Perform tasks on an entire document or database at a time, such as saving or closing a document or creating, copying, or deleting a database. Also use the File menu to handle database replication, manage mobile use of Notes; import, export, or attach non-database files; print from databases, manage your user preferences, SmartIcons, and user ID; administer Notes servers (if you have administration access); debug LotusScript; and exit Notes.
Edit	Change selected elements of a document or a database by cutting, copying, clearing, or pasting. Also use the Edit menu to find and replace text, check spelling, and manage the marks that identify unread items in the current database.
View	Display elements in: ■ The workspace, including information on icons such as server names and unread document counts. You can also switch to view agents, the database design, or specific views. ■ The current view including a search bar, horizontal scroll bar, display of only certain documents, collapsing or expanding levels, and a preview pane. You can also switch among agents, folders, or views or the current document (ruler, page breaks, hidden characters, horizontal scroll bar, field help, preview pane, collapse-expand for sections, and form switching).
Create	Add elements to the current database, such as views, forms, folders, or agents; or add elements to the current document, such as tables, pictures, or hotspots.
Actions	Perform tasks on selected elements. For example, when a document is open, use this menu to categorize the document or move it to a folder.
Window	Perform tasks on selected elements. For example, when a document is open, use this menu to categorize the document or move it to a folder.
Help	Get guidance on your current task, open the Help database for more detailed information, find Release 3 menu equivalents, or see the About and Using documents for the current Notes database.

processes, forms, and policies used by a department such as customer service. Most databases are shared, though individuals can set up their own databases for personal use.

Database sharing is one of the keys to Notes's ability. Workgroup members who have access to shared databases can:

■ Contribute comments and ideas to a discussion database

■ Participate in a workflow process in which documents are routed by e-mail to those who must act on them. They arrive just in time for the necessary action.

On the computer, a Notes database is a single file containing multiple documents.

More than a typical record

In traditional database terms, each document is something like a record, but a Notes document is more sophisticated. It can present such enhanced contents as formatted text, pictures, objects, and many other types of information. A document can range from a short comment on a coworker's suggestion to a sophisticated market study with graphs and statistical analysis.

To work with a database, you add its icon to the workspace. You can use a database only if you have the proper access.

Most Notes databases are stored on servers, where they are available to all members of the group. You also can create a local database, stored on your own system.

Using database libraries

New to Notes 4, a *library* is a database containing lists of other databases. You can use a library to identify databases and help find the one right source among what eventually will probably be many possibilities.

The main view in a library lists databases alphabetically by title and gives a brief description of each database (Fig. 1.4). Each library document gives the title, an abstract, and the replica ID number of a database. It also contains buttons you can use to add and open a database. You also can get a preview by opening the database without adding it to your workspace.

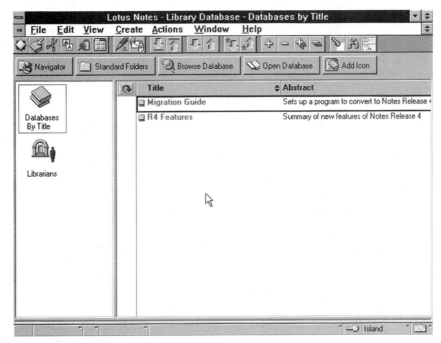

Figure 1.4 A library provides quick access to related databases.

Unlike a database catalog, which lists all the databases on a server, a library lists whatever databases the librarian publishes in it, on one server, or on several servers. There can also be more than one library on a server. For example, your organization may store databases related to several departments all on one large server, and people from each department may find the databases related to its work in libraries such as Marketing Library or R&D Library.

You can be your own librarian, creating a local library for your own use, listing databases on your own hard drive as well as databases on servers. The only difference between a local library and libraries on servers is that no other users can use your local library or become librarians for it. A local library is also a useful backup resource for rebuilding your workspace if your desktop file is damaged.

Views, Panes, and Folders

Users of Notes Version 3 and earlier will find only a little that's familiar in the interface of Version 4. The new Notes interface uses objects like views, panes, and folders. By no coincidence, these elements are more familiar to those who work with cc:Mail.

Database designers managers have a lot to say about how you can use these elements. Much depends on what specifications they put into the design, and what level of access you have been assigned. Even so, these features give you a lot more flexibility than they take away.

Viewing a view

One of the less endearing concepts in computer instruction is the idea that when you complete an operation you are supposed to "view" something. Don't analyze it or try to understand it, and certainly do not attempt to do anything useful. Just sit there and look at it for a while.

Database views, including views of Notes databases, are something else entirely. They represent different ways to organize and present data. One view might present a group of documents organized by their subjects (Fig. 1.5). You can create views like this by assigning documents to categories. A different view of the same contents might be organized by author (Fig. 1.6). In this case, the author's name is probably a field within the document.

Views can also show many types of information about the documents listed in them, such as author's name or date of creation. A view need not show all the documents in a database; it can display only a selected assortment.

From a view, you can:

- Select and open documents

- Copy and paste documents

- Delete documents

- Print documents or the view itself

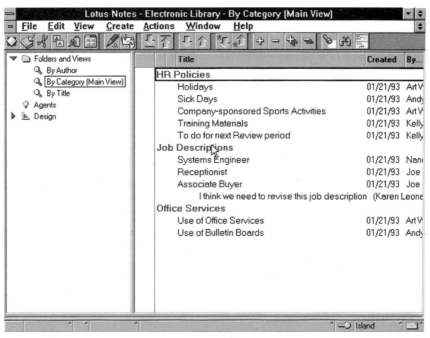

Figure 1.5 A document view organized by subject.

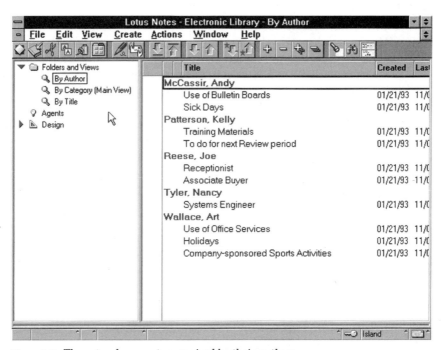

Figure 1.6 The same documents organized by their authors.

- Forward selected documents to other Notes users
- Refresh the view to see new documents
- Search for documents that contain specific text

The view pane is about as close as Notes comes to a conventional tabular database. It contains:

- One row for each category or document title
- One column for each type of information, such as author's name, displayed for that document

A database might include an *action bar,* a row of buttons you can click as shortcuts to perform common tasks in the database. If there's an action bar, it appears above the column headers.

The left edge of the view pane may contain view icons identifying the status of each document. These icons include:

- Check marks identify documents that have been selected
- Stars identify documents you have not yet read or have marked as unread because you want to review them later
- Trash cans identify documents that have been marked for deletion
- Diamonds identify replication conflicts that should be resolved

Assigning categories

Views often assign documents into categories. You can use and assign these categories to identify the documents that deal with a particular subject, have been issued since a particular date, or come from a particular source.

Categories help you organize data in views that contain large numbers of documents and move around in these views more quickly. Categories often are sorted alphabetically.

Not all views use categories, but most do. In these, you can categorize your own documents in any way that makes sense to you. You can also:

- Create new categories and put documents into them
- Create subcategories and put documents into them
- Put documents into existing categories
- Remove documents from a category
- Rename a category
- Delete a category

Window panes

When there are windows, there can also be window panes. Notes 4 has lifted that logic from cc:Mail, and it now displays information in three panes:

- A navigation pane
- A view pane
- A preview pane

One pane is always selected, usually when something within the pane is selected. You can identify the current selection by a thick black highlight. Notes menus use the selected pane as their context for displaying relevant selections. If you can't find the task you want to perform in the available menus, click on the pane where you want to work, and look at the menus again.

The navigation pane (Fig. 1.7) displays the names of all views, folders, and agents in the database. If the database design allows it, the navigation pane may also show design elements of the database.

A view pane (Fig. 1.8) contains a list of documents. Often, the first column will display an icon to help you identify the type of document. There also is a *gutter* to the left of the document listing. You can click there to select a document. If you decide to delete a document, it remains in the view until you

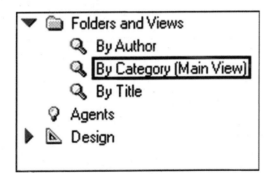

Figure 1.7 A navigation pane.

	Title	Created	By...
	HR Policies		
	Holidays	01/21/93	Art Wallace
	Sick Days	01/21/93	Andy McCassir
	Company-sponsored Sports Activities	01/21/93	Art Wallace
	Training Materials	01/21/93	Kelly Patterson
	To do for next Review period	01/21/93	Kelly Patterson
	Job Descriptions		
	Systems Engineer	01/21/93	Nancy Tyler
	Receptionist	01/21/93	Joe Reese
	Associate Buyer	01/21/93	Joe Reese
	Office Services		
	Use of Office Services	01/21/93	Art Wallace
	Use of Bulletin Boards	01/21/93	Andy McCassir

Figure 1.8 A view pane.

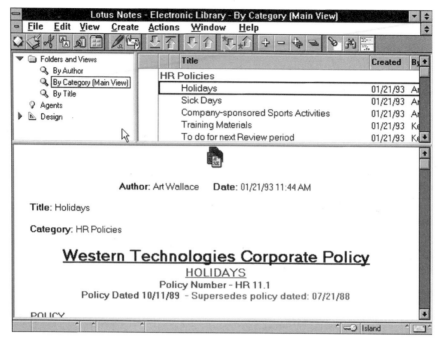

Figure 1.9 A preview pane.

close the database; an icon in the gutter indicates it has been marked for deletion—and that you still have time to change your mind.

The preview pane shows you a quick preview of a selected document. Select **View,** then **Pane** to display the document as in Fig. 1.9.

Filing in folders

Folders are a new feature of Version 4, also adapted from cc:Mail. They are alternatives to making category assignments. Assigning to a category requires that you place a category field within a document. When you establish a folder, you can assign documents to it, using drag and drop techniques as you wish. In Fig. 1.10, several documents from a database of corporate policies have been copied into a folder of documents to be presented when orienting a new employee.

You can keep a folder private, or you can share it with other users of a database. No one else can read or delete your private folders.

When you create a private folder, Notes stores it in one of two places:

- If the manager of the database has allowed it, your folder is stored in the database, letting you use the folder at different workstations.

    Note: To see whether a database allows folder storage, select the data-

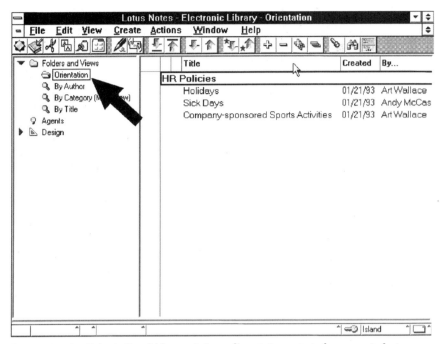

Figure 1.10 An Orientation folder contains policy statements to be presented at a new employee orientation.

base, choose **File - Database - Access,** and see whether *Create personal folders/views* is turned on.

- If the manager has not allowed storage of folders in the database, Notes stores the folder in your desktop file. Among other things, that means you can't use full text search in the folder.

You can put documents into folders by dragging the documents, or by using the menu. You may want to use the menu if it's not convenient to drag, or if you want to manage a large number of documents at once.

Creating views and folders

There are several ways to create views and folders, and only one involves starting from scratch. This is one place where piracy is a virtue. You can copy designs, or parts of designs, from other databases, including the samples that came with Notes. Even if you do not use one of these models, you will start with a default design, and you can create your own default design.

If a view or folder already exists in the database that is similar to the one you need, you may be able to use it with only minor modifications. If a similar view or folder already exists in another database including templates and example database, the procedure takes a few more steps but has the same result.

Delivering Documents

A Notes document is a special kind of database record. Like a more conventional database, a Notes document is made up of fields. A field can contain information like the document's subject, its author, when it was created and revised, and to which categories it is assigned. There is usually one field that simply contains a large block of text. Each document is based on a *form* which defines and arranges the fields.

You can read a document, or you can display it in an edit mode that lets you change its contents. You also use edit mode when you create a new document.

The types of information you can enter depend on the types of fields in the form. For example, you can enter text in text fields and numbers in number fields. Notes also has a field type called rich text. It lets you include formatted text, graphics, and Notes features such as links and file attachments. Keyword fields let you assign documents to categories. When you enter a keyword field in edit mode, you can press Enter and select a keyword from the list Notes displays. You also can add new keywords to this list (Fig. 1.11).

A Notes document can contain many other features, too, including those in Fig. 1.12.

When you create or edit a document, you can:

- Create a bulleted or numbered list automatically by adding bullets or numbers to paragraphs.

- Create a table.

Figure 1.11 You can create and assign categories by writing and selecting keywords.

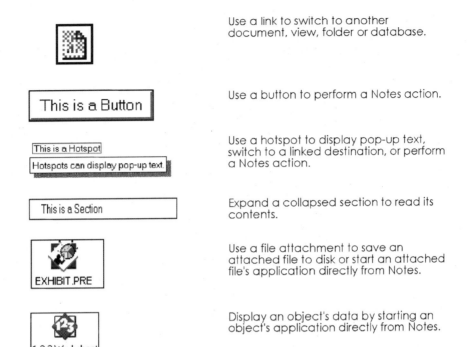

Figure 1.12   These features can appear in a Notes document.

- Create a collapsed section that readers can expand when they want to read its contents. You can collapse one or more paragraphs into a single line.
- Create a link that lets readers switch to another document, view, folder, or database.
- Create a button that lets readers perform a Notes action such as sending a mail message or opening a database.
- Create a hot spot that lets readers display pop-up text, switch to a linked destination, or perform a Notes action.
- Create special characters, such as international currency symbols.
- Add a picture.

Collapsing categories and sections

The categories in a Notes view are much like the topic headings in an outline with subcategories and individual document titles appearing as subtopics. You can expand or collapse the view to display only the main categories, or expand it to display all or part of the subcategories and documents. Depending on the database design, both the navigation and view panes have this ability. Figures 1.13 and 1.14 show the difference.

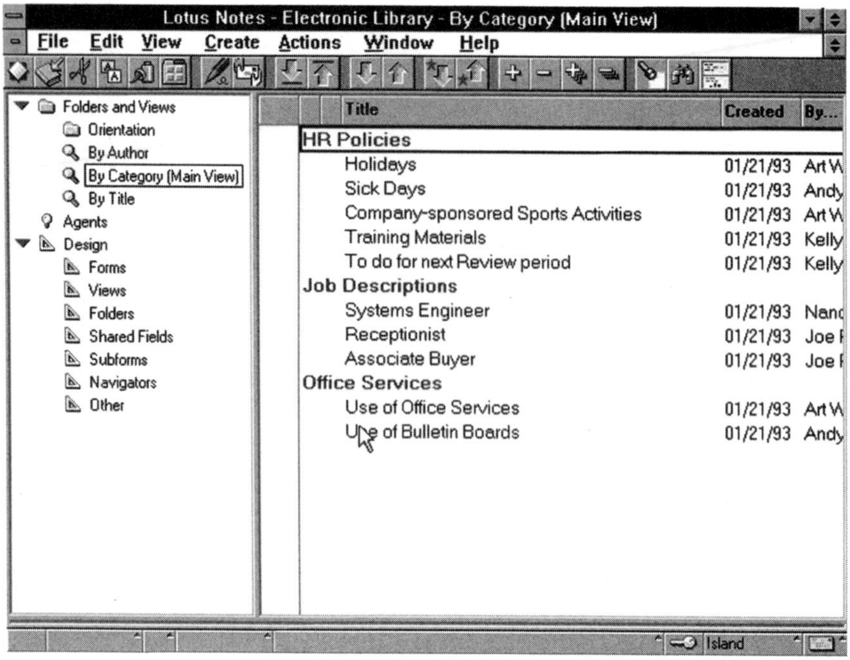

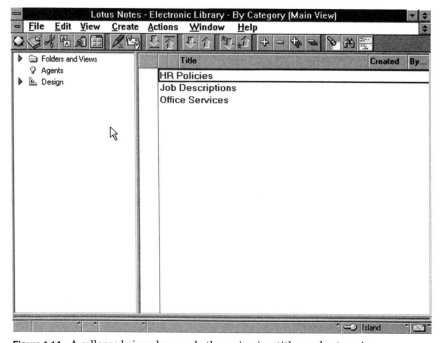

Figure 1.13 An expanded display shows all views, categories, and documents.

Figure 1.14 A collapsed view shows only the main view titles and categories.

Notes 4 takes this feature even further, giving you the power to collapse sections of a document itself. This is a useful way to help readers find the information they need in a long document.

Checking spelling

Creating a document is largely a word processing function. To help this process, Notes provides a spelling checker comparable to those available in dedicated word processors. Like all spelling checkers, Notes compares the words it finds in the document with those contained in one of two dictionaries: a main dictionary of common words and a personal dictionary to which you can add things like proper names and professional terms. It flags any word that does not match a dictionary entry—a suggestion, though not always a conclusive one, that the word is misspelled.

In addition to misspelling, the spelling checker looks for repeated words. It does not flag numbers or single-character words like *a* or *I*. It also gives up— as should you—on any word more than 64 characters long.

Styling paragraphs

Another feature borrowed from word processors—in fact, it originated in desktop publishing—is the use of named paragraph styles. These let you save combinations of paragraph attributes like type faces and margins. You can use paragraph styles to create a uniform type specification for subheads. Or, if you often use indented paragraphs for extended quotes from other publications, you can create a style that establishes a standard indentation.

One style that is always available is called None. You can use this style to create a new style without altering any of your existing styles. Give None the properties you want to assign to the new style, then save it under a new name.

Searching for Information

Notes offers two ways to search for information within a database:

- A standard search is the simplest but least flexible
- A search using a full text index gives you added abilities

Standard searching

The standard search function is available in all Notes databases. You can:

- Search for text in the current document, and replace the text you find with a different text string.
- Search for document titles within a view. This type of search will find all documents whose titles contain a specified word or phrase.

■ Find all documents that contain a particular word or phrase anywhere in the document.

Indexing the text

You have the option of creating a full text index for a database. This takes time and uses some disk space, but it grants you the ability to:

■ Save your search criteria for later reuse

■ Make your search case-sensitive

■ Include synonyms and varied forms of the search words

■ Search for pairs of words or phrases that are close to each other within the document

■ Sort the results of the search

■ Extend the search over multiple documents

Building a search

A full text index also gives you the ability to use the Search Builder. This is a tool that helps you create formulas that specify the criteria for your search. The Search Builder (Fig. 1.15) gives you a fill-in-the-blanks method of constructing a search to find documents that meet one or more conditions. These conditions can include specific words or phrases, author names, dates, and the contents of specific fields.

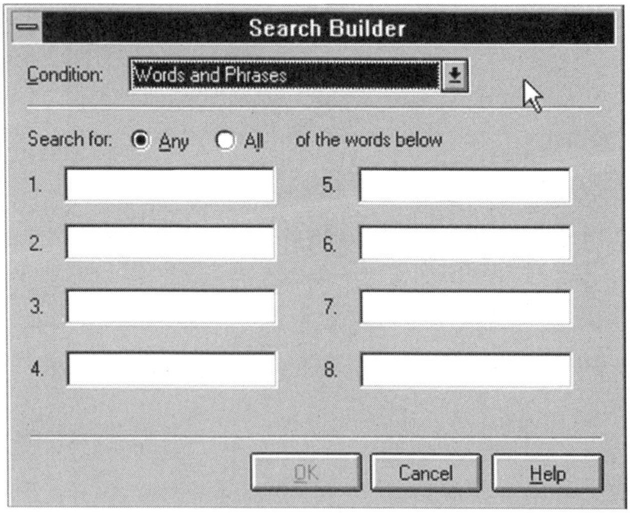

Figure 1.15 The Search Builder helps construct a sophisticated search.

Using the Mail

Notes combines e-mail with database management, but the two major components don't exist separately. They are interlocked in a way that makes the program's group dynamics possible. One indication of how they are mixed: the Notes mail component is really a specialized kind of database. Your messages, both coming and going, are documents within that database.

In its most basic form, Notes mail lets you communicate electronically with other Notes users. It also lets you exchange messages with users of other e-mail products. You can connect either by network or by telephone from field locations.

In fact you don't even have to use Notes as your e-mail package. If you have cc:Mail or any other product that uses the Lotus Vendor Independent Messaging (VIM) standard, you can use it as an e-mail front end to Notes. Since Notes 4 has adopted its interface from cc:Mail, however, there now are fewer reasons to do so.

A notes mail message is just another Notes document, and you can treat it accordingly. You can change fonts and colors, attach files and images, and include tables and graphics. You can also add buttons, hot spots, and doc links. Like every other Notes user, you have a mail database in which to store your messages.

Using mail folders and views

Notes mail comes with several installed mail folders and views. Users of cc:Mail will find them familiar:

- The *Inbox folder* automatically stores all messages you receive. The messages remain in the Inbox until you delete them or move them to a different folder.

- The *Drafts folder* stores all messages that you save without sending. This folder gives you a place to store an unfinished message you can go to later. Then you can complete the message, make any changes you want, and then send it. After you send the message, it no longer appears in the Drafts folder. If you save the message when you send it, Notes places it in the Sent folder, unless you select a different folder for the message.

- The *Sent folder* automatically stores all messages that you save when you send them, unless you select different folders.

- The *All Documents view* shows all the messages that are currently in your mail database, regardless of their status.

- The *Trash folder* lets you store messages you want to delete. After placing messages in this folder, you can later finish the deletion, process them, or recover them.

- The *All by Date view* shows all the messages in your mail database sorted by date.

- The *All by Person view* shows all the messages in your mail database categorized by person.

- The *To Do view* lets you assign and track tasks for yourself and others.

- The *Discussion Thread view* groups messages that are part of the same conversation. It shows the original message grouped with any replies.

You can create as many additional folders and views as you want, treating them the same way you do in any Notes database.

Taking Notes on the Road

Remote use is becoming an increasingly important e-mail feature. Mobile Notes lets you connect with your Notes server over a telephone line, as an alternative to a local area network (LAN) connection. You can use mobile Notes in situations like these:

- On a laptop when you work at home or on the road. You can call a Notes server and gain access to your mail and other databases. When you return to the office, you can switch back to your network connection.

- On a mobile workstation when there is no network-based Notes installation. If you work at a small branch office, for example, you can use a modem to call a server in the home office.

Using Notes interactively

There are two ways to use remote notes:

- *Interactively,* calling a server and maintaining the connection while you work.

- *Locally,* by creating database replicas on your own system, contacting the server only to replicate and update the information and to exchange accumulated messages.

Interactive use saves disk space, an important advantage to laptop users. The database remains on the server; you don't need to create a copy on your own system. Since you are working directly with the main database, you can be sure the information is up to date. In addition, when you send or receive a mail message, you do so immediately. Should you make a mistake in the address or routing, you will be informed right away.

Working with replicas

On the other hand, working locally has much to recommend it. The power of Notes to replicate its databases, and to update information from the replicas, is a powerful ally here.

The big saving in local mode is in connect charges. When you are working with a local replica, you can place one call to replicate the database, and another when you are through to send the updated information. In addition:

- Performance is usually quicker, since you are working with your own hard disk.

- You can prepare all your outgoing mail, then send it all at once in a batch process. This is sometimes more convenient than sending messages individually.

- Should the server go down, you can still get your work done.

Using mobile mail

When you use mobile Notes in local mode, you work with database replicas. That applies to all your databases, including the one that handles your mail. When you are finished using the replica, you can use the Replicator to send and receive your mail by exchanging documents between the replica and the mail database on the server.

If you are working in remote mode, Notes creates a replica stub of your mail database. This is a replica of the database structure, but with no documents. To use the replica stub, you replicate the documents in your mail database to it.

Notes also creates a local copy of a mailbox database. Like its street corner equivalent, this is a temporary storage place for mail waiting to go to the post office. When you dispatch mail from a local replica of your mail database, Notes temporarily stores the outgoing mail here. When you make a replication connection with your mail database on the server, notes sends the mail and leaves the mailbox database empty.

If you use a local replica of your mail database, Notes automatically displays a symbol for the replica on the Replicator workspace, along with a *Send outgoing mail* icon for the mailbox (Fig. 1.16). When you are using mobile Notes, you can use these Replicator symbols to send and receive your mail.

Addressing mail

When you address mail that you create in a local replica of your mail database, Notes looks for the recipient (the name you entered in the To: field) in your Personal Address Book. If the recipient is not there, Notes assumes the server will look for the recipient in its Public Address Book when the document is sent during replication. If the server cannot find the name, it sends a nondelivery report to your mail file on the server to let you know the mail was not received.

You may not see this report until the next time you replicate your mail file, so make sure that recipients you enter are listed in your Personal Address Book or the server's Public Address Book.

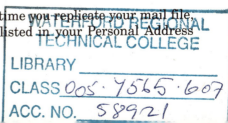

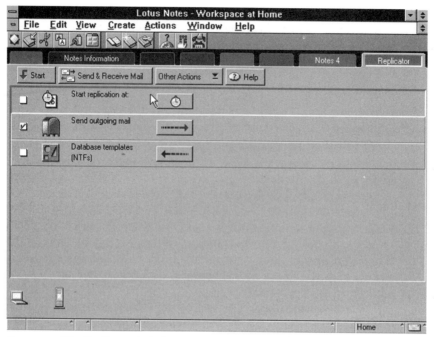

Figure 1.16   The Replicator includes an icon for sending mobile mail.

Making server connections

A *server connection* is a document in your Personal Address Book that contains information, such as a server's phone number, that Notes uses to connect to a server. There are four types of server connection documents.

- A dial-up server connection tells Notes the phone number you want to use to connect to a server over a modem. Notes saves the phone number so you can use it whenever you call the server.

- A network server connection tells Notes the network port you want to use to connect to a server on a local area network. This is useful if you need to use a port with a specific protocol driver to connect to a server.

- A pass-through server connection tells Notes the pass-through server you want to use to connect to another server. If you have access to a pass-through server, you can set up a server connection for each server to which the pass-through server leads.

- A remote LAN server connection tells Notes the remote LAN server you want to use to connect to another server. If you're using a remote LAN service, such as Microsoft Remote Access Service (RAS), you can set up a remote LAN connection for each server you want to use on the remote LAN.

Listing locations

A location is a document in your Personal Address Book that contains communication settings you use when you work with Notes in a particular place. For example, you might use a network port at the office to connect to Notes servers on a LAN and use a remote port at home to connect to Notes servers over a modem.

In each location document, you specify settings such as the network or remote port you want to use, whether your mail file is local or on a server, phone information such as dialing prefixes, and replication schedules.

When you install Notes, the program automatically creates four location documents in your Personal Address Book:

- Island (Disconnected)
- Home (Modem)
- Office (Network)
- Travel (Modem)

You can edit these documents and customize them, or you can create your own new location documents. When you use Notes in a different location, you choose the location document that contains the settings that apply to the place you're working. You can set up locations in several ways:

- A typical arrangement is to set up the Office location to use a network port and your mail file on the server when you're at the office, and set up the Travel location to use a remote port and a local replica of your mail file when you're on the road.
- If your home and office are in different area codes, you can set up the Home location to use 1 and your office's area code as a dialing prefix. Then when you use Home and call a server, Notes automatically dials 1 and the area code before it dials the server's phone number.
- If you use a calling card only when you make long-distance calls from hotel rooms, you could create a location called Hotel and include your calling card number. Then when you use Hotel and call a server, Notes automatically uses your calling card number.

Figure 1.17 shows a typical location document.

The Replication Process

Replication is at the heart of nearly everything Notes does. Replication lets you keep multiple replicas of a single database, on multiple servers or workstations. This gives users on all kinds of networks in a variety of locations access to the same information.

Once the replicas are in place, the replication process exchanges modifica-

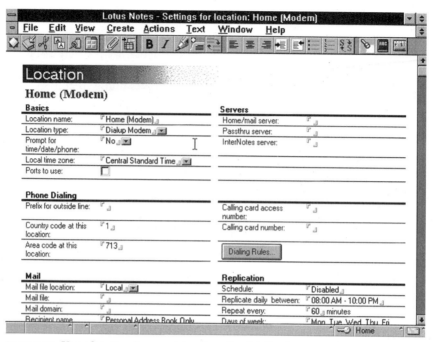

Figure 1.17 Use a location document to set up the details of a remote location.

tions between replicas. Through frequent replication, you can keep all of the replicas essentially identical over time. For example, employees in one office might make changes to a replica on their server. At the same time, people in another office make changes to a replica of the same database on their server. When the databases are replicated, each can receive updates from the other, and all contain up-to-date information. Of course, the more frequent the replication process, the better the two databases are coordinated.

You can replicate databases between two servers or between a workstation and a server. A key to mobile use is the ability to replicate between a laptop and a server. You can replicate databases in one or both directions. You can set up the replication process so two replicas receive updates from each other, or so only one replica receives updates from the other.

Notes lets you choose the databases you want to replicate and when to replicate them. You can call for automatic replication according to a schedule you set up, or you can do the job manually through server or workstation commands you specify. Replication between servers generally takes place automatically on a schedule specified by a database manager or network administrator. Replication between a workstation and a server generally occurs manually when an individual needs to process updates.

Creating local replicas

Notes lets you create copies of server databases on your workstation called local replicas. Local replicas are useful because you can work with them when you're not connected to a server over a network. With mobile Notes, you can call servers over a modem and exchange updates between local replicas and databases on servers.

To perform workstation to server replication, you must first create a local replica. Then you can work in it locally and replicate changes between it and the database on the server.

A replica can take any of several forms:

- A *full replica* contains all of a database's documents and design features (such as forms and agents).

- A *partial replica* contains only selected documents, shortened documents, or selected database features. This is useful if you need only part of a database and want to save space on your hard disk or reduce the time and expense of remote replication.

- A *replica stub* contains a database's design features but no documents. This is useful if you need to fit a replica on a diskette to copy to a remote workstation; you can replicate documents to it later.

After you create a local replica, you can make changes to it and send your changes to the original database on the server. You can also receive changes that have been made to the server database. Notes also lets you perform selective replication. For example, you can specify that your local replica receive only documents created after a certain date. Like creating partial replicas, this is useful if you need only part of a database and want to save disk space or reduce the time and expense of remote replication.

Foreground and background

You can conduct replications as foreground or background tasks. When you replicate in the foreground, you must wait until Notes finishes replicating to do other work. Upon finishing replication, Notes reports information in the Replication Statistics dialog box.

When you replicate in the background, you can do other work while Notes replicates. Notes displays messages about replication events in the Replicator status bar and upon finishing replication. When you replicate in the background, Notes also opens a background replication window that displays messages about replication events; the window closes automatically when you exit Notes. The messages displayed in this window are also stored in your local Notes Log database.

Using the Replicator

The Replicator is a special Notes workspace page; its tab appears at the far right side of the display. The Replicator is a command center that lets you manage replication of your local databases in one place.

With Replicator, you can replicate multiple databases with different servers with a single command. When you use Replicator, Notes replicates in the background so you can do other work while Notes replicates. When you use Notes away from the office, you can have Replicator call each server you want to replicate with automatically. If you're using a pass-through server to reach another server, or if you are using a remote LAN server, you can have Replicator make a single call and replicate all of your local databases at one time, even if they're on different servers.

Replicator also lets you customize replication depending on where you're working. You could set up a local database to receive full documents when you replicate at the office on a network and receive shortened documents when you replicate away from the office using a modem. Replicator also provides additional ways to replicate; for example, you can assign high priority to selected databases and replicate only those databases.

The Replicator page

The Replicator is always the last page on your workspace, and you cannot delete it. Figure 1.18 shows a page with these types of standard entries:

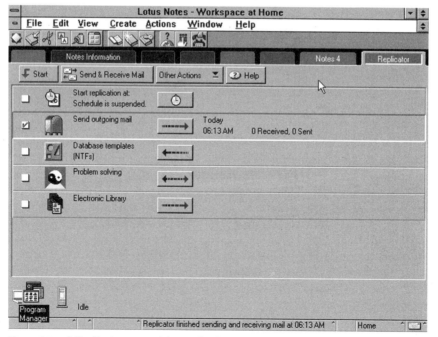

Figure 1.18 A Replicator page with standard entries.

- *Start replication at.* Use this entry to set up and activate a replication schedule.

- *Send outgoing mail.* Use this entry to send all pending messages from your mailbox database.

- *Database templates.* Use this entry to update the designs of databases based on templates.

- *Database.* There is an entry for each local replica you have.

None of the standard entries can be deleted. In addition, you can create some entries of your own for mobile locations:

- *Call.* Use a call entry to connect with a server.

- *Hangup.* Use this entry to end a server connection.

Action buttons

Most types of Replicator entries contain action buttons you can use to specify Replicator options. For example:

- You can use the clock button on a *Start replication* at entry to specify a replication schedule.

- You can use the arrow button on a database entry to specify the replication direction.

- You can use the phone button on a call entry to specify the server you want to call.

The status bar at the bottom of Replicator displays current replication information, such as call attempt information, the database currently being replicated, and the number of documents that have been replicated. After a replication is finished, Replicator displays replication statistics for individual entries such as the server used and the date and time of replication.

Accommodating multiple locations

A mobile employee can set up Replicator in a different way at each of several locations. That avoids the need to change Replicator settings with every move to a different location. For example:

- You could set up a database entry at your Office location so that it sends and receives documents when you're at the office. You could delete the same database entry at your Travel location so it never replicates when you're on the road.

- You could replicate all of your local databases on a schedule at your Office location and replicate only your mail on an as-needed basis at your Home location.

■ You could arrange database entries in one order at your Travel location and arrange them in a different order at your Home location so that Replicator replicates in a different order at each location.

Conflict resolution

A problem with any shared database is that of resolving conflicts between different users who need to change or retrieve the same information at the same time. This can be a particular problem with replicated databases, since simultaneous changes are being made to different copies. Sometimes these changes come into conflict.

In Notes replication, that conflict can take one of two forms:

■ You can experience a *replication conflict* when two or more people edit the same document in different replicas.

■ You can encounter a *save conflict* when two or more people edit the same document in a database on the same server at the same time.

Notes deals with replication conflicts by setting priorities. If employees try to replicate different copies of the same document, Notes designates the document that has been saved most recently as the primary document. It displays any other documents with a diamond symbol in the left margin. This indicates that there is a conflict involving these documents.

In the case of a save conflict, Notes designates the document that was saved first as the main document. Should someone else try to save the same document, Notes prompts the user to save it with the conflict noted. If the individual does so, Notes displays it as a response to the main document, with diamond symbol in the left margin.

Maintaining history

Notes maintains a replication history of any database that has successfully replicated at least once. Notes uses this history to determine the dates of documents to include in the database's next replication with a particular server. For example, if a database successfully replicated with a particular server 24 hours ago, Notes will only replicate documents added, modified, or deleted in the replica on that server during the last 24 hours.

Before replication starts, Notes checks the replication history stored with each database to make sure they agree. If they don't, Notes performs a full replication.

The first time a database replicates successfully with another server, an entry appears in the replication history. If the database replicates with additional servers, an entry for each server is added to the history. On subsequent replications with a server, no new entries appear in the list; instead, Notes updates the date and time to the most recent replication with that server. If a database doesn't replicate successfully, Notes doesn't update the replication history.

Scheduling replication

A replication schedule lets you replicate local databases automatically at fixed intervals. You specify replication schedules in location documents in your Personal Address Book. This way, you can specify different replication schedules for different work locations. For example, you could specify a replication schedule for your Office location only, or specify different replication schedules for your Office and Home locations.

Notes administrators can also specify replication schedules for server to server replication. For more information, see Notes Administration Help.

When you start Notes, the program checks to see if scheduled replication has been set for the current location. If it is, Notes performs replication in the background based on the location's schedule. For example, suppose you have scheduled replication for 8 a.m.–6 p.m. Monday through Friday with a 360-minute repeat interval. If you start Notes at 9 a.m. on Tuesday, Notes immediately attempts to replicate, and then attempts to replicate again 360 minutes later. If a scheduled replication attempt fails, Notes tries to replicate again each minute until the attempt is successful.

Because of the time and expense of replication, you should schedule replication for local databases only if they contain time-sensitive information. If they do, it may be useful to:

- Schedule replication shortly before you normally start using Notes and shortly before you normally finish using Notes at a particular location. This way, you can get the most up-to-date information from servers at the beginning of the day and provide information you've updated to servers at the end of the day.

- If you replicate over a phone line, schedule replication during the middle of the night when telephone calls are cheapest and servers are not as busy.

Replicating selected items

It isn't always necessary to replicate an entire database. Sometimes, you can replicate only selected parts of it, saving time, cost, and disk space. Selective replication also lets you display only the database fields and records in which you're interested.

For example, you could create a local replica of your mail database on a laptop, replicating only documents less than 3 months old. This way, the replica takes less time to create and uses less disk space on the laptop.

Another use of selective replication would be the case of a database with information that affects various departments of a business. You could selectively replicate only those documents that apply to your department.

2

Changing the Way You Do Business

To start with, there is no such person as an end user. Never has been. Probably never will be.

Of course, *end user* is a term that's been kicked around pretty often by computing professionals. It's not been a term of endearment, and the kicking around is no doubt part of the problem. One otherwise respectable and respected columnist recently equated *end users* with *great unwashed*.

But put it this way: have you every met anyone who referred to themselves as an end user? If you need more formal proof, call the Human Resources departments of any five major employers and ask for the job description of an end user. On second thought, don't bother. You already know what the results will be.

The people called end users really are accountants, and engineers, and clerks, and—yes—even computer professionals. When they envision their roles, they don't think in terms of their relationships to computers. They think in terms of their relationships to their jobs, goals, and responsibilities. It is in these results-oriented roles that they are helping to make electronic mail one of the hottest applications in client/server computing today.

There are no end users

- People relate to their jobs
- Not to their computers

E-mail is turning them into workgroup members

Furthermore, these people are taking e-mail far beyond the basic idea of text-based telephone tag. E-mail is rapidly maturing into a messaging platform that can communicate just about anything to just about anybody. Humans are not even essential to the process. Applications can exchange messages just as readily as people can. Messaging applications can schedule processes, automate tasks, and support business decisions. More important, these super forms of e-mail are helping people work together in a true sense of teamwork. With constantly improving ways to exchange information, the people who never were end users are being transformed into *workgroup members*. They are important parts of active teams, relating not just to their equipment or even their job specialties, but to their roles in a more dynamic organization.

E-mail Grows Up

Originally, e-mail was a way to send electronic memos, often over the limited range of a LAN. According to estimates by the Yankee Group, the number of e-mail recipients in the United States has been growing at a rate of about 60 percent a year, and that growth is likely to continue (Fig. 2.1).

Growth can bring both opportunities and problems. In a company of any size, there can be as many e-mail systems as there are LANs. One of the major challenges in adapting a more expansive view of e-mail is to link these diverse networks into an enterprisewide messaging system.

Modern e-mail does much more than provide communication among a limited group of people. Even a small workgroup can be a cross-functional team whose members work in different departments, and on different networks. This requires that e-mail span the enterprise, an undertaking that has more than its share of rough spots.

As an enterprisewide undertaking, e-mail is becoming the basis of a host of enhanced communication services. These services will greatly affect how you

E-mail spans the enterprise

- Integrated communication
- Mail-enabled applications
- Workflow management
- New management styles

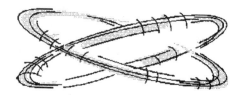

Growing at 60% a year

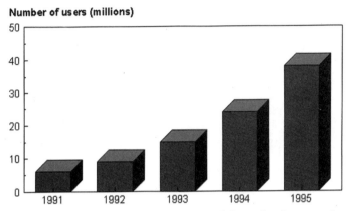

Number of users (millions)

Figure 2.1 The number of e-mail users in the United States has been growing at a rate of 68 percent per year. (*Yankee Group.*)

and other organizations do business. Companies have integrated fax and voice mail with their e-mail systems. E-mail has also become the basis of an entirely new class of applications called groupware, or mail-enabled software. Yet another growing class, workflow management, claims e-mail as an important ancestor. Innovative organizations are using e-mail to support activities like total quality management.

Electronic agent of change

Even ordinary e-mail can start to transform an organization. It quickly becomes a vital part of the communication process. When advanced e-mail

The changes aren't just technical

- Flatter structures
- Better project tracking
- Quicker response
- Improved processes

Not just an application

■ A foundation for:
- – Messages
- – Faxes
- – Data
- – Schedules
- – Documents

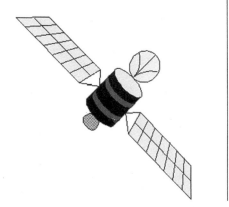

arrives, it brings more than technical change. Organizations that already have had the experience report outcomes like these:

■ Flatter management structures

■ Better project tracking

■ Quicker responses to markets

■ More efficient work processes

E-mail is not just an application, nor is it just a way to send messages. It is a foundation for other applications like:

■ Multimedia messages

■ Fax routing

■ Database access

■ Scheduling

■ Document sharing

Where e-mail comes from

E-mail has its roots in the office automation (OA) systems of the 1970s. Predating most personal computers (PCs) by several years, OA systems were usually based on midrange systems, but there were a fair number of mainframe-based systems as well. Some of the holdover systems from that era, like IBM's Profs and Digital Equipment Corporation's (DEC's) All-in One, can still elicit a little nostalgia.

The arrival of PC LANs late in the 1980s held a promise of low-cost electronic communication. LANs were slow to catch on, though, and their func-

Today's challenges

- Technical: link the organization
- Human: overcome resistance

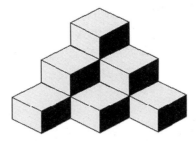

tions were limited. The earliest versions of Netware were designed mainly to share file and printers. Other functions like e-mail came along later.

Nevertheless, e-mail became the first type of application to be specifically designed for a LAN. There were approximately 6 million e-mail boxes in 1987. Within 3 years, the total had reached 17 million. As this growth continued, people learned that e-mail is not just a simple medium of communication. It can multiply the value of a network, and it can grow as the network grows.

Technical developments have also contributed to the growth of e-mail. A standard set of protocols labeled X.400 has helped standardize e-mail systems. A companion X.500 standard provides for advanced directory services. Vendors and their customers have come to accept these standards, making e-mail a day-to-day business tool instead of an add-on.

There's a difference, though, between standards and universal standards. The spirit of proprietary systems lives on, and you can often find a variety of semicompatible e-mail systems in even a modestly-sized enterprise. If e-mail is to become a truly valuable tool, it must let workgroup members exchange information and ideas, regardless of who or where they are. That requires an enterprisewide system. To create such a system, there are now two options: replace the individual systems, or find a way to get them to work together. Neither is easy.

Architectural change

Accompanying e-mail's new role is a change in its basic architecture. The old OA-based systems used a host-dumb terminal layout, a formation that has all but given way to client/server systems that emphasize the desktop instead of the central host.

On the client side of the new e-mail configuration, newer systems can support the full variety of desktop devices you'll find in the typical office. They also let people customize their desktop systems to suit their personal needs.

Meanwhile, the server component provides three important services:

Client/server e-mail

- On the client side:
  - User interface
  - Ability to customize
  - Other services

- On the server side:
  - Directory
  - Message store
  - Transport mechanism
  - Filters

- *The directory.* Also called an address book, this function holds information on where to find other people by e-mail. Expanded versions include more personalized information. For example, a directory listing might note the type of word processor on each person's system. The system could use that information to transmit data in an appropriate format.

- *The message store.* This is the repository for the actual messages. An e-mail system can forward messages immediately to the recipients' mailboxes, or it can store them for forwarding in a batch. In the case of long-distance transmission, the messages might be held until night when telephone rates are lower.

- *The transport mechanism.* This is the service that routes a message to its recipient.

A server can also have a filtering mechanism that ranks messages by their importance. When you see a list of your incoming messages, you can identify the one that comes from the boss or an important client, and save the rest for later.

The Example of Notes

Lotus Notes is by far the best-known and most influential example of how to energize a work group by way of e-mail. It's not that Notes is the most powerful product of its kind. It falls much closer to the desktop than to servers or larger systems, and some of its best applications involve ad hoc collaborations among relatively small groups.

One key to Notes's success is its ability to span open platforms and to adopt the client/server model. In that role, Notes works on both the client and server sides. As a client, Notes makes it easier for both workgroup members and third-party developers to build links with other systems and other applications. In server duty, Notes can tap the expanding power of network operating systems and multiple server platforms.

The more important key to Notes, however, is imagination. It is an imaginative product in the first place, and in receptive hands it inspires more imagination among workgroup members. It is a tool people can use to improve the way they work together, and growing numbers of people are

How Notes expands e-mail

- Unifies small groups
- Spans multiple platforms
- Acts as client and server
- Expands network power

Inspires imagination

doing exactly that. The impetus behind Notes has come outward from the workforce, not downward by way of large-system hosts.

E-mail and the Organization

Except when routing messages between mixed systems, e-mail is an uncomplicated technology. That's part of its appeal. There's not a lot about basic e-mail to inspire the high-tech specialist, but there is much to inspire managers and their employees who value the ability to communicate in new and more pro-

Supporting working relationships

- Building teams
- Improving quality
- Serving customers
- Supporting re-engineering

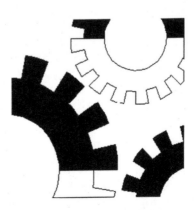

ductive ways. The secret of e-mail's success is that it supports new and better ways for people to work together.

Few applications have done a better job of serving an organization by serving its people. Modern business structures demand better forms of personal communication. E-mail meets that demand. It supports the kind of working relationships the modern business environment requires. This environment includes:

- Flatter, more team-oriented structures
- An emphasis on customer service
- Organizational reengineering

Flattening the pyramid

The traditional organization has a familiar pyramid shape. At the top, there's one chief, and below there are a great many Indians.

In truth, Native American tribes were seldom organized that way. More commonly, a war party was truly an all-volunteer army, led by the person who could command the greatest following. Meanwhile, the leading civil authority was usually the person who could best handle the office's most important duty: resolving disputes. Order was maintained more by force of tradition than by force of authority.

Modern business organizations are evolving toward that kind of pattern. A leading example is the self-directed work team, an ad hoc group formed to meet the needs of the moment. Leadership may be just as informal.

Managers have learned that their most effective roles are as mentors and facilitators, not authority figures. In his book *Among Schoolchildren,* Tracy Kidder described a school year in the life of a sixth-grade teacher. The principal, who regarded the teacher as superior, wisely chose not to try to tell her how to teach. Instead, the principal saw his mission as supporting the teacher's work in the classroom.

This style of structure and leadership relies on information and quick communication. One of the reasons e-mail has become so popular is that it meets that need. Its enhanced versions, including workflow management and mail-enabled applications, can do even more.

In large part, organizations have implemented these new organizational forms in the quest for quality. They establish such institutions as quality circles and total quality management, both of which rely less on organizational authority and more on information and quick communication. E-mail fills that need, and advanced mail-enabled applications can contribute even more.

Serving the customer

Another major goal of the 1990s corporation is better customer service. In fact, customer service is an integral part of the same movement that includes total quality and flatter organizations. Good service often requires that you empower employees to make decisions and take responsibility. If employees are to have larger decision-making roles, they need more information. That, in turn, requires better communication—another role for expanded forms of e-mail.

Customer service is internal as well as external. A common slogan of the customer service movement is, "If you aren't serving a customer, you should be serving someone who is." This has had serious implications for information systems (IS) professionals, whose functions increasingly require that they serve the internal customers they prefer to call end users.

Reengineering

No one engineered the corporation in the first place, but a process called reengineering overlays these other changes in organizational structure. Reengineering is a methodical process of streamlining the enterprise. It implies that the organization and its data will be reshaped in tandem. E-mail can have a key role in enabling this process. It helps break down organizational barriers and supports the kind of communication and teamwork modern organizations must have.

Managing success factors

A modern organization also must be able to constantly define, manage, and redefine its critical success factors (CSFs). These can include:

- Sales growth
- Market share
- Internal growth

Critical to success

- Management must measure
  - Sales growth
  - Market share
  - Internal growth
- Databases provide snapshots
- *Notes plays the video*

The ability to plot and manage CSFs is critical to a company's ability to achieve its objectives. It is critical, that is, until the next CSF comes along. It is nearly a law of modern business that not only must you continue to measure and manage CSFs, but at the same time you must also hit a moving target. The reward for managing a CSF is that a new CSF takes its place. You often will find that the original CSF was only a part of a new, larger CSF.

There are few tools to do this job. Client/server databases can record and report much of the information you need to monitor a CSF, but it still provides a static snapshot. In addition, some people try to alter their work processes to fit their database models.

What you really need is a tool that focuses on the ongoing process rather than its status at any one time—in other words, workflow management. That is where products like Notes come in. You can use forms to track the workflow. Within these forms, you can write business rules. You can write these rules to fit the job, not the data. You need not worry so much about tools, and you can focus instead on the tasks.

Doing it yourself

Perhaps one of the most far-reaching features of e-mail is to free small workgroups from depending on central IS staffs for their computing welfare. Notes is gaining fame as a platform for developing some fairly serious but home-grown client/server applications. It's fairly easy to build a database application that relies on e-mail links instead of remote procedure calls (RPCs) and other tricky features of distributed databases. There are some things Notes can't do well—transaction processing is one of them—but there are many things it can.

Of course, there are IS folks who doubt this is a good idea. They point out that small home-grown applications can grow in use and importance. Eventually, some reach the exalted status of mission-critical, but without the controls and protections the professionals would provide for applications in this class.

Nevertheless, e-mail has been a bottom-up phenomenon, answering people's needs to communicate with each other.

E-mail all the way

To fulfill its function in a flatter, more flexible organization, e-mail must be fully accessible. That means it must be more than a separate function, and even more than a few mail-enabled applications. It should bring information to an employee, no matter what kind of application that employee is using. In other words, everything an employee does should be mail-enabled. That should be true whether the employee uses a PC, a workstation, or any other kind of function.

From the employee's point of view, an application should include mail as a utility, much as a word processor incorporates a spelling checker. E-mail should also be transparent. Neither the individual nor the application should

What employees need

- Transparent communication
- Multiple messaging
- Integration with applications

have to know the details of how a message is routed, whether it is to an adjoining LAN workstation, or through multiple connections over a wide area network (WAN). Execution should be as simple as a pull-down menu.

A fully functional e-mail system should also have these qualities:

- It should be integrated with fax, voice transmission, and other forms of messaging.

- It should be seamless, letting you transmit files from their native applications. For example, you could transmit a spreadsheet that includes all its formulas, not just the resulting numbers.

In more advanced life forms, applications use e-mail as their foundations, building on such present-day functions as calendar and scheduling utilities. These are being expanded into broader functions like workflow management and electronic conferences.

Not long ago, features like these were described as a future form of e-mail. Most are now part of the present. Application suites can exchange data with each other and include quick-connect links with e-mail systems. In particular, the Lotus suite is tightly integrated with Notes and its workgroup functions. When you link applications in this way, people can use them while working together instead of alone.

To accommodate these applications and make best use of them, modern forms of e-mail must:

- Adapt to changing organizational structures. Host-based systems have some serious weaknesses here.

- Build on e-mail's many strong points while making up for its weaknesses.

The Enabled Application

The mail-enabled application might sound like something that escaped from the language of political correctness. What the term really describes is e-mail's most recent evolutionary form. This is a process through which e-mail is gradually replacing many of the single-purpose applications now used on personal computers.

In its simplest form, a mail-enabled application is a Windows program that has a Send command in its File menu. For example, the familiar draft horse Word 6.0 has such a command, which sends a mail message with a Word document attached. The command is available only if you have installed Microsoft Mail, but it is also one of the more primitive forms of mail enablement.

Later examples, including many still to come, are much more advanced and much less limiting. E-mail is evolving into new forms that support networked and group applications like workflow management, document routing, process scheduling, and electronic conferences. One step in this evolution has been the development of application suites, whose components can exchange information with one another. The logical next step, though a giant one, is for the applications on multiple desktops and systems to talk to each other just as readily.

Two classes

Mail-enabled applications are designed to capitalize on e-mail. At the outset, at least, these are familiar spreadsheets, word processors, and other individual desktop applications that have e-mail features built in. There is another class of message-centered programs that are built specifically around e-mail functions.

An ordinary application can become an enabled application simply by adopting either of two prevailing e-mail standards:

- MAPI (Messaging Application Programming Interface) from Microsoft

- VIM (Vendor-Independent Messaging) from IBM/Lotus

Considering their sources, it's only natural that these competing methods are slugging it out in the e-mail marketplace. An application that uses either, though, can place a Send command in its menu system, probably not far from

Heavyweights battle it out

- MAPI, developed by Microsoft
- Vendor-independent messaging, in Notes and other Lotus products

the Print command. A dialog box opens, asking you to enter a recipient's e-mail address. When you send the message, a file from the host program is automatically attached.

At the receiving end, you can retrieve the transmitted file and open it in the host application. Don't have the application? With most e-mail systems, no problem. Viewers let you read the file.

Connecting with Notes

Naturally, Lotus uses its Notes and VIM to link as the enabling force for its applications. For some time, mail-enabled versions of the Lotus 1-2-3 spreadsheet have included a Version Manager feature that makes it easier to share worksheet data. You can create a named range of cells and e-mail it to a colleague, with attached information such as version number and your name. The recipient then could incorporate it into a worksheet on the receiving system. These high-powered ranges can also become separate Notes entries.

With this technology, workgroup members can study each other's work, incorporate it in their own, and roll up data from various spreadsheets. Changes are visible as members make them; there is no need to wait for an end-of-process consolidation. The WordPro word processor, successor to Ami Pro, takes this process further with features that let members mark up and compare each other's documents, store them in a Notes database, and even apply the electronic equivalent of a yellow highlighting pen (Fig. 2.2).

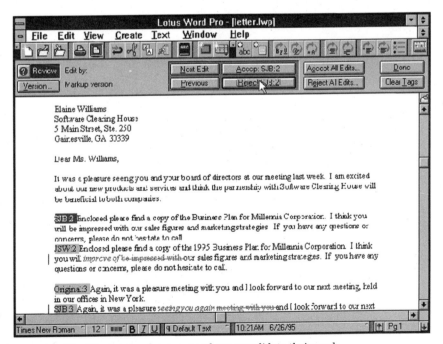

Figure 2.2 WordPro lets workgroup members consolidate their work.

In the view of Lotus officials, their product line is going well beyond enablement. Using Notes as a centerpiece, Lotus is building what it calls a whole new way for people to work with each other.

Synchronizing work

Yet another popular e-mail adaptation is the use of workflow technology to schedule work activities. For example, one large oil company uses e-mail to coordinate employees' activities when a tanker pulls into port. A diverse group of employees, including the ship's crew, headquarters staff members, and even sales representatives must synchronize their work. The company uses the e-mail system to send assignment notices and updates to the employees. By avoiding mistakes and delays, the company is trying to cut down on overtime charges that may run as high as $10,000 per hour.

The firm has found other uses for the system too, including advertising job openings, sending notices of policy changes, and advertising company events.

A midwestern paper products firm uses e-mail to manage portable computers in the field. The e-mail system can upgrade software, change menus, and distribute new e-mail directories. The system also gives managers a way to verify that the changes have been implemented properly.

Managing workflow

The oil company's job synchronization system is an example of another type of application whose roots are at least partly in e-mail. This is workflow management: coordinating the multiple steps of a business process.

Workflow management also claims ancestry in document management, and many typical workflow applications involve managing the flow of paper, or its

Smoothing the flow of work

- Workflow management:
  - Part e-mail
  - Part document management
- All part of making a process flow more smoothly.

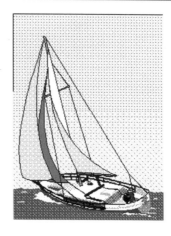

electronic equivalent. A typical example is processing an employee's expense report:

- The employee fills out an electronic form reporting the month's expenses.
- The form is automatically routed to the employee's manager for approval.
- The form then goes to accounting for payment.

The workflow management system doesn't have to end here. It could continue through the process of issuing the reimbursement check. It could also provide for multiple approvals, perhaps observing a rule that a senior manager's approval is necessary if the voucher exceeds a certain amount. That rule can be built into the application.

Though much of workflow management originated in document management, e-mail has become the enabling infrastructure that allows further development.

Scheduling meetings

Another fast-growing offshoot of e-mail is scheduling meetings and appointments. When you want to call a meeting, you can not only check your schedule but also those of the people you want to attend. When you find a suitable time, you can send e-mail messages to other group members, inviting them to the session.

Applications like these have been around for a while. The most ubiquitous is probably Microsoft Schedule+, shipped as an application with recent versions of Windows. Novell's Groupwise and, of course, a Notes application, are more sophisticated variations on the same theme. If you like, these products will search for a time when everyone is free, though if you don't set this feature correctly you may be summoned at 6:30 on a Sunday morning (Fig. 2.3).

Even this relatively simple product contains some features many want, like the option of declining a meeting invitation (whether you decline, and if so for what reasons, is between you and the person who called the meeting). You can also set aside committed blocks of time to work on important projects.

The expanded electronic conference

In offices throughout the land, regular meetings are being held on how to reduce the number of meetings people have to attend. Not only do meetings take time, but also people often have to spending even more time traveling to them. One subject that often arises at these sessions is electronic conferencing. Instead of meeting face to face, you can see each other's smiling faces on your computer screens.

This is an idea that is not yet ready for prime time. Electronic conference applications do exist, and people actually use them sometimes. Nevertheless, critics point out that the video quality still needs work, and it is not the same thing as being there.

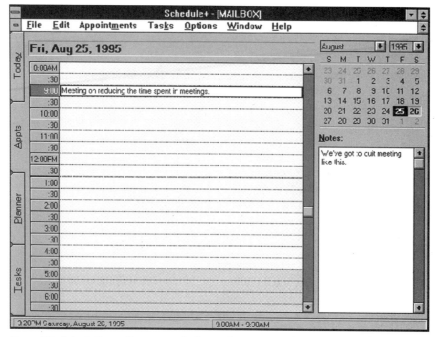

Figure 2.3 Scheduling software can find out when everyone's free for a meeting.

The no-meeting meeting

- Post a topic on the discussion database
- Exchange comments at your leisure

In the short term, at least, if e-mail is to replace the conventional meeting, it will be more like a bulletin board service, or an electronic exchange of memos. In fact, a discussion database is a Notes staple. You can use it as a model to exchange ideas and comments about any job a group undertakes. For example, the design team on a software project could use this template to suggest ideas and seek solutions to problems.

With e-mail as a foundation, conferencing becomes the corporate equivalent of the electronic bulletin board. You can select the topic of a conference and post it on the e-mail system. Other workgroup members can add their comments and reply to others in a freewheeling electronic discussion.

In fact, you can conduct an entire meeting by e-mail. You don't have to coordinate schedules, and you don't have to spend inordinate amounts of time that everyone knows is unproductive. There's no requirement that everyone be there at the same time, or even at the same place. Another advantage is that the e-mail system maintains a record of the entire exchange—electronic "minutes" of the meeting. There should never be any serious question of who said what.

Electronic communication will never replace face-to-face human interaction, but it can streamline the communication process.

Some Problems Still Exist

Just as e-mail has both technical and organizational benefits, it has both technical and organizational problems.

- The main technical problem is to create an e-mail system that spans the multiple types of systems and networks found in many organizations. Before the people can talk to each other, their machines must talk to each other, and progress in that area has been slow to develop.

- The organizational problem is an old, familiar one: wherever there is change, there is also resistance to change. This is a human problem that requires human responses. No technical innovation will overcome this one.

This new technical challenge will eventually yield to new forms of technology. In fact, some solutions are available, though they are expensive and hard to use.

E-mail still has some problems

- Technical:
  - Linking diverse systems
- Human:
  - Resistance to change

For example, the headquarters of a major casualty insurance firm has more than 36,000 employees using five different e-mail systems. These include older large-system installations like IBM Profs and DEC All-in-One, plus newer desktop networks like Lotus cc:Mail and Microsoft Mail. Each has its own file formats, directory structure, and transport mechanism, and application programming interface (API). In addition, the company maintains e-mail connections with large policyholders and other outside organizations.

Reducing this diversity has helped. The existing five types of systems are down from nine a few years ago. The company has also installed a messaging backbone from SoftSwitch (Wayne, PA) to connect the internal systems. An X.400 gateway maintains connections with the outside companies.

This solution works, but managing it is not easy. Due to high employee turnover, system managers must constantly make sure multiple types of directories are up to date. It is a labor-intensive task; there's no automated way to do it. Further reductions in diversity will not come easily, either. There is a mixture of entrenched legacy systems and those beloved by individual departments. Trying to make people abandon familiar systems brings up the second obstacle—resistance to change.

Electronic junk mail

Another problem with e-mail is its lack of selectivity. People tend to send too much e-mail. They write e-mail memos on trivial subjects, then load up the cc: line with the names of everyone who might be interested or influenced, or send copies to everyone on an internal mailing list. The result is that to find the worthwhile messages in your e-mail box, you have to wade through megabytes of electronic junk mail. This problem only gets worse when you return from a business trip or vacation.

E-mail overload

- Too many messages
- To too many people
- With too many copies

One solution is to set up an electronic filter to sort and classify your messages. For example, Notes and many other e-mail systems let you sort your messages into categories you have established. Within each category, you can include instructions for handling the mail in that class. You can ask the system to delete automatically the mail that falls into one group, to forward another class of messages, or to send a standard response to another group.

Suppose you're about to leave on vacation—happy thought. Before you leave, you could ask your e-mail system to:

- Forward immediate-action messages to your vacation replacement

- Reply to routine messages that you're away and expect to be back on the 20th

- Automatically delete all messages generated from internal mailing lists

You even can filter mail before it reaches the desktop. A server-based filter can manage the complete mail system by setting up systemwide standards. For example, you could set up the system to delete all messages sent before a certain date, or to notify an employee that his or her mailbox is becoming clogged with a backlog of unread messages.

Making judgment calls

The drawback to this type of filtering is that no amount of computer logic will replace human judgment. Artificial intelligence will always remain artificial, and computer logic still accepts nothing more complex than yes/no questions. A filter's operation is automatic and nondiscriminating.

Take, for example, that vacation time instruction to delete all messages from internal mailing lists. This gets rid of one class of junk mail, but it also could cause you to miss something important. Messages circulated by mailing list might include the general announcement of attractive new options in the benefits package, or important new requirements for claiming expense reimbursements.

Education needed

There's a better solution: educate people on how to use e-mail correctly. There is plenty of training available about how to compose and send a message in a standard e-mail package, and how to read the messages the system sends to you. What these courses usually fail to teach is what to say in these messages, and who to send them to.

One problem is that while many employees are good at what they do, only a few are accomplished writers. That's one reason why the typewritten smiley face has become such a staple of e-mail communication. Lots of people don't know how to express themselves otherwise.

Here are some things good e-mail communicators should learn:

- Limit your messages and copies to people who really need to know. Though e-mail may give you the power to send a message to the company president,

How to use e-mail correctly

- Keep messages relevant
- Don't avoid personal contact
- Be brief
- Avoid accusations

don't deluge the president with your thoughts on how to run the company. Save the privilege for times when you can offer something truly useful. Think, "Would the boss really want to know about this, or am I just showing off?" Take the same approach to lower-ranking employees. Don't swamp them with information they don't need or problems then can't solve.

- Don't use e-mail when the subject calls for face-to-face communication. Granted, these subjects are often the hardest to discuss. The reverse is also true. Make sure you read and respond to important messages; don't try to dodge unpleasant subjects by filtering them out.

- Don't ramble. Keep your messages brief and to the point. Stick to the relevant facts. You may be surprised at how many people consider your opinions irrelevant.

- Choose your words carefully. Avoid accusations, or even words that might be taken for accusations. One good way to do this is to start a critical statement with "I." "I am disappointed that the report has not yet completed," sounds a whole lot better than "You failed to complete the report." At first, using I-statements may sound self-centered, but in truth when you focus on yourself and your reactions you are less likely to direct harsh words at others.

Does E-mail Pay?

It's hard to calculate the payback from any personal computer technology. Well-publicized studies strongly suggest that all the PCs in all the offices in all the communities of all this nation have done next to nothing to improve personal productivity. One such study found the greatest concentration of PCs in service industries. These are the same industries where productivity growth has been slowest.

Yet hardly anyone would trade a computer for the old methods that seem so inefficient in retrospect. Even if the studies cannot find it, there's something in our common sense that says computers really are more efficient.

E-mail is an important test of that belief. It is such a nice fit with modern business practices that it must be doing some good. That unsupported belief won't be very convincing, though, when the bean counters ask for an accounting of your beansmanship.

Streamlining the wrong tasks

The first PC applications concentrated on automating individual tasks like writing and calculating, plus some specialties like publishing. Few of these activities are directly related to management's most serious challenges: coordinating, communicating, collaborating, and negotiating. These are things you do in and with groups: employees, customers, suppliers, and the like. The early PCs, then, were tools of lower-ranking employees. They did little to raise productivity at the top, where it would have the greatest impact. The senior executive with an unused computer on the desk is still more than a stereotype.

Even though the PC won a well-deserved victory over the mainframe mode of thinking, it has still largely been a personal productivity tool, not one that enhances the effectiveness of the group as a whole. Ironically, it is the service sector, with its heavy concentration of PCs, that could make best use of better workgroup productivity. This is where it is particularly important to organize people, information, and documents. These are often unplanned and ad hoc activities, in contrast to the well-established process of the manufacturing assembly line.

Does Notes boost output?

Lotus offers Notes as an answer to the problem of energizing workgroups. There is a lot of theoretical support for the idea that products like Notes can improve group productivity, but there are few hard facts. Most of the studies to date have focused on relatively simple forms of e-mail, ignoring the added workgroup dynamics that products like Notes can achieve. Other studies have assumed, without really proving it, that using Notes's groupware features automatically translates into better coordination, shorter meetings, and quicker access to information.

Another leading theory is that the improvements brought by products like Notes is incremental, not revolutionary. It does not arrive with a big bang but accrues slowly over time. It's hard to find major short-term improvements in productivity.

To look for answers, a Lotus-backed research team interviewed a sample of Notes users who had long, substantial experience with the product: at least 200 nodes in service for at least a year. Initial screening cut the group nearly in half. In some cases, the companies had kept too little data to support valid conclusions; in others, factors like reorganization made it impossible to isolate the effect of Notes on productivity.

Among the remaining users, who could measure their benefits, the median 3-year return on investment, before taxes, was 353 percent; the proverbial worst-case scenario was an improvement of 163 percent. The typical project paid for itself in less than 4 months. This was a limited study with a small sample, but the research is continuing as other customers gain more experience and benefits.

These and other studies may yet answer the productivity paradox. There still are many issues to be resolved, though. Many of them are accounting questions, such as how to allocate the costs and benefits of a network or its software among various parts of the organization. These issues become particularly important as e-mail becomes an enterprise rather than just a departmental institution. Even organizations that have existing e-mail systems want to know whether an enterprisewide backbone-type system would justify its costs.

The real question

For most organizations, the real question is not whether to install e-mail—they probably already have it—but how to provide the most cost-effective system. In the usual case you are also considering the costs and benefits of consolidating departmental e-mail systems into an enterprise network. This requires that you make a cost analysis of two types of factors. First, there are technical factors like these:

- The cost basis of an e-mail system, compared with possible alternatives for providing the same service

- The long-term cost-effectiveness of an e-mail system, most likely a backbone system that serves the entire organization

Factors to analyze

- Technical:
  - Initial cost
  - Long-term cost-effectiveness
  - Technology options
  - Media mix
- Organizational
  - Business value
  - Chargebacks
  - Funding incentives
  - Expected return

- The most efficient mix of e-mail, voice mail, fax, pagers, and other communication media

In addition, there are organizational factors to be analyzed, including the following:

- The business value of e-mail to the organization
- The appropriate methods and amounts with which to charge back computing costs to various parts of the organization
- The justification of corporate funding for workgroup projects
- The expected return on investment

Time is not on your side. Change in computer technology is so quick, and so inevitable, that new technology appears at your doorstep nearly every day. It's easy to rush into these new devices without adequately analyzing their impact. It's important that you understand exactly how far you should go, and the bottom-line impact of making that trip.

Tortoise and hare

If technology is a fast-changing field, accounting is not. Many accountants like the apparent security of methods and standards that change slowly, if at all. Not only are accounting methods failing to keep up with technical change, they aren't even in the same race. To properly account for the impact of technology requires a different way of thinking. A savvy technical manager can help the accounting department achieve it.

For example, many department heads approach financial executives with the idea of "justifying" their expenses. This mode of thinking assumes that there is something wrong with what you propose. Your request will be denied unless you can overcome the presumption that these costs are an excessive drag on the bottom line.

Profit from e-mail

Nina Burns, head of Creative Networks (Palo Alto, CA) suggests a more positive approach: present e-mail as a profit-making activity. Combine a business structure with a financial model through which management can see e-mail as a product line—one whose output will improve the organization's profitability.

The first step is to identify the cost basis of an e-mail system (Fig. 2.4). This includes three major categories:

- Acquiring equipment and facilities
- Personnel costs
- Operating expenses

Within each of these categories, some expenses will be fixed. These are one-time costs that should produce returns for longer than a year. Other costs are

Identifying costs

- Equipment and facilities
- Personnel
- Operating expenses

These can be fixed or recurring

Typical first-year costs

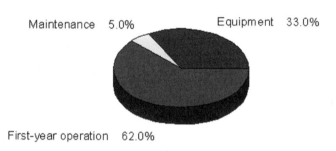

Maintenance 5.0%   Equipment 33.0%

First-year operation 62.0%

Operating costs include personnel and software development

Figure 2.4 Operating costs are often the major share of the cost.

recurring. These are the variable costs you incur each year, month, or hour as long as the system is in service. In-house systems tend to have higher fixed costs. Outsourcing usually involves higher recurring costs such as monthly service costs.

Compute the profit

The next step is to establish the profitability ratios of the e-mail system. Table 2.1 shows several ways to calculate these ratios for an e-mail system. All measure the earning power of a project, in this case the e-mail system. This is a key to demonstrating the benefits of e-mail. Instead of trying to defend the cost, you are describing the likely return on the e-mail investment.

TABLE 2.1.   These Ratios Help You Sell the System as a Source of Profit, Not Expense.

Typical Profit Ratios for an e-Mail System	
Gross profit margin	Gross profit/Number of users
Operating profit margin	Pretax earnings/Number of users
Net profit margin	Net income/Number of users
Return on investment	Net income/Total sales

In conventional use, these ratios usually are calculated per customer or per dollar in sales. In the case of e-mail, you can calculate the ratios per internal customer using the e-mail system. You can use these ratios to compare alternatives, such as the long-term cost of developing your own system versus outsourcing. You can also use them to determine what to charge your e-mail customers for the service. Determine how much the customers would be willing to spend for the service, both in up-front installation costs and for continued service and support.

Though the object of this exercise is to present e-mail as a profit-making activity, this is not the place to try to maximize the profits. Set pricing levels that would encourage internal customers to use the system and boost their own efficiency.

Calculating benefits

It's easy to calculate costs. The value to the organization and its internal customers' orders is often intangible. This is the main reason it has been so hard to quantify the benefits of computerization, even when common sense tells us they exist. Nevertheless, if you can readily measure costs, you can also calcu-

Calculating the savings

- Less employee time
- Lower telephone expenses
- Less use of fax
- Fewer overnight services

Benefits you can measure

- Increased customer contacts
- Increased orders
- Reduced risk of outdated information
- Greater processing volume
- Fewer errors and returns
- Quicker response times

late reductions in cost. The possibilities include reduced costs for items like these:

- Employee time
- Telephone expenses
- Use of fax machines
- Overnight and courier services

Don't consider the direct costs alone. In the case of telephones, for example, the costs include not only the phone service itself but the time employees spend on the phone, including the common sport of telephone tag.

It's also possible to quantify many e-mail benefits. Some companies have found results like these:

- Increased number of customer contacts, with reduced advertising costs
- The ability to use automated ordering systems, which increase sales volume without requiring additional staff resources
- The reduced risk of using outdated information
- Increased number of applications processed per day
- Improved success rate of sales calls, attributed to the availability of up-to-date account information
- Fewer returns caused by errors in order handling
- Improved customer satisfaction and reduced service costs, brought about by improving the response time on customer service inquiries

Let the system measure itself

The e-mail system itself can be a source of the data you need. You can use it to make calculations like these:

E-mail as a data source

- Average message size
- Number of messages
- Error rate

- To determine the average message size, divide the total number of bytes transmitted by the total number of messages.
- To determine the average number of messages, divide the total number of bytes by the average message size.
- To calculate the average error rate, multiply the total number of failed messages by 100.

There are several other units of measure you can use, such as calculating the amount of paper it would have taken to transmit the same amount of material, or the amount of time spent to produce an e-mail message compared with a paper memo. (Remember, though, that many people print their e-mail.)

Go figure

Though you are presenting e-mail as a profit-making enterprise, the goal is not really to achieve maximum profit. You probably will want to minimize the charges you apply to your internal customers to encourage them to use the system and realize their own efficiencies.

It is important, though, that you present the system in terms of opportunity, not cost. Instead of trying to justify an expense, demonstrate how much added value the system can bring to the organization.

How Organizations Use Notes

One advantage of Notes is that it lets ordinary people build simple but effective applications. For example, employees of a small manufacturing firm used

Notes to build a proposal development application. At about the same time, the company was acquiring four smaller firms. The Notes application helped all four boost their revenues and improve their competitive positions. The highlight came when the combined companies won a $6 million contract, a feat company officials believe would not have been possible without Notes.

One reason is that Notes links more than 100 people from four organizations that until recently were independent companies. The software helped them coordinate efforts in preparing their bid. In addition, they used Notes to coordinate with clients and vendors, exchanging drawings and information, and maintaining current information on the project status.

In the case of another large contract, to a public agency, the customer was given a connection to the firm's Notes database, so it could review information and status reports at any time.

Saving paperwork

A state government agency has used Notes to reduce that unfortunate symbol of government operations: paperwork. This agency is responsible for collecting fees and taxes, often generated by other agencies. The agency introduced Notes to help meet a reduced budget while improving its levels of service.

For example, the agency often must resolve citizen complaints involving discrepancies between its own records and those of other agencies. The process involved:

- Thirty boxes of printed database information received each quarter from the other agencies

- Separating and filing this information in individual citizens' records

- Analyzing the paper data for mismatches in data among the involved agencies

- Preparing and mailing letters notifying citizens of the problems

Typically, a citizen who received such a letter would contact the agency to try to resolve the problem. Analysts who took these calls could rarely offer on-the-spot responses. If nothing else, they needed time to look up the citizen's file.

The Notes application directly reads and combines the information in multiple agencies' databases. This data is immediately available on-screen. Now, the analyst who receives a call is usually able to resolve the problem on the spot.

At this agency, officials say Notes has become a particular favorite of non-IS employees. They've found they can go so far as to design their own databases.

Larger firms save, too

An international electronics manufacturer has maintained more than 300 Notes databases at its headquarters alone. Notes first came into the company as a way to implement product development controls, replacing a database that had "exploded." Instead of expending the time and money needed to rewrite the old database, the company was able to develop a replacement nearly overnight—the prototype was available in less than a week.

More recently, the company has made particularly good use of Notes in quality assurance. Originally, the company's quality assurance process had involved manual recording of product lots that were accepted or rejected. The company had the means to inspect individual items, but the recordkeeping burden would have been too great. Instead, the company was often rejecting lots, at an average added cost of $200 each lot.

With Notes, the company was able to establish a mix of lot- and component-level decisions, with a significant reduction in the number of rejected lots. Notes also helped the company manage its vendor relationships and track the performance of individual vendors.

3

The Power of Groupware

People working together usually are more effective than people working alone. Such is the principle behind Notes, the first and leading groupware application.

Notes is hardly a breakthrough in technology. It uses e-mail and database methods that are familiar and well established. Notes's genius does not really lie, either, in its combination of these two functions. The essence of Notes is not its technology but in the way that technology is used to help people work together. That means they usually also work better.

Since Notes was the first groupware product, it more or less defined the field. More or less, because many people still are unsure exactly what groupware is. They express their confusion by asking, "What is Notes good for?"

One reason for their confusion is that conventional databases employ a logic that confounds even people who are experts in other areas of computing. Another reason is that Notes is an unconventional database. Yet another reason is one some computer professionals wish would go away. When it was introduced, Notes was almost unique among software products. Instead of just a human interface, it offered human interaction. That is the essence of groupware, and it is the soul of Notes.

A rare combination

- An ordinary e-mail service
- An ordinary databasesystem
- An extraordinary combination

What groupware can do

- Integrate functions
- Store documents
- Provide an application foundation
- Share data
- *But what does all that get you?*

What Can Groupware Do?

Business has been busy lately, flattening organizations, boosting teamwork, and expressing the need to capture and manage an organization's "knowledge base" to achieve competitive advantage. In response, the computer industry has focused attention on software specifically designed to support a team approach. This is groupware, software that enables teams of people to integrate their knowledge, work processes, and applications to achieve improved business effectiveness. Groupware integrates messaging, document storage, and application development. At the same time, it supports the sharing of all types of data across disparate networks and computing platforms.

There is continuing debate about what constitutes a true groupware product. It is more important, though, to answer another question: "What can groupware really do?" Does groupware offer a basic return to the bottom line? If so, can it be quantified in ways that justify implementing a new kind of client/server-based system?

A process, not just communication

If groupware is to achieve a measurable return to the bottom line, it must do more than simply improve communication. In fact, in Lotus's experience, groupware applications that are designed from the start based on a loose idea of "better communication" often fail. Notes customers have found, for example, that groupware is least successful where it is implemented primarily as an e-mail or bulletin board system. Instead, groupware is used most successfully to address a specific business process.

A *business process* is a set of work activities that involves multiple people

Processes, not things

- Developing products
- Managing accounts
- Serving customers

performing multiple steps, usually in multiple areas. These people can come from inside or outside a physical workgroup, or even outside the organization itself. It is the mission of a segment of the company, described in business terms, not computer terms. In a functioning team, each member has an expertise or skill which can contribute to the overall success of the process. There are many common types of business processes including the following:

- Developing a product
- Managing client accounts
- Serving customers

Groupware should not only improve communication among team members, but it should also make business processes more effective.

Everyone a candidate

Every organization can benefit from improvements in at least one business process, whether it's creating a product or a service, handling customer requests, or supporting some other corporate operation. A typical business process might involve receiving a call for help from a customer, logging that call for tracking, checking records to see if the problem has occurred before, then working with other groups in the organization to find a solution and report back to the customer.

Processes like these take place every day in almost every organization. They are strategic to the ongoing success of the business. Furthermore, they existed long before computers were invented. This raises the question: If this activity is critical to organizations, why haven't makers of computer systems found ways to address them? The answer is connected to the ways in which today's companies have evolved to differentiate themselves, and to the ways in which computer systems are evolving to help support strategic business goals.

New mission-critical systems

The first organizational software systems, developed nearly 30 years ago, were designed primarily to automate operational processes like payroll, general ledger accounting, and budget management. In the mainframe-based environment of the 1970s, and later in the minicomputer-based environment of the 1980s, such systems were dubbed "mission critical" because they were essential to the basic operation of an organization. Operational systems capture and analyze data from business transactions, such as entering orders or managing inventory. These tasks are typically part of back office operations. Their focus is on the data they capture, and on maintaining the integrity of the data's relationships in a consistent, real-time state. Examples include:

- Keeping a customer's name associated with all of his or her orders and payments
- Performing electronic funds transfers
- Making airline reservations

With the implementation of client/server systems, organizations have been under increasing pressure to downsize operational systems. That way, they can take advantage of less expensive processing power, better application development tools, graphical user interfaces, and other improvements in technology.

Where's the revenue?

Client/server systems have produced some impressive cost savings. Yet, it has been nearly impossible to show any reliable return on investment in the form of revenue gains. There is a reason for this. While client/server-based software packages may allow applications to be developed more quickly and inexpensively, you cannot increase revenue if you continue to automate the same types of processes you used before. Computerized or not, the same processes will continue to produce about the same results at the familiar bottom line.

To increase revenue, an organization must apply client/server technology to a different set of business processes, such as product development, account management, and customer service. These processes tend to have unstructured, qualitative data, which usually appears in documents. Operational systems are known for their structured, quantitative data. Client/server computing lets organizations build applications that make these processes more efficient. It is possible to redesign them altogether.

Where Does Groupware Come From?

Though it was not obvious at the time, until recently computers have been used in only two types of situations:

- Automate transaction-heavy back office applications. This has been the traditional mainframe task.

- Improve personal productivity. The PC has done this very nicely, particularly through its real "killer app" word processing.

Groupware is an entirely new class of products. Its function is to improve group productivity. Lotus defines groupware as "software that uniquely enables organizations to communicate, to collaborate, and to coordinate business process." Groupware includes e-mail, but it also offers more. It goes beyond messaging to act as an integrated platform for developing and deploying a new class of client/server applications. These applications guide the flow of both structured and unstructured information to enhance business relationships. These enhanced relationships can extend across a team, a department, a company, and even linked enterprises.

An organization that adopts groupware can share knowledge across time zones, geographical boundaries, and networks. It taps the collective intelligence found in documents, e-mail messages, faxes, and other unstructured data sources.

The unstructured nature of this information is probably part of the confusion about what Notes and groupware can do. Those who like their information in neat packages will not be happy with Notes. Neither will those who see Notes as a combination of components instead of a coordinated and coordinating whole. In particular, some people look at the e-mail component and assume that's all there is.

Understanding groupware dynamics

A groupware process has three basic parts:

- A *common task*.   The system should allow many people to work on the same task, as in a software development or document editing system that lets many developers, writers, and editors contribute to the finished product.

- A *shared environment*.   This element keeps people in contact. It lets you know where a project stands, what fellow team members are doing, and what your next activity should be. An e-mail system that simply sends messages back and forth is a primitive form of a shared environment. A

The three parts of groupware

- Common task
- Shared environment
- Time and space

Communication takes place...

Same time, same place	Different times, same place

Same time, different places	Different times and places

more advanced system might be like a training application that provides a bulletin-board type of database for electronic class discussion.

- The *time and space* element emphasizes when and where the interaction takes place and accommodates communication accordingly.

The time and space element includes several possibilities:

- *Synchronous* interaction takes place at the same time and place—a face-to-face meeting is the most familiar example.

- *Asynchronous* interaction takes place at one place but at different times. Groups working on different parts of a project may share office space but complete their tasks on different schedules.

- *Distributed synchronous* interaction takes place at one place, but at different times. Electronic conferencing is a growing example of this kind of contact.

- *Distributed asynchronous* interaction takes place at different places and times, such as when contributors from across the country add entries to a discussion database.

Cooperative examples

One fruitful area for group cooperation is the collaborative writing project. Here, teams of writers, editors, and production specialists produce a magazine or report that includes the work of all.

Such a system collects the work of contributing writers and parcels them out to appropriate editors, sending the text by e-mail. The editors make necessary corrections and assign each article to a place in the finished publication. Then it all can be e-mailed to a desktop publishing specialist who assembles the product into a completed layout. It now is often possible to transmit that product electronically to the printer.

Another major area of collaboration could be group decision making. We all know how a camel is supposed to be a horse designed by a committee. That joke overlooks how well suited the camel is for its native environment. Notes lets workgroup members critique documents, add their comments, and contribute to discussion databases. Also available is a Notes link to Intel Pro Share, a kind of electronic whiteboarding product that supports a kind of conference call. Each participant can mark up a copy of a document, and the results are immediately displayed to other participants. A hookup like this elevates the asynchronous communication of a discussion database to a distributed synchronous process in which people from different localities can participate in the process at the same time.

Operational vs. Strategic Systems

Operational systems are rarely strategic. Companies seldom differentiate themselves based on how well they handle operational processes such as order inventory or accounting. Companies can certainly fail by poor budget management, but they seldom thrive on the execution of their operational systems.

Running a complex organization involves more than executing operational systems. It involves business processes: teams of people coordinating, collaborating, and negotiating, often with large groups of employees, outside vendors, suppliers, and customers. In contrast to the operational systems, an organization's success is often tied directly to how well it executes its business processes. How quickly can a company create a new product or service? How well does it sell to and support the customer? How effectively does it manage teams? The pages of business magazines are filled with tales of companies whose strategies center around addressing these challenges head on.

Business processes involve different types of problems than the operational processes of the back office. Salespeople must know how to close a deal, not just how to enter the order. In fact, truly effective sales and account management involves several multistep business processes: developing a proposal, tracking client status, managing credit, and collections. Product development is another example of a process-intensive activity. Engineers need to know more than just how to put pieces together. They also must assess customer needs, collaborate on problems, execute engineering change orders, and conduct quality assurance testing.

Business processes are inherently complex; they are information intensive; and they most often require the input and contributions of several people. They involve more comprehensive processes than operational systems were ever designed to support. It is these processes that have become mission critical, because today they are at the heart of business. They often mean the difference between failure and success for an organization.

Process management models

- Workgroups
- Communication
- Information

Points of difference

There are major architectural differences between the new systems for strategic business processes and the operational systems that are designed to handle back office automation. These differences can be illustrated by examining how the new systems enable three key new models:

- A new model for workgroups
- A new model for communication
- A new model for information

Workgroup model

The new systems are designed with extended workgroups in mind. These groups are no longer fixed, immobile groups of people working within the walls of a single company. They encompass a much broader collection of people. Extended workgroups cross organizational boundaries and can include business partners such as vendors, suppliers, and contractors. In addition, they can include occasionally connected users: salespeople, executives who travel, people who work at home or in remote offices, and others who may not be continuously connected to the company network, but who still are an integral part of a business process.

Whatever the process, people are working together. Take the familiar process of handling customer service inquiries. The people involved in this process may work in different departments and buildings, are at times linked to customer sites, and include users worldwide who are only occasionally connected to the network. This model differs dramatically from traditional back office applications, where users work continuously on-line, or form a fixed, easily defined workgroup. The new model is specifically designed to address the ad hoc nature of teams which may be constantly changing depending on the nature of a project.

Communication model

The new strategic systems also require a new model for communication. To be an effective knowledge base, the new model must present users with the means to tap important information, without necessarily knowing the names or locations of the people with whom they wish to communicate. E-mail starts the process. It provides an excellent message transport and is a good model for sending and receiving information from one person to one or more others.

That isn't enough. To truly share information, users need a new model. This form of information sharing is like a newspaper's classified advertising section. Rather than sending direct mail to thousands of people, the seller posts a notice in a place where interested parties know how to find it. One need not know the names of the target recipients; all that is needed is a database where people know where to look.

Data model

Strategic systems share information that is fundamentally different from the type of data stored in operational systems. The data types used by a workgroup performing a business process do not necessarily fit neatly into rows and columns. Business processes involve all types of data, much of it unstructured. The data may include memos, customer profile forms, or engineering change orders. There may be news feeds from outside information sources, faxes from customers, reports from operational databases, e-mail, scanned images, resumes, policy documents, or virtually any kind of information needed to make a business process work effectively.

The rows, columns, and records of relational databases are appropriate for operational systems such as order entry, but they don't fit most business process applications. The rich collection of information a salesperson uses to win against tough competition goes well beyond structured forms. This kind of information is usually captured in documents, and it requires a document-centered model for storage. This kind of document database can be viewed as a container for objects that can include information of all types. To find useful information in this rich collection of unstructured data, a new model for information access is also essential. Content-based search methods, such as full text search, are more suitable to this new model than the structured query language (SQL)-based search methods of operational systems.

Putting the Group in Groupware

As thousands of organizations have found, the hard part of installing Notes is not putting it on the network. The more difficult, and more important, task is to install the right mode of thinking within the group. More than a few efforts at group dynamics via Notes have foundered because the organizations paid more attention to the "ware" than to the group.

Keys to success

- Reward teams, not individuals
- Get management support
- Help employees think as a group
- Identify a specific program
- Let employees know they can take risks

A major New York advertising agency attempting a large-scale Notes installation encountered a typical pair of problems:

- One large class of people was so anxious to get up and running, their demands overwhelmed the ability of the technical staff to get the network in place. People became impatient when it took several months to get them hooked up.

- Another equally difficult class was made up of people who had no idea what Notes was supposed to do for them. One subclass of this group had no knowledge of Notes's potential; another group had no interest. In the first group was an employee who suggested that Notes would be a great vehicle for preparing periodic status reports—not understanding that Notes automatically generates such reports and there is no need to create them.

Rebound to reality

When an organization starts to look at a product like Notes, the idea can look very attractive. The organization may already be going through a process of downsizing and reengineering. In those circumstances, groupware can look like the ideal way to connect new, ad hoc, organizational structures. In fact, the very appeal of Notes is that it empowers people to work together in these new organizational forms.

Notes lets individuals share information freely and easily. It also lets them customize their own views of the workgroup's information so they can use it in the most effective way. An individual can create a personal database, which could be a personal contact list or a system to manage an involved business process. Notes also can be linked directly to corporate databases; an individual can extract information from an Oracle or Sybase server, and transmit it around the network in a full multimedia presentation.

These are high expectations, and it is necessary to prepare people for the inevitable rebound to reality. Most organizations are ill prepared for the cultural changes and new ways of working Notes encourages. Groupware encourages flat, flexible organizations and emphasizes group productivity. Many companies still maintain highly structured organizations with every role delineated on an organization chart and an emphasis on individual performance. Notes does not fit well in such organizations.

For reasons like these, many companies have had to scale back ambitious Notes projects, or accept longer implementation periods than they had anticipated.

Many executives interviewed a few years ago at a workgroup computing conference actually said they were afraid to put Notes in their organizations. "I don't want everyone empowered," said one. "Notes is like a virus," another declared. "Once it gets in, it spreads by itself." The second comment is at least apt. Notes has something in common with early PCs and more recent Macintoshes. If people can't bring them in through the front door, they will come in through the back. Or, as a Lotus executive put it more gently, Notes is an evolutionary product, not a revolutionary one.

Individual resistance

Individuals can be just as resistant as organizations. Some people believe the information they hold is the key to personal power. Government is characterized by this attitude, but the private sector is not far behind. When groupware knocks down barriers to information, it also deprives these people of a sense of power.

There was one case in which a group of employees refused to use Notes for anything other than e-mail. Some of these employees did not want to share information with their colleagues. They feared they would lose a competitive edge within the organization. Some simply did not want to take the time to learn Notes because it cut into their billable hours.

Hard to accept

There are many reasons organizations are not enthusiastic about adopting groupware, among them:

- Few organizations devote as much effort to improving their ability to collaborate as they do improving their business processes.

Danger signs

- Rigid structure
- Lack of focus
- Information is power
- No evaluation tools
- Few technical resources
- Employees evaluated as individuals

- Few managers understand exactly how technology can help build their organizations' collaborative processes. Few expect collaboration to happen whatever the circumstances.

- Few technical professionals know enough about workgroup interaction to propose technology that will improve that process.

- Most groups that deal with organizational issues have enough to worry about already.

- The problems with implementing groupware are overwhelmingly people-oriented, not technical.

- Groupware is a new, fast-changing technology in which today's truth can be tomorrow's—make that tonight's—historical relic.

Barriers to groupware

For all the promised advantages of groupware, there are some places where it just hasn't worked out. Other environments are visibly cool to the idea. Yet other organizations have rushed into groupware development without really thinking things through. They find that a seemingly simple software product has a huge impact on the way people work together within their organizations. Early users encountered problems like these:

- *Cultural conflict.*   Organizations that inject groupware into organizations that are unaccustomed to shared work and responsibility are courting danger. They must address their organizational needs at least as early as they do their technical requirements. Large numbers of companies have failed to do this. "The success of groupware projects depends on people, not tech-

Barriers to groupware

- **Cultural conflict**
- **Inadequate human resources**
- **Underestimated cost**
- **Underestimated effort**
- **Information overload**
- **Poor incentives**
- **Support needs**
- **Duplicating others**

nology," says one Notes consultant. "It's incredible how few companies seem to understand this."

- *Inadequate human resources.*   Through mergers, reengineering, and downsizing (if there's a difference between any of these), many organizations have cast key employees adrift. Much could be written (and increasingly has been written) about the economic and social damage corporate America has caused by casting out employees to serve the instant gratification of stockholders. Where groupware is concerned, these personnel practices often have left organizations without the key people they need to help institute a groupware system.

- *Underestimated cost.*   Implementing a major Notes application can require millions of dollars in expense for both technical and human resources. Lotus can cite some instances of huge returns on these investments, but the investments still can be massive—and the returns are not guaranteed.

- *Development effort.*   Except for its e-mail component, Notes is not a finished piece of application software. Like any high-end database product, it is an application development platform. You still must get up on that platform and develop the applications.

- *Excess information.*   Like the Internet, a Notes network can grow to contain a large accumulation of sometimes esoteric information, available from a variety of unseen sources. The resulting body of information can be so large and diverse it's hard to find what you want. People who once had too little information now have too much—and are no better off.

- *Misdirected incentives.*   Even when a company preaches group collaboration and implements Notes to provide it, pay and appraisal practices continue to reward individual performance. Stories abound of workers assembled into work teams, then subjected at year's end to traditional performance appraisals that emphasized their individual accomplishments. In that atmosphere many worry with good reason that someone else may take credit for the effort and ideas they shared with the group.

- *Support requirements.*   A major Notes installation requires a large, well-designed network. It requires continuing support, particularly to keep servers alive and pumping.

- *Me-too implementations.*   Many companies see their competitors adopting workgroup systems and rush to do the same thing. They don't stop to determine either the problems or the advantages they will bring to the unique environs of their own organizations.

There Are Solutions

One solution for the professional firm might have been a compensation plan that rewarded an employee when a colleague made a sale based on information the employee provided. There's nothing like the smell of extra money to send people digging through a database.

Those who have been there also say it's important to ensure that Notes is part of a revised business process, not the cause of it. If you are reengineering, introduce Notes at the same time, not before or after. Groupware can help an organization make the transition to a modern, more flexible, organi-

It takes the right formula

- Offer the right incentives
- Focus on a business need
- Involve management

zational style. In such an environment, an employee can gain power by sharing information rather than keeping it secret.

Offer incentives

If you want people to work together, don't just hand them a disk of software. Give them the right incentives, too. No one is going to post important information in a Notes database if there's reason to believe someone else will make use of it and take all the credit. It's an old management truism that the behavior you reward is the behavior you get.

One solution for the professional firm might be a compensation plan that rewards an employee when a colleague makes a sale based on information the employee provided. Management can easily reward individuals whose work is cited or downloaded. You can come from the other direction, too. Managers whose workers do not contribute to the network, or draw resources from it, should suffer black marks on their appraisals for failing to encourage professional development.

Concentrate on need

Another key to successful Notes implementation is to draw a clear distinction between the technology and the business need it is expected to answer. The Association for Information and Image Management (AIIM), an industry group based in Silver Spring, MD, has been conducting an active campaign to get prospective workgroup customers to concentrate first on what they want their applications to do before deciding what they should buy. AIIM has been spreading this message through a series of trade show conferences.

This is old advice, which has been given to prospective computer users for as long as there have been computers to use. Nevertheless, the advice is often still necessary. Organizations become enamored with new technology, or try to imitate other organizations without fully analyzing what a product like Notes can do for them.

One reason lies in the fluid definition of workgroup computing. Ray Ozzie, the creator of Notes (ironically, an individual invented the world's leading group action software), points out that previous PC software products emulate familiar objects. The spreadsheet, word processor, and database management systems have physical counterparts in the ledger sheet, the typewriter, and the file cabinet. Notes emulates a process, not a product, so many people find it hard to grasp it.

Information Management Consultants (McLean, VA) says Notes requires that you take a different view of your business requirements. For example, the conventional approach to automating a loan processing would be to ask questions like these:

- How many loan applications are processed per week or month?
- What critical information do these applications contain?

- How much storage is required?

From a workflow point of view, you should ask questions like these:

- Which processes are triggered when a loan application is received?
- Who must read and respond to the application?
- After the application is filed, will it be needed again in the process?

Involve management

It's also important to get the support of top management. That may be a business cliché, but it has special meaning in a workgroup setting where many applications are home-grown by individuals and small groups.

To interest management, cite a specific goal for the project. In the loan application case, the goal might be to improve customer service by reducing the turnaround time for loan applications. At the same time, provide a way to measure the results, so you can demonstrate—you certainly hope—that the project has been worth its cost. The most direct measurement in the loan application case would be an increase in customer satisfaction with your speedier processing times. Less direct but certainly just as important would be to demonstrate increased revenue, reduced costs, or both.

Implementing a Workgroup System

A good workgroup application is not imposed top-down from the IS department. Neither is it an entirely home-grown product, created by a lone user. In the spirit of working together, a good workgroup installation comes from both resources.

The impetus often comes from line managers responsible for particular products or functions. These individuals know the details of the business process

Get going

- Identify a business need
- Get management involved
- Start a pilot group
- Expand the pilot
- Get commitment

and are in a position to recommend ways to make that process run more smoothly. The department resource also is the person who is in the best position to evaluate the results.

You cannot achieve the best results, though, without the involvement of technical specialists. These are the people who will have to provide the networks and software to make the workgroup project happen. The ideal development team is a mix of department-level and technical people, working together to explore the potential of the technology to expand the potential of the process. Not incidentally, this is an opportunity for IS professionals to practice what has been so widely preached: to become more involved with business processes.

Steps to success

Unlike some earlier forms of computing, including the PC itself, workgroup computing can achieve tangible, quantifiable, results. But if you are to have something to quantify, implementation must be a planned, orderly process that proceeds through a series of steps:

- *Define the business objectives.* Know what you want to accomplish. Don't implement workgroup computing on a vague notion that something good will come of it.

- *Select a workable pilot project.* Identify a realistic product that can produce measurable results.

- *Assemble a team.* In other words, create a workgroup to deal with workgroup computing.

- *Identify the group.* Determine the size and scope of the group to which the project is applied.

- *Identify the benefits.* These must be tangible benefits you can measure and report to management.

- *Analyze the process.* Make sure you understand how it works now, and how workgroup computing can improve it.

- *Improve the process.* Determine how you can achieve your objective and attain the benefits by enhancing the process.

- *Get management commitment.* Few good things happen without this.

- *Select vendors.* Decide what kind of outsourced help you need, and the best places to find it.

- *Schedule the implementation process.* Set a schedule and deadlines for key steps.

- *Check up on yourself.* Conduct a postimplementation analysis to determine what went well, what did not, and how you can apply that knowledge to the next project.

Defining goals

You need not start out with a comprehensive set of clearly defined goals, though establishing those objectives is a goal in itself. It is better to start with general statements. Say, for example, you want to improve the productivity of a customer service group. The natural next thought is to define what you mean by improved productivity. Then you could begin to assess exactly how an improved workgroup process could accomplish that. As you proceed, your objectives become more detailed until they can stand alone as final statements. By starting with general statements you improve your chances of making rational, realistic decisions.

Once the initial goals are set, sort them into two groups: strategic and tactical. You'll probably find that meeting the strategic goals will require substantial change; achieving the tactical goals will be relatively easy.

These initial steps will help you understand what you hope to achieve, and what you realistically can achieve. In the process, you will also begin to gain an understanding of exactly what it will take to get there.

Picking a pilot

There is no rule which says you must implement a single application at a time. Many successful programs have simultaneously applied workgroup computing to more than one project. There is a rule, though, that says it takes more than twice as long to do two things at once.

It's important, though, that in selecting a pilot project you avoid one that could become too successful. A pilot that proves a crashing success could eat up resources as hordes of employees clamor to take advantage of it. From the originator's standpoint, meanwhile, it could prove to be a tough act to follow. Try instead to pick an important application with strong support among the people who will use it. Then, set realistic expectations and ask management only for reasonable resources.

Assembling the team

The implementation team for your chosen pilot project should be a diverse group. There should be a mix of people representing IS, management, and the client department. Furthermore, the group should be well balanced so no one discipline can dominate the rest. One of this group's most important tasks is to gain an understanding of the process with which they are working.

Identify the group

Another important group is made up of the people who will work with the completed project. A good group is small enough to work cohesively but large enough to give the pilot project a good test. That may mean 100 people in a large organization; half a dozen in a small company.

If you must err, do so on the side of selecting too small a group. Identify a compact group of well-motivated people, and draw the boundaries of the project around this group. This makes it easier to conduct a successful pilot. You can always expand the project later when it proves successful.

Network resources are another consideration. Don't let the project fail for technical reasons. The group should have an established network capable of supporting Notes. This is no time to be making technical changes, too. Also make sure the group has enough technical support—they should not have to rely on a harried IS employee who already has too much to do.

Consider, too, the types of jobs represented. Almost by definition, groupware involves multiple job skills and specialties. The fewer of these you include in the pilot group, though, the lower the training and implementation effort.

Measure the benefits

Management is all about measurement. Some results are easier to quantify than others, but you must provide some measure of achievement and added value to the organization.

Establish baseline measurements before you start the project. Track such things as the time needed to complete a document or to respond to a customer service call. Also consider counting the number of requests for support. Measure these factors again when the project is in place.

Intangible results are harder to measure, but they can be just as important. Include measurements of:

- The general knowledge gained by participants in the implementation process
- Improved morale
- The ability to complete cross-training between job specialties
- Improved communication
- Greater access to information

Employee surveys can provide measurements of some of the factors like morale. Measure information access by the length of time it takes someone to find information. As a rule of thumb, if group members spend more than 25 percent of their time looking for information and retrieving it, they can benefit from a workgroup automation process.

Analyzing the process

To make sure you understand the process you are trying to improve, construct a series of charts. One should describe the overall activities to be accomplished, as they are now being done. A second chart should describe the same process, as it would exist in an ideal world. A third chart should show the worst-case analysis, with Murphy's law in full force and effect.

Then, take each step in these charts and break it down into a series of tasks. Look for the common tasks—those that are performed regularly and by large numbers of people. Talk with the people who perform these tasks. Determine the value of each step. You may well learn that the process that takes place at the work site is much different than management thinks it is.

This process can help you build a list of requirements for the revised version. In particular, it can help balance the client department's desire for more features with the system's ability to provide them. Identify the specific need for each feature, then compare it with the cost and time needed to produce it.

Selecting vendors

As the process proceeds, many organizations will need professional help. This can take many forms, including:

- Systems or software vendors
- Systems integrators and VARs
- Consultants
- Internal resources

You can use any of these, or a mixture, as suits your needs. Considerations include:

- Whether the project is strategic or tactical
- The availability of internal resources
- The nature and scope of the pilot application
- Current and future network resources
- Anticipated growth of workgroup technology

If your resources are limited, and your objective is to meet tactical needs, some combination of VAR and consulting resources may be best. If your interest is strategic, and you expect a high growth rate, consider a software or systems vendor.

Scheduling implementation

The implementation process will move through many steps, including:

- Application design
- Pilot test
- Training
- System testing
- User acceptance testing

- Feature and function review
- Final application development
- Second pilot test
- Second round of training and testing
- Establishing support
- Signing off

Initial plans should include preparing a schedule of these activities. Make sure all these issues are addressed, and at the proper times.

Postmortem

No, the job is not done when the project is finally implemented. Was it ever otherwise?

About 2 or 3 months after implementation, take a good look at how well the project has succeeded. Look back at the list of expected benefits. Are you actually getting them? Can you measure the results?

Also review the implementation process itself and determine how it can be improved.

4

Getting a Handle on Workflow

Everyone talks about the weather, but nobody does anything about it. Mark Twain didn't say that (it was his editor friend Charles Dudley Warner), but many developing categories of computer technology are something like that.

Take workflow management. Everyone seems to know what it is, but hardly anyone can give you a precise definition. The definitions of workflow management and its component parts tend to be indistinct, arbitrary, or both. That may be just as well, though, because you can write your own definition. Then you can put it to work, improving the way your organization works.

Why Workflow?

In today's competitive marketplace, business strategy must focus on the concept of a business as a set of core capabilities, linking customer needs to customer satisfaction through a chain of value-adding activities. These activities and processes are inherently knowledge-based as most organizations focus on creating and managing intellectual property. The model for managing this new type of organization is no longer top-down, but network and team-oriented.

Bigger job for information systems

With shorter life cycles for products and services, companies are placing greater value on anticipating market trends and customer needs. Information systems (IS) can no longer just support business functions like accounts receivable or order entry. Now they must link all of an organization's activities. In marketing alone, these computerized activities can include lead generation programs, sales prospecting, account management, marketing research, and product design and development. The process must manage them as connected parts of a closed loop. The voice of the customer must pass through the organization with a minimum of filtering. This process of turning customer needs into delivered products must be managed both for maximum effectiveness and minimum process time.

Information systems must deliver all the information, not just operational data, required for doing all jobs in the chain. By managing information across organizational boundaries and treating related but separate activities as part of a coherent process, companies can compress the time involved in these critical business cycles. New IS must also manage the sharing of critical information, expertise, and knowledge that leads to effective decision making by members at all levels of the organization. This shared information makes it possible to create team-oriented organizations.

Supporting the new model

Workflow software is designed for this new organizational model. Workflow applications support specific business processes and are tied closely to the roles played by individuals in the workgroup. At each stage individuals will add value to the process by evaluating and making judgments, or by adding and editing new information. A workflow application provides an environment that both captures information and moves it through a work process, ensuring that each member of the workgroup can find the pieces of information needed to do this individual's piece of the job.

Workflow systems also provide a context in which work is performed, allowing individuals to concentrate on the work at hand, rather than on the process itself. By tying information directly to business processes, workflow software has the potential to return significant value on the investments that have been made in information technology.

Step by Step

In its elementary form, a work process is the sequence of steps that gets a particular job done. The process is not the job itself. It is the way the job is accomplished. Every business has processes. General Motors has a standard process for assembling a pickup truck. At the other extreme, an individual running a one-person business often follows a standard, if unconscious process, when screening the day's mail. Regardless of size, when you manage a process, you make it more predictable. Usually the process will also be more efficient and effective.

The process need not always follow exactly the same steps every time. It can vary depending on conditions. For example, you might create separate processes for resolving customer complaints about product quality, as opposed to complaints about service. An early step in the process of resolving a complaint would be to classify the complaint. On that basis, you would assign it to one resolution track or the other. The critical point is that you manage the variations depending on the conditions you encounter. You don't just choose different methods at random.

Automating the process

Workflow automation automates these processes. In its elementary form, you computerize the process of paper-shuffling. Instead of manually tracking a document as it flits from desk to desk, you monitor and manage a series of e-mail transactions. Typically, a server-based mail router moves documents between database files or electronic mailboxes.

A rules-based system can automate the process of managing which variations on the basic process are in order. For example, in the two-track customer service process, a workflow management system would apply a set of rules to determine whether the complaint concerned a product or a service; then it would route the complaint accordingly.

Understanding Workflow Management

For openers, *workflow* is one small syllable removed from *workgroup*. That's more than a linguistic accident; the two words are close companions. If *workgroup* describes the work the group does, it stands to reason that *workflow* deals with the flow of that work. That's an important distinction. When you manage workflow, you manage a *business process*.

The International Data Corporation defines workflow management this way:

> Workflow empowers individuals and groups of individuals in both structured and unstructured work environments to automatically manage a series of recurrent or nonrecurrent events in a way that achieves the business objectives of the company. At the same time, workflow software should allow feedback to management, ensuring it the opportunity and ability to extend or modify these basic processes as the business environment changes.

Document routing is a common form of workflow management. You manage the process of getting an invoice or a purchase order to all the parties who must

What is workflow management?

- Managing a business process
- The process, not the job

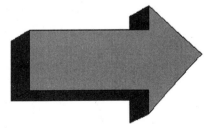

Popular workflow projects

- Multiple processes
  - Help desk
- Different forms and views
- Monitoring progress
- Spotting problems

approve or process it, making sure it passes through all the right hands, in the right order, and within the allotted time. In fact, many workflow processes involve routing paperwork through a chain of approvals by higher authority. Approvals aren't a necessary part of the process, though. Publishing a newsletter is the kind of business process that lends itself well to workflow management, but instead of tracking approvals, you route the newsletter through writing, editing, printing, and other steps of the publishing process.

What you can automate

Applications like document routing are fast becoming the kindergarten blocks of workflow management. Nearly any workflow application gives you the means to manage basic and well-known processes. Workflow management can handle those chores plus many more like these:

- *Managing multiple operations.* A PC help desk may log several calls during a day, and several problem resolution processes will be in various stages at the same time.

- *Providing different information to different people.* Different people in the process need different information to perform their roles. A workflow management system can present different forms and screen displays, each emphasizing the information the recipient needs.

- *Helping management monitor progress.* Managers can keep track of resource use, individual workloads, production cycles, and delayed projects.

- *Providing access to corporate information systems.* A workflow management system often includes links to client/server and legacy databases.

Advanced uses

- Monitoring resource use
- Approving applications
- Enhanced document management
- Hiring

- *Flagging and correcting problem areas.* A workflow management system can be designed to check regularly for delayed projects, resource shortages, or overloaded employees. You can go further, and insert rules that automatically resolve these cases, such as by reassigning a task to a less busy employee.

Expanded functions

As new workflow management systems are developed, they expand this basic list. Many of the newest systems involve more sophisticated forms of document management: large-scale imaging or document management tools with database access and full production capacity.

Advanced products start from familiar foundations and add additional functions. In particular, high-end systems are making it possible to establish more precise kinds of control over more complex processes. In this context, document routing is an elementary process. The more advanced products give you the power to manage a high-volume transaction load.

Some of the processes to which workflow management products have been developed include:

- A form of project management that monitors human and physical resources throughout a business process. Management can identify overloaded and underused resources and spot bottlenecks.

- Vertical market applications for such activities as processing mortgage applications and insurance claims.

- Enhanced document management products that monitor documents as they move between workstations.

Look around

As a workflow management user, you can also expand your own horizons. Vendors and consultants tend to concentrate on the most obvious uses. To get full value, look for the less obvious workflows that could profit from better management.

Take the process of hiring a new employee. Do you advertise the opening, and if so where? A rule-based system could respond to the type of opening being filled and help you direct your recruiting efforts where they will be most likely to attract the right kind of person.

Then, you must set up interviews, often more than one. Again, you can incorporate rules that schedule interviews with the right people, at times when these people are available. If several people will then participate in the hiring process, you can get them together and display the criteria for making their judgments.

When the employee is hired, another workflow process begins. The new hand must go through certain processes such as establishing a personnel file and signing up for health insurance. You can route the individual through the process, making sure nothing is missed. The process can continue, assigning the new employee to a desk, procuring a computer and software—and making sure the software is properly licensed.

Types of workflow applications

Workflow applications come in various types, so naturally several authorities have tried to categorize them. Just as naturally, various authorities have used various classification schemes. A composite of the leading methods might look like this:

Types of workflow applications

- Production
  - Static
  - Dynamic
- Ad Hoc
- Collaborative

- *Production applications* are repeated from time to time. Often, the times are very short. For example, you would follow a similar process every time you evaluate a loan application. Processing insurance claims or credit applications are typical applications in this class.

- *Ad hoc applications* are often one-time projects whose processes are created for the occasion. You might use this kind of application to plan a product announcement or conduct a survey. Even if you reuse this process, it may not be for a few months or longer. An ad hoc application is not necessarily a small one. Preparing the architectural plans for a new building would be a very large ad hoc project.

Production applications can be subdivided into two types:

- *Static applications* are relatively simple and routine. You follow a well-established process every time. Claims and credit processing both would fall into this class.

- *Dynamic applications* tend to be complex and often rely heavily on rules and conditional responses. They often require that you coordinate many varied activities. Common examples include sales tracking, processing purchase orders, and managing customer service requests.

Typical of most classification systems, there is not total agreement on the system itself. For example, some people recognize the two types of production applications as separate classes. Others recognize yet another class, administrative workflow, which combines elements of both production and ad hoc systems.

Wherever you drill your pigeonholes, any process in which work flows through a great number of people is a candidate for workflow management. The main value of classification is to help you understand just how that flow progresses. Understanding the process is the necessary first step to managing it.

New developments

In addition, the field is expanding so rapidly new types of workflow management applications are appearing all the time. For example, some new products have been classified as *collaborative*. This small but growing classification consists of high-value, nonrepetitive transaction processes. In fact, the research firm BIS Strategic Decisions predicts this will be a growing form of workflow management (Fig. 4.1).

Products in this group tend to be high-end document and collaborative process management tools. Examples include:

- New product development
- Sales force automation
- Document assembly

Workflow's Growth Potential

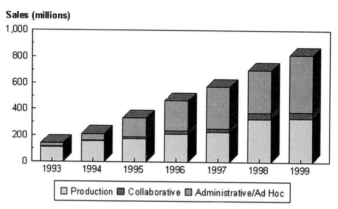

Figure 4.1 Ad hoc applications will form an increasing share of workflow development.

Two product levels

- High-end
  - Based on document management
- Desktop
  - Based on e-mail

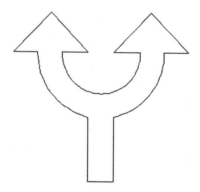

Types of Workflow Products

Just as there are several types of workflow management applications, there are several types of workflow management products. As usual, there is disagreement about which classifications to use, but conventional wisdom recognizes at least these two:

- High-end products, usually rooted in document management, that handle complex processes enterprise-wide in a client/server system.

■ Desktop systems, usually with e-mail origins. These are standard PC applications like Microsoft Exchange or Novell's Groupwise. These typically run at the small workgroup level over local area networks.

Notes falls between these two classes. Initially, it fits at the high end of the desktop group. It is increasingly being used, though, as a front-end product for higher-end tools.

Workflow architecture

Workflow systems can be built on any of three technical architectures:

■ Electronic messaging systems

■ Distributed document management systems

■ Relational database systems.

Each of these architectures includes unique ability to handle the process logic of workflow applications. Each is appropriate for a different type of workflow application.

Electronic messaging

Because of its store-and-forward architecture, e-mail is suitable for some routing applications, where information is passed from point to point in a standard sequence. The administrative forms routing that used to be done with paper is ideally suited for mail-based systems. Examples of mail-based workflows include travel authorization or expense report approvals. A more advanced example might include a credit approval process, which would take a sales order, route it to various people who could perform standard credit checks, forward those records to the manager responsible for approval, and finally route the approval back to the sales administrator, who could then confirm the transaction. This type of workflow application is generally easy to install, set up, and administer, and requires minimal system resources and cost.

Mail-based workflow applications add process logic through macros or scripts that determine routing sequences and build in latitude for action by players in the process. Macros embedded in the mail form can determine what information to display, what to prompt the user for, and where to mail the form next. Since mail is essentially a delivery technology, workflow applications that use a messaging foundation carry all information about the process in the individual mail message or routed form.

Distributed document management

This type of system, which includes Notes, often appears as a compromise between extremes. Document management combined the flexibility and user accessibility of mail-based systems with the security, concurrency control, and sharing of database management system (DBMS)-based systems. Since the Notes architecture is based on a shared document database with integrated messaging, information can be both routed and shared as part of a process, depending on the nature of the work. Users can query the system about the status of the work and the process itself.

This technology is best suited for applications that require collaboration among members of a group. For example, a collaborative application could involve a process such as tracking incoming customer service calls, where logging a single call might generate both a mail message to the salesperson for that customer, as well as an entry in a database that records and tracks the resolution of the customer's problem.

Notes' client/server architecture lets it monitor the workflow process from an agent on the database server, ensuring the integrity of the process. This agent can be programmed to monitor events such as receipt of new documents, user actions, or elapsed time, and also to trigger actions such as changing field values or mailing out messages. Unlike messaging or other file-based systems, this server-based agent can be used to manage a workflow process through to completion. In a customer service application, the workflow agent can be programmed to automatically update fields in the tracking database to reflect the changes in status as the problem is worked through its various phases before resolution.

Relational databases

Structured databases and traditional transaction processing systems are built to manage structured and high-volume workflow processes. Relational database management systems (RDBMSs) are very good at handling transactions through a centralized data store, so RDBMS-based workflow applications are useful for centrally managed processes that require real-time precision and data handling. While centrally managed processing guarantees strong data integrity, it also places significant demands on a network infrastructure, requiring interactive access by all users at all times. DBMS-based approaches are also weak in supporting the compound documents that contain the work itself.

DBMS-based systems are generally used for structured, repetitive processes such as insurance claims processing, inventory handling, and other back office business operations. These applications generally are written by IS professionals, have little room for exception handling, and do not allow for user customization. Workflow process logic that includes work-oriented variables such as user roles, elapsed time, and work documents is beyond the data definition and manipulation capabilities that characterize most database applications. These systems also do not offer a conventional way of embedding workflow process logic into the server's native execution environment.

Workflow problems

Like any new and growing field, workflow management suffers some areas where it still needs help. They include:

- *Lack of a standard definition.* This makes it harder to evaluate products and their vendors' promises and to understand exactly what workflow management can do for you. A Workflow Management Coalition, composed of leading vendors, has been working on some common standards, including a basic definition of their product class.

- *The nature of workflow management products.* By and large, these are application development tools, not finished applications. A prospective customer cannot open a box and see exactly how a product would manage a specific in-house process.

- *Resistance to change.* To get the full benefit of workflow management, you often must change established procedures. Whenever someone brings change, some employees naturally fear and resist it. Delphi Consulting, a Boston market research firm, conducted a survey which found that cultural resistance was the single biggest obstacle to adopting workflow management. The need to reengineer business processes was next. Technical issues like cost and immature technology were reported as much less significant (Fig. 4.2).

Inside a workflow application

An authorization for travel expenses is an example of a fairly static process. The process can go something like this:

Workflow problems

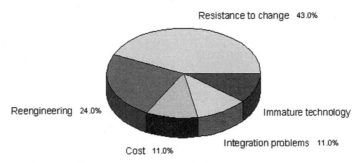

Figure 4.2 Human problems outnumber technical difficulties.

1. Either the traveler or a support staff member fills out a request for the authorization.

2. The request travels by e-mail to each person who must approve it. The request document is sent as an attachment to each e-mail message.

3. Each approving authority reviews the request, and clicks on a button indicating his or her decision.

4. When all approving authorities have completed their forms, the request is marked as approved or disapproved.

5. The decision is forwarded to the requester.

6. A daily progress report updates management on the status of each request.

If you want a more sophisticated system, you could include rules that flag exceptions to established criteria, such as maximum allowable rates for hotel rooms or rental cars. An approving authority may decide to approve the request anyway—perhaps the hotel is in a resort city where lower-priced rooms are not available. In any event, the system could call attention to the exceptions. It could also go further and impose a rule that requires the approving authority to justify any expenses that exceed established levels.

Workflow and Notes

Notes is more a workgroup than a workflow product. But since a workflow usually proceeds through a workgroup, Notes can serve many of the basic workflow functions. Its message-based architecture and comprehensive database management abilities make it attractive for many types of applications.

Leading roles for Notes

- Basic, forms-based processing
- E-mail processing
- Link to high-end systems

A popular use is to build message databases for transmissions over enterprise networks.

Notes has several features that lend themselves to workflow processing including:

- Forms-based action buttons
- Standard form templates
- Signature controls
- Document version control

These features are often all you need to implement a basic workflow application.

Notes may be even more valuable as a transport mechanism for other workflow tools. In that respect, Notes is an enabling technology. Notes can make it possible, or at least easier, to implement workflow projects that go far beyond Notes's basic abilities.

The basic approach

For example, when a northeastern consulting firm installed Notes, one of its first projects was to improve the process of ordering systems and software for its 15 remote offices. Under the former system, orders were transmitted to the main office by fax.

The firm now handles the entire procedure in Notes, using forms built from standard Notes templates. The only thing necessary to set up the process was to modify some of the document templates that were shipped with the product.

Enabling role

A Florida-based insurance company added workflow ability to Notes by adding a third-party project management package (QAW from Quality Decision Management Inc., North Andover, MA). Like many recently produced workflow products, QAW can run in conjunction with Notes. The combined package runs on a network that initially served 85 employees.

The business objective was to improve the firm's responsiveness to internal requests. It might take some time, for example, for headquarters to respond to a request for a Human Resources service. There was no system of feedback or progress reports. To an employee, the request would seem to disappear into a black hole. Even though work may be progressing, the employee could see no visible signs that anything was happening.

The new Notes-based process provides more feedback. The request is submitted as a Notes document. At any time later, the originator can call up that document, which then will include a log of everything that has taken place so far.

Son of e-mail

Though workflow management is primarily seen in terms of imaging and document management, e-mail is also an important ancestor. As demonstrated by Notes's popularity as a workflow management system, e-mail can be the foundation of many workflow management systems, particularly the ad hoc variety where the actual flow of work may follow no predetermined pattern.

Certainly, the popularity of e-mail has helped spur demand for better workflow management. A typical e-mail system uses forms, similar to familiar paper documents. It is fairly easy to add some form of document management to the everyday e-mail system. Since workgroup members are working with a familiar process, they need little further training to participate in the workflow management system.

There's another advantage to this kind of system. Some IS departments have been slow to implement workflow management on an enterprise level. A workflow system based on e-mail is easy to implement department by department. The obvious downside is that the organization may find itself with a multitude of workflow systems. If these are based on an enterprisewide e-mail system, though, this should be of little consequence. The individualized systems will usually be confined to small groups working on ad hoc projects.

With its database management feature added to its e-mail component, Notes takes this process a large dimension further. A Notes-based system not only offers e-mail, but also makes it easy to manage the forms and documents involved in the typical workflow management system.

Workflow alternatives

Workflow management is a bureaucratic system in a way: it depends largely on processing forms. Notes's built-in forms lend themselves to workflow processing; if you need heavier duty from a Notes-based product, Lotus Forms operates in a mixed-system e-mail atmosphere. Each form in this system holds its own routing logic, letting it travel in a prescribed routing path from creation to approvals. Each form can also contain fields that can be given any number of attributes.

The Lotus products and others like the newest versions of Novell's Groupwise, are based on e-mail. Newer, higher-end products are moving workflow management into the client/server area. There is a natural fit here: both workflow management and client/server systems usually involve reengineering business processes. A workflow-enabled client/server application brings a high level of automation to business processes. As such, it becomes an engine for redesigning the processes it manages.

Workflow Examples

Travel authorization is one example of a simple, but useful, type of workflow application you can use from within Notes. This database is a central repository for travel authorization requests as they travel the route through creation, approval or rejection, and tracking. You can use this database to track and update the status of travel authorization requests. Traveling employees can use the views in the database to check the current status of their requests. Supervisors whose responsibility is to approve travel requests can use the database to check their pending work, and to approve or reject requests.

The process

The process begins when the traveler or an assistant fills out a travel authorization request (Fig. 4.3). A lower part of the form includes database fields in which the initiator can specify the authorities who must approve the request (Fig. 4.4).

When the initiator saves the request in the database, each manager who must approve the request receives an e-mail message. This message reports that the request has been initiated and includes a document link to the request document. The manager can double-click on the doc link to call up the request form.

Customer service: a more complex process

Customer service is a more complex application. It can use as many as five databases:

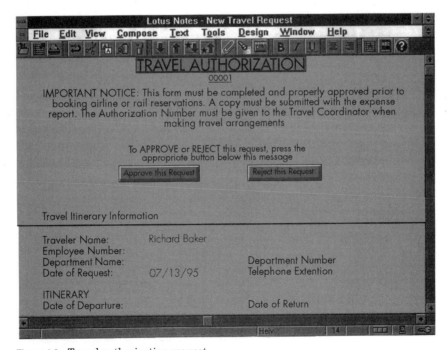

Figure 4.3 Travel authorization request.

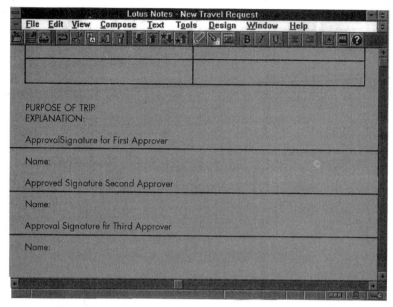

Figure 4.4 Signature blocks.

- A call tracking database
- A database of information on the company's products
- A collection of previous problem reports, and solutions
- A list of customer requests and suggestions
- A keyword list that stores key phrases with which to search records

Customer service applications vary, but the workflow process can go something like this:

1. A customer service representative receives a call and opens a call report in the call tracking database (Fig. 4.5).

2. The representative makes an assessment of how serious the problem is and rates it on a scale (Fig. 4.6). If the rating exceeds a preset number, designated managers receive e-mail messages alerting them to the problem. These messages include doc links to the call report.

3. The call report presents the representative with a list of standard problem types. Depending on the selection from this list, the problem will be assigned to a support specialist in the appropriate department. If the representative feels it is better to assign the problem to someone outside the standard list, it can be done manually. For example, the representative may know of a specialist who is uniquely qualified to deal with the problem.

4. If the caller suggests a solution or problem improvement, the representative can route the call report to the product suggestion database as well as

Caller Information

321-95-143 - Subscribers
Nathalie Beautz ("Nat")
[Submitted by Esteban Garcia on 04/09/94]

| Edit Document | Print Document |
| Call Statistics | Research |

Short Description: Wants author's address

Problem Details:

Wants to know where she can write to the author of "Night Falling" from the March issue.

Severity Level: Low impact

Product Fields: Kic Poets Monthy / Magazines
Other

Call History:

1 : Esteban Garcia 04/09/94 01:27:42 PM
Gave her our mailing address and said we would forward letters to the author.

Date of Call: 04/09/94 12:23 PM
Assigned To: Esteban Garcia   **Work Group:** Customer Service

Call Status: Resolved

Figure 4.5 Call tracking form.

the call tracking list. The representative can select a priority level for implementing the suggestion.

5. If the caller provides information that might be useful in responding to future calls, this information can be routed to the customer suggestion database.

Decisions, decisions

Count the number of decisions being made here. Most, including assessments of severity and priority, are made on the spot by the representative who receives the call. There are other instances, though, in which the system makes the calls, such as when it routes particular problems to particular departments. Note, though, that even this automatic process has provisions for a manual override.

Designing a Workflow Application

In a standard business school exercise, the instructor builds a figure from toy blocks, then challenges students to duplicate it. The fastest time wins; the clock starts when you move the first block. The invariable winner is the student who plans every move before making the first one.

Nowhere is planning more valuable than in creating a workflow management application. It is vital that you understand the business process you are trying to improve before you start devising an application to make the improvements.

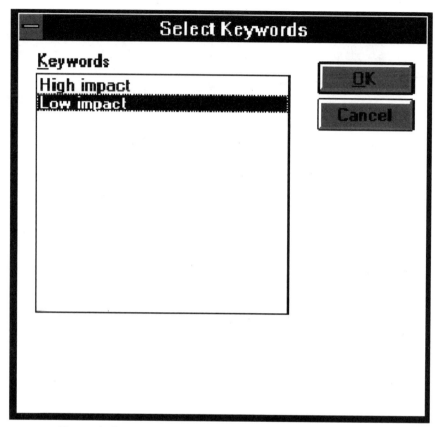

Figure 4.6 Keywords denote the severity of the complaint.

Designing a workflow application

- Define the business process
- Develop the application
- Put it into service

That's why the successful development of any workflow management system must begin with defining the business process you want to improve.

The complete process goes like this:

- *Define the business process.*   Find out how the current process operates. Look for problems and their causes. Define a new process that addresses these problems, then sketch in the specific details.

- *Develop the application.*   Start by building and testing one or more prototypes. Design the forms and views that will make up the application. Construct any macros or other programming elements you want to include.

- *Put it into service.*   Conduct a pilot test and smooth out any rough spots. Establish access controls. Provide for documentation and training, and develop a plan for long-term maintenance.

Defining the process

To understand and improve the process:

- *Learn how the present process works.*   That usually means interviewing people on all levels, from the managers responsible for the total process to the individuals who implement the details. Review existing forms and reports, both paper and electronic. Make sure you understand how the organization is structured and how work flows through it now.

- *Look for problems and areas for improvement.*   No doubt, the managers involved and other employees will be glad to point many of these out; you probably will discover others on your own. When you identify a problem,

Learning the business process

- How does the present process work?
- How can it be improved?
- What new process would work better?

probe further to discover its causes and effects. Be particularly alert for problems that originate in the work process.

- *Define a new process.* Establish goals, and review them with both management and workgroup members. Decide which parts of the current process, if any, you want to keep. Define the objects, actions, and roles that will exist within the new process, and draw a diagram of the ideal workflow. Submit these ideas for review and revision by management and affected employees.

- *Design and build the application.* This is now the easy part—relatively speaking, anyway.

Developing the application

That's not to say application development is quick. To build a dynamic application like workflow management will probably mean working through several prototypes, revisions, and refinements. You may go through this sequence, or parts of it, several times:

- *Build a prototype.* Concentrate on your primary goals and key features. Let a representative group of testers use it, and provide a form for their feedback. Don't be satisfied with bug reports alone. Ask the testers to report usability problems and areas for improvement. The main focus at this early stage should be to design an application that responds to your needs and goals. You can fix bugs later. Don't make the mistake of giving these prototypes solely to technicians and power users. They often overlook problems that become serious to less sophisticated clients.

- *Design the forms.* A well-designed form makes it easy to enter information, and more important, easy to enter it correctly. Readability is just as important. Like any on-screen display, a good form is not just the one that

Development steps

- Build a prototype
- Design forms and views
- Provide automated help

crams the most information into the available space. The best forms enhance the communication process.

- *Design the views.* Well-designed views let employees find and group the documents they need without excess effort. A view is not just a reference resource. It should make action easy. It should help employees complete their work properly with a minimum of supervision. Remember, too, that managers and approval authorities mentally classify their documents differently than those who originate the forms. The two groups may need different views of the same material.

- *Provide automated help.* Macros, functions, and other forms of coding give developers the means to help less experienced workgroup members. A clearly labeled button is a vast improvement over a block of wordy instructions. If entries must be from a certain list, provide the list in a drop-down box. If the application must send data to another application, make the transfer automatically. If your audience is limited to technically experienced people—and you are sure of that—you can simplify some of the instructions. The larger and more diverse the audience, though, the more likely it includes some beginners who will need help.

Managing the finished product

Implementation is another process that cannot be rushed. Start with a pilot test, again with a representative sample—ordinary employees as well as the technically knowledgeable. Again, too, concentrate on usability issues as well as bug fixes.

Changes and repairs you might have to make include:

- Reducing the number of forms and views
- Adjusting data validation procedures
- Improving screen displays
- Improving labels on fields and buttons
- Providing additional prompts
- Adding pop-up help

You also must provide for:

- *Security.* Make sure the application provides enough access control to prevent outside access to sensitive information.

- *Documentation and training.* Teaching people to use an application will be costly, both in direct expenses and indirect costs like lost time. Documentation should include clear instructions for new users as well as maintaining a record for future application maintenance. If you are producing a major application, a training professional or technical writer can save much more in grief than the services cost.

- *On-line help.* Take advantage of Notes's ability to maintain a help file as a database. You can also use doc links and popups to provide instant, on-the-job reference. Effective user aids can include:

  - Field help for quick reminders
  - Help buttons on forms
  - Pop-up annotations

- *Maintenance.* Appoint someone to take charge of this application, assist employees, and shoot troubles. This individual should have a manager's level of access to the database. If the application is large or critical, assign one or more assistant managers. The application's designers are good candidates for manager's positions, but remember, good Notes developers are in demand. The creators may not be here tomorrow.

Defining the Business Process

Workflow management is not really about software; it is about the business process you want to manage and improve. Don't confuse the business process with the computer application you create to manage it. The purpose of the application is to improve the process, make it easier, more efficient, and better managed. The application is a tool; the process represents the work you do with that tool.

One of your first assignments is to understand the process as it exists now. Find its strong and weak points. This understanding is your key to building a better process through workflow management.

The questions you must answer include:

- Why does this process exist?
- What starts this process?
- How do you know when it is successfully completed?

You can get the answers from the people most directly involved in the process: the managers who set the goals and standards, and the lower-level people who make the process work. Set up a series of interviews with representatives from all the people who make the process work. Include managers, technical users, and the not-so-technically-inclined.

The management perspective

There's a familiar proverb about distinguishing the forest from the trees. In workflow management, you need to keep an eye on both. The forest-wide perspective comes from the managers who use and supervise the current process and who will oversee the use of your application tool.

Tip: Carry a portable recorder and tape your interviews. Key people might not be available later to refresh your memory or fill in details.

Questions to ask include:

- What are the goals of the business process?
- What do you see as its strong and weak points? Why?
- What is the organizational structure of the group that uses this process?
- How is it managed and controlled?
- Which is more important: top performance, or ease of use and management?
- What do you expect from the new application? What are your criteria for its success?

Workgroup members as trees

If the managers are the foresters, workgroup members concern themselves with individual trees. Look to these people for the fine details of how the process works. Talk with at least one person who represents every role that is played in the process. The list can include people with different jobs, or even people from different departments. Find out what they do, and more important, why they do it.

Ask questions like these:

- Do you use this process regularly, or only occasionally?
- How much experience do you have with computer applications? How comfortable are you with computers?
- Do you use a networked computer?
- What steps do you perform? Why do you perform them?
- Are there steps that seem unnecessary?

For example, does the employee prepare reports that are rarely read?

- Are there any trouble spots in this process? If so, why do you think they arise, and what do you think we can do about them?
- Why do you perform these steps?

Tip: Answers like "We've always done it that way," or "I was told to," suggest that a procedure has become obsolete or inefficient.

- Is the information you need readily available?
- What do you think is the most important improvement we can make in this process?

- If you were making out a wish list, what other improvements would you include?

Don't rely on verbal descriptions alone. Ask your sources to walk through their roles in the process, noting what works well and what does not. Look for inefficiencies, like having to enter the same data in two different places. Also note the key terms the sources use. Apply these terms to the application's forms and controls, so they speak the employees' language.

Check the paperwork

Not all your information sources are human. Workflow processes are built around forms and reports. Check out those that are currently in use, both paper and on line. As you examine each form, look for:

- Information that is essential to the process
- Information that is not essential but might be useful
- Information that is useless
- Additional information that is needed

Make an evaluation

Don't mess up the workflow of your own project by collecting information you don't use. The last step—often omitted—in the research process is to use the collected information to make a thorough evaluation of the process as it exists now. Make sure you understand these factors:

- All the objects, roles, procedures, and human interactions that make up the business process.
- Areas where you have found inefficiency, redundancy, or confusion.

Ask a few key workgroup members to review your work. This might also be a time to begin sketching a diagram of the workflow to be managed.

Design the New Process

When you fully understand the current process, its strengths, and its weaknesses, you have the necessary solid foundation on which to start designing a new process. Focus on:

- The process
- Needed information
- Limits and constraints

As you proceed, these factors will shape themselves into an overall design. Let this process happen as it will; don't try to force a design to materialize. Ideally, this will not happen until you begin building a prototype.

To design a new business process:

- Establish an overall process of what the new process should look like.
- Sketch in the details.
- Draw a diagram of the expected workflow.
- Begin to write design specifications.

Establish an overall process

If you are building the new process on an existing process, decide which elements of the existing process you will:

- Keep
- Modify
- Discard

Using your earlier evaluation of the present process, look for ways you can improve efficiency, remove restrictions, and avoid problems. Then:

- *Identify a focal point for the application.* This is usually a single object—an application form, for example—that is central to the process, and is used by most of the people involved. Your application may have several workflows. In that case, each workflow should have its focal point, which can be unique to that workflow or shared with others.

- *Write a description of the new process.* Have management and key employees review it.

Sketch in the details

This is the tree-planting part of the forest/trees model. Using the overall plan you developed in the previous step, you can begin defining the details of how this scheme will go into operation. There are three kinds of elements to define:

- *Objects.* Forms and the information they contain.
- *Roles.* Who does what in the course of the process. Include every person and every action.
- *Actions and interactions.* What every person does and why. How objects affect the application.

Draw a diagram

Often it's easiest to understand a workflow process by drawing a diagram of it. This is particularly true when the process involves many branches, decisions, and conditional actions. It could take you several pages of text to describe what you could show in a simple diagram—and the diagram still would do the job better.

Later, you will learn several standard ways to prepare a workflow diagram, but the basic standard is that you identify:

- How the process is launched.
- Each step in the process.
- Which roles each person performs.
- The actions an individual can take at each step. For example, a person in a management role could approve or disapprove an action; someone in an advisory role could only comment on it.
- The actions an individual cannot take at each step.
- Which actions should occur automatically.
- When the process is complete.

Write specifications

Writing design specifications is not a one-time activity. No doubt you will find yourself starting to write specifications in the early stages of planning. There is equally no doubt that you will still find yourself writing specifications long after the application has been put into service. Unlike many data processing projects, specification writing is not a separate activity. It is part of the overall workflow. That's because most computer applications are designed to manage data. Workflow management applications are designed to manage action.

Your organization's requirements and the nature of the process will dictate many of the design details. These details should include:

- How to incorporate each object, action, and role within the application.
- What forms, databases, and other elements are needed.
- Whether the application is to be based on e-mail, a central database, or some combination.
- Whether workgroup members are connected all the time, or only occasionally as in a remote dial-up system.
- Provisions for security and access control.
- Design details for forms and views. Write these as you establish them. You may know some of these details very early. You also may find late in the process that you need an element you had not anticipated.

Again, have management and key workgroup members review and approve this work.

Workflow Planning Points

Good design can make the difference between a workflow management application that works well, or one that never seems to go quite right. It also can be the difference between application that works well and one that merely works.

Your application will work better if you optimize:

- The number and use of databases
- Access control
- Types of approval authority
- Notification to people involved in the next step of a process
- Access by dial-up users
- Database replication
- Status reporting

Database design

The rule of thumb for designing a relational database is to provide a single table for each subject. That rule is only partly true in a nonrelational system like Notes. Here, a key factor is the number and nature of the lookups you will need to retrieve information from other databases.

Some principles to follow include:

- If yours is a simple application with no lookups, you usually can use a single database.
- If there are only a few lookups, you probably can work with a few databases contained in a single view.
- If there are many lookups, consider a separate database just to hold all the lookup information.
- You may need a separate database for mail-in forms.
- A database that is too large can also be too slow to be useful.

Controlling access

While it is important to control access to a database, it is just as important to provide enough access. Make sure you give people enough access to do their jobs. For example:

- Be sure everyone has access to all the lookup databases they require.
- If one part of the process will be handled by a single department or group, grant access only to this group.
- If one group of people needs access to the full content of every document, define that group as a role in the access control list. An example would be editors who need to review and correct documents in a publishing process.
- If separate groups need access to documents created with specific forms,

give each of these forms a Compose Access list of people or groups who are allowed to create documents based on the form.

■ Don't automatically give managers full access to modify the database or its contents. You open the door to errors that could cause a great deal of damage.

Getting approval

A workflow process often requires that someone approve or edit a document. Effective use of group names helps make that process easier. When the inevitable personnel changes occur, you need only add and delete individuals from their assigned groups; you need not make regular changes to the documents or the access control list.

Other points to consider include:

■ Use role or group names to provide flexibility and allow for changes in workgroup membership.

■ Whenever an application requires an approval, provide space on the form for it.

■ When you create groups of approval or editing authorities, you can provide additional access control by checking individual names against a lookup list of authorized group members.

Providing notice

If a workflow process is to proceed without delay, people need timely notice when they are expected to perform their roles. Often that means sending e-mail notices that a particular document is available for review by a particular date or time. In other applications, workgroup members might be expected to log into a central database for information on their coming tasks. Remember, though, that this system depends on each person faithfully checking in on schedule.

These tips can help you smooth that process:

■ If each person must check with a central location, you can use a share model application.

■ If each approval authority has easy access to the central database, you can send e-mail notifications that include doc links to the document to be reviewed.

■ If an approval authority is a dial-up user, send the entire document, not just a doc link. Remember: the changes this member makes will not automatically update the original document. Consider a mail-in database to manage transactions of this type.

Providing dial-up access

Dial-up patrons rely on replicating databases from a server to their own systems. That can be a time-consuming process if the database is large and the dial-up employee is not selective in the number of records retrieved. The database could easily exceed the capacity of the remote hard disk.

There is an allied problem, too. If the application relies heavily on lookups to a large database, the data needed to support those lookups may also be too large a the remote user's time and system.

To relieve these problems, you can:

- Design lookups so they are not refreshed during an editing session.

- Place views in the current database for use in lookup formulas.

- Require only limited connect time between server and remote system. Require connections only in the parts of the process that require them, and let employees know what these are.

- Help employees devise selective replication schemes that will retrieve only the needed information.

Diagramming Workflow

If a picture is worth a thousand words, it is undervalued in the modern era of visual communication. A workflow diagram displays the objects, roles, actions, and interactions of the process you want to manage. It also gives you a good way to spot errors, omissions, or awkward spots. It helps you, and others, understand how the application works. A diagram can help both to understand the present process and to visualize an improved one.

A workflow process has four major elements:

- The status of the process
- Individual roles
- Data and forms
- Actions and interactions

There are four general types of workflow diagrams. Each concentrates on one element:

- State, or work-centered
- Role
- Data/form
- Action

Whatever the type, a workflow diagram consists of boxes, circles, and interconnecting lines that show the interactions within the process. While you could diagram a workflow in all four ways, one is usually enough. Pick the type of diagram that in your opinion best reflects the kinds of relationships needed to make the process work.

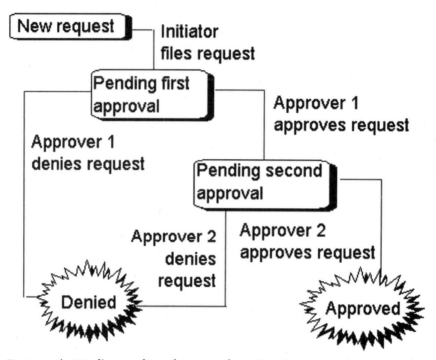

Figure 4.7   A state diagram shows the status of a project at any step.

State diagrams

A work-centered diagram like Fig. 4.7 shows the status of the work at each step in the process. Lines describes the actions made by people in various roles, moving the process to its next state. This type of diagram is strongest at showing how work is coordinated. On the other hand, it can be hard to read and understand.

This kind of diagram can easily become more complex. For example, the diagram shown here depicts a yes-or-no process in which each approval authority has only the choice of accepting or denying the request. Perhaps one of more of these authorities also has the option of returning the application for modification or more information. The number of lines and actions involved can easily produce a complex, confusing chart.

Role diagrams

A role-centered diagram like Fig. 4.8 also follows the process step by step, but at each step emphasizes the major role being played at each stage. This kind of diagram concentrates on how participants interact with each other. It also tends to be more readable than a work-centered diagram.

A role-based diagram can have its own kinds of entanglements, though. Often, more than one role is played out at a given step. For example, at any

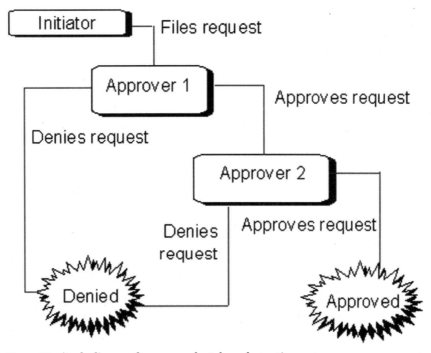

Figure 4.8 A role diagram focuses on who takes what action.

approval step the initiator might have an option of asking for a status report or modifying the request. In that case, both the initiator and the approval authority have roles at that step, and that can be hard to depict in a role-centered diagram.

Data diagrams

Another approach is to follow the paperwork. In a data/form diagram like Fig. 4.9, each box shows what happens to the information—usually a form—used at each step. The lines depict the links to the next action that involves this particular form.

This type of chart is best suited for relatively static workflows that do not require a lot of coordination, multiple paths, or requests for changes.

Action diagrams

In an action diagram (Fig. 4.10), the actions are in the boxes, and the lines show how these actions are linked. This type of diagram effectively shows how actions are coordinated, and it can be combined with other information. For example, an information block could list the forms used during the process. The action technique is hard to use, though, when an activity does not automatically move the process to another step.

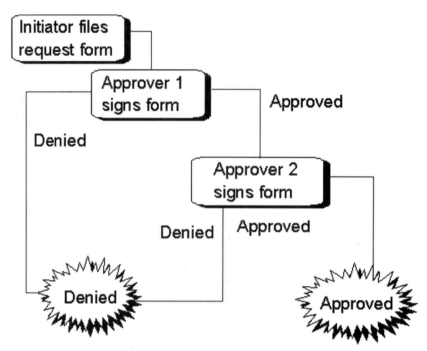

Figure 4.9 A data/form diagram follows the paper trail.

Alternatives

These aren't the only possible ways to diagram a workflow process. There are many alternatives, perhaps including those of your own design. The possibilities include:

- A multiple focus where each block contains an action, plus the roles, forms, and objects involved in that action.
- The traditional programmer's flowchart.

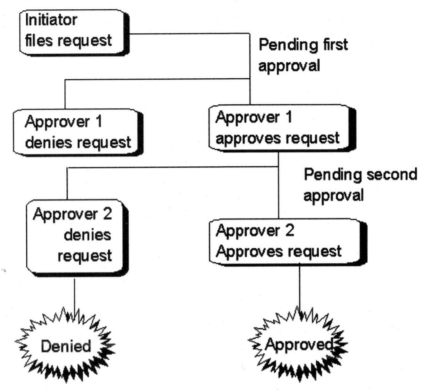

Figure 4.10 An action diagram shows how steps are linked.

Building an E-mail Network

Computer time is the 180-degree opposite of geologic time. Therefore, it's been only an eon or so—one or two years—since e-mail was just simply a way to exchange text messages among a few people on the same LAN.

Today, e-mail has evolved from a limited-purpose tool into an all-purpose messaging system designed to spread information throughout an enterprise. The technical demands of building and maintaining such a far-flung system have increased accordingly. Even though every messaging system has more or less the same components, the way these are designed and implemented varies widely among individual packages. And though Lotus has published an overall messaging strategy, there are significant differences in approach and technology between its two messaging products: Notes and cc:Mail.

The Building Blocks of E-mail

All messaging systems have these major components:

- A *user agent* (UA). This is the client-side program that produces the screen display and lets individuals create, send, and receive messages.

- A *message store.* This is the post office function that provides temporary storage for incoming messages not yet received, and for outbound messages to be transferred to another post office.

- *Message transfer agents (MTAs).* There may be one or more of these MTAs involved in any given transmission. These route the messages from origin to destination.

- A *directory,* which keeps track of patrons' names and e-mail addresses and tells the MTAs where to route a message.

Postal monopoly

Legally, the U.S. Postal Service has a monopoly on first class mail. In practice, the post office has lost that edge and must share this function with overnight

Sum of the e-mail parts

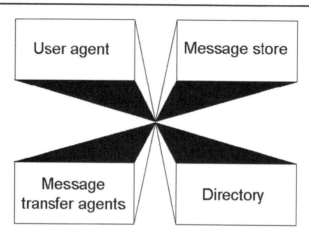

services, fax, and e-mail. E-mail itself has undergone a similar change.

Traditional host-based systems were relatively simple. There was a single post office and a single directory. Everything was routed locally through a single type of system. The early LAN e-mail systems were organized the same way. Even when additional post offices came on line, there were few problems as long as all used the same e-mail package.

A fully evolved e-mail system is likely to be a mix of different packages and technologies. A Notes post office has trouble handling even a message from its corporate cousin cc:Mail, much less competing systems like Office Vision, Groupwise, or Microsoft Mail. Each has its own directories and MTAs, and these are essentially useless to any other system.

Simple systems have complex problems

Even something seemingly as simple as the message header can be unexpectedly complicated. The header is modeled after the familiar corporate memo, with fields labeled *To, From, Subject* and so on.

These headers are not as simple as they might seem. A memo circulated to everyone in the company, or even a large division, could have thousands of names in its *To* field. The directory might maintain a mailing list which itself takes in a large group. Worse, the mailing list might be made up of several subgroups, plus some individual recipient names. When even a simple structure does not translate well to another system, something this complex is a disaster that is not just looking for a place to happen. It has found one.

There are other potential complications as well:

- Some systems allow longer entries in *Subject* fields than other systems do.

One e-mail size does not fit all

- ■ File sharing for local area networks

- ■ Client/server for heavy-duty use

- ■ A system of priorities for dispatching messages may or may not carry over to a different package.
- ■ Though the body of an e-mail message is simple text, more and more patrons are attaching other files to their messages. These may or may not make it into another system in their intended form.

Then there's the headache of trying to manage these growing, diverse systems without dragging network performance back to the covered wagon days.

Two Basic Systems

E-mail systems come in two basic forms.

- ■ File sharing systems designed primarily for LAN use
- ■ Client/server systems intended for larger, more diverse networks

It's a measure of e-mail complexity, though, that until recently each of Lotus's messaging products used a different form. Notes was a client/server system; cc:Mail was a file sharing system.

Sharing files

In a file sharing system, everyone shares the services of the same post office, which holds their e-mail messages. The post office consists of a group of files on a network server whose main e-mail purpose is to store patrons' messages. Most activity takes place at the desktop. This e-mail component manages the display, handles reading and writing from message files on the server, performs text searches, and executes any of the rules that organize incoming mail. The instructions that travel to the server tend toward the basic: opening and saving a file, for example.

File sharing systems represent a simpler era of e-mail. They are among the easiest to install and use, and they adapt easily to different server platforms. They have another big advantage, too: they are independent of any single network operating system.

Nevertheless, file sharing systems have their limits as an e-mail system expands to enterprise scope. They don't accommodate growth easily. A few dozen people can overwhelm a single post office, requiring that you set up multiple post offices with links between them. The post office files can grow to disk-cramming size, preserving every piece of e-mail—the junk e-mail as well as the good stuff—that ever passes through them. The only real cure is to shut down the post office for periodic housecleaning. As luck certainly will have it, that will be the exact moment when an overseas dial-in client desperately needs to get onto the system.

Notably, even cc:Mail has lost its file sharing orientation and has gained client/server characteristics.

Client/server allows for growth

In a client/server e-mail system like Notes, the front end handles only the presentation and display. Everything else is done by the server at the back end. The instructions sent back by the client tend to be more sophisticated: retrieving a particular message, for example. The server then translates these instructions into the more primitive file management commands.

This setup can accommodate growing numbers of users and traffic volume. Properly implemented, a client/server system can perform better and handle higher volumes.

Client/server systems also give better support to mobile users. With most file sharing systems, a heavy processing load is shifted to the remote station, with accompanying heavy traffic over slow, cumbersome connections. They also require a lot of management attention. In a client/server system, most of this workload is handled at the server. The remote connection by telephone is almost as simple as the network connection from a desktop.

Contacting the post office

A messaging application exchanges data with its post office by way of an API. Initially, these APIs have been proprietary, but more recently they have begun to take on the appearance of common standards. The leading APIs include:

- MAPI is Microsoft's mail application programming interface.

- VIM, or vendor-independent messaging, is Lotus's in-house technology.

- CMC, or common messaging calls. This is a spin-off of the X.400 messaging standard.

Most recent e-mail products, including Notes, support MAPI, and it is becoming nearly a universal e-mail API. In addition to supporting MAPI, Windows 95 and Windows for Workgroups also work with CMC.

Some standard APIs are appearing

- MAPI
- VIM
- CMC

In a client/server system, the API manages the split between front and back ends. This also makes some integration possible. Notes can use MAPI, for example, to exchange messages with a Windows 95 mail agent.

Linking with Other Systems

Even if they can converse only with themselves, today's collection of proprietary e-mail systems are adequate for most uses. Each product creates and maintains its own directory system.

In addition, messaging abilities are increasingly being built into network operating systems. Windows 95 is shipped with client versions of Microsoft Mail and Exchange; there also is an integral user messaging agent. Novell has integrated the directory for its MHS with Netware Directory Services (NDS). Novell also has coordinated, but not really integrated, the directory services for Netware and Groupwise.

While the APIs of client/server systems allow some interaction between diverse e-mail systems, transferring messages from one system or network to another is still a major challenge. This is where you enter the world of backbones and gateways.

Stumbling at the gateway

A gateway is a classic necessary evil. It's necessary, because you need one to get from one network or messaging system to another. Yet a gateway is a doorway to many kinds of evils including clogged traffic, garbled signals, and security problems. If anything goes wrong with a transmission, chances are it happened at a gateway.

Gateways are mixed blessings

- You need them to link diverse systems
- But each gateway is an obstacle

Often, when you must link Notes with some other protocol the natural solution is to build a gateway between the two. In isolation, the single gateway may make sense. But this is a network, not a single installation. In practice, the aggregate total of individual systems can erect an obstacle course of gateways. To get to its destination, a message must operate like a video game hero, constantly running, dodging, climbing, and jumping to avoid gateway gremlins.

You can't entirely eliminate gateways from your life, but you can minimize their numbers and influence. The first step is the simple decision that you will manage gateway traffic instead of just letting it happen. Your e-mail network should be a planned system in which the greatest number of messages, the greatest number of times, are routed through the least number of gateways.

Getting some backbone

Backbones give you the opportunity to minimize gateway traffic. A message backbone provides a unified message transfer system that includes routing and directory services. Each divergent system has a single gateway to the backbone. At most, a message traveling through this system must pass through two gateways: one to get onto the backbone and another to get off. And these are only the messages that must travel between diverse e-mail systems. Local messages, which still make up the bulk of all e-mail traffic, never need reach the backbone at all.

A backbone can be based on one of three standards:

- The X.400 protocol
- The Simple Mail Transfer Protocol (SMTP), the language of Internet e-mail
- The Novell Message Handling Service (MHS)

The X.400 standard

X.400 is a recommended standard accepted by many of the world's largest telecommunication firms. Products based on this standard exist mainly on larger computers: mainframes, minicomputers, and Unix systems. X.400 has several things going for it:

- It is widely accepted by those whose opinion matters.
- It is an open standard, not tied to anyone's product line.
- It has a close relationship to the X.500 directory standard.
- It has a wide range of customization opportunities, such as expiration dates and a feature which verifies that a recipient has not rejected the message.

On the other hand, there are some weak spots:

- X.400 comes in several editions, including 1984, 1988, and 1992 vintages. These are not always consistent with each other.
- X.500, which adds necessary directory services, has not yet appeared in many commercial products.
- Getting the most from an X.400 system requires strong technical services, a requirement that extends to consultants and vendors as well as your own staff.
- Because they run mainly on larger systems, X.400 products sell at large-system prices.

E-mail via the Internet

SMTP defines the operation of MTAs. It comes from an extended family of related parts and accessories including:

- Multipurpose Internet Mail Extensions (MIME) provide for extended data types in a message body.
- The Post Office Protocol version 3 (POP3) defines mail submission and retrieval transactions between user agents and local message transfer agents.
- The Domain Name Service (DNS), used by SMTP to route messages.

Using the Internet, any two people who have e-mail systems can probably manage to communicate with each other. Thanks in large part to the access provided by commercial service providers like CompuServe and America On Line, the Internet has become what many organizations strive to achieve: a universal e-mail backbone. Except for the relatively new MIME, the Internet standards are widely used and well tested.

Among the advantages of the Internet:

- Its structure is already in place.

- Nearly anyone, on nearly any kind of system, can send and receive Internet e-mail messages.

- Internet mail access is standardized.

- The Internet standards have been adopted by many products, a good number of them in the shareware class.

There are, of course, some drawbacks:

- Internet mail requires Transmission Control Protocol/Internet Protocol (TCP/IP) access from the desktop. This can be both a technical and an administrative chore.

- Internet security is suspect. Some of the greatest fears have proven to be overstated, but there still are some legitimate soft spots.

- You have little control over how Internet services are managed. That makes it hard to take such steps as avoiding peak periods with routine messages.

The Notes SMTP gateway

On some server platforms, Notes provides an SMTP gateway, an add-in that links Notes to the Internet e-mail system. This gateway lets you communicate with Internet users, plus other Notes domains that maintain Internet connections. The gateway is designed to let you exchange mail over a public mail backbone while preserving the integrity of the original message. The gateway encapsulates the message within an SMTP format, transmits it over the network, and extracts it at the recipient's gateway.

It redirects incoming mail from an SMTP course, converts it, and passes it to the Notes mail component. When sending a message from Notes, the gateway acts as a foreign domain, collecting and converting messages and sending them on via SMTP.

The SMTP gateway converts each address of a message from one environment to its corresponding form in the other. The conversion preserves enough address information to preserve full, automatic reply service. Since the two systems use different message formats, the gateway also converts the messages themselves. It also overcomes formatting obstacles like the inability of an SMTP message to carry attachments. The gateway uses MIME to represent a multipart Notes message as a single SMTP text transmission. The gateway also works in reverse: it recognizes incoming MIME and breaks them down into the multiple parts used by Notes.

Joining the Netware fraternity

Netware isn't normally mentioned among possible backbone technologies, but it is a familiar, widely used system with a hard-to-ignore customer base. These people are equally loyal to MHS as a way of handling e-mail.

Netware lends itself to a store-and-forward type of service. In past Netware versions, MHS servers routed messages based on their own directories. With Netware 4.1, MHS gained the ability to use that system's NDS.

Corporate users who already have Netware installations have implemented many home-grown applications based on MHS. Its advantages include:

- In many organizations, the network already exists.

- So does a directory system.

In short, it's possible to use Netware as a backbone without a great deal of effort. Novell does not have a strong record of backward compatibility, though, and there is some doubt if Netware has the necessary capacity to sustain itself as an enterprise backbone.

Getting the Network Ready for Notes

They tell of the major law firm that decided to jettison an old mainframe-based system in favor of a LAN and a client/server system. The firm installed a Novell network and a suite of basic applications such as word processing, spreadsheets, e-mail, and scheduling. Then, partners in charge of such things decided it would be a good thing if the lawyers could use Notes to collaborate on cases.

Big mistake. Not in the choice of Notes, but in failing to anticipate the impact this decision would have on the rest of the network. This was early in the history of Notes, and the version available at the time ran only on the Netbios protocol. There were major problems getting Notes to work with Netware's IPX packets. An Operating Systems version 2 (OS/2) server had to be reconfigured to communicate with the Netware server so applications could read and write each other's files. Attorneys at half a dozen overseas locations often had to use leased lines so slow they could not take advantage of Notes at all.

Notes itself cost the firm $162,000. New cables, switches, and other hardware cost a little more than the software: $165,000. Then, there was another $210,000 for WAN installations so the overseas offices could tap into Notes. The cost of expanding the network to accommodate Notes totaled $375,000—more than twice the cost of the software.

Hindsight says this firm should have waited for a later version of Notes, which no longer required Netbios and could better coexist with Netware. But the real problem is that the partners who decided on this installation made a business decision that did not adequately acknowledge the technical issues involved. They didn't really know what it would take to make their network ready for Notes. Networking entails many hidden costs that management often fails to anticipate. If your Notes installation is to succeed, you must first account for these needs and costs.

Groupware or gropeware?

Organizations that install major network applications like Notes certainly demonstrate a need for groupware. Management and IS should work together

Networks have hidden costs

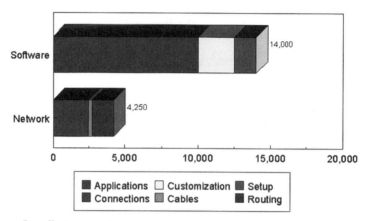

Figure 5.1 Installation costs for a typical 200-person network.

in planning projects like this. Instead, their only contact often is to blame each other for the things that went wrong.

Consultant Daniel A. Gasparro describes a "technology deficit" which, he says, "is draining the resources of corporations worldwide. It's not a shortage in hardware or software. It's the lack of understanding on the part of upper management about how to oversee, budget, and come to grips with the real expense and value of the enterprise information infrastructure."

Like the law partners who suddenly decided to add Notes to their network mix, the business managers who usually make these decisions are mainly concerned with the financial details. They aren't always well versed in the technical issues they are raising. This ignorance can have a profound effect on the bottom line they are trying so hard to protect. Getting a network up to speed for Notes or any other major network application can entail many hidden costs (Figs. 5.1 and 5.2). These costs cannot be managed as long as they are hidden. Management needs to learn to involve IS people in these decisions as automatically as they involve their financial aides.

I'd rather be pushing a Mac...

Meanwhile, IS staff members have a well-established reputation for making their decisions solely on technical grounds without adequately understanding how their actions will affect the business.

They have other less-than-endearing habits, too. One is a fanatic brand loyalty exceeded only by owners of pickup trucks—the kind whose bumper stickers proclaim that they'd rather be pushing a Ford than driving a Chevy, or vice versa. In IS, these obsessions take such forms as Mac versus IBM, Netware versus Windows NT, or Unix versus anything else. These excessive

Even more hidden costs

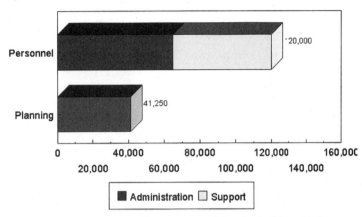

Figure 5.2 Personnel costs outstrip the expenses of the physical installation.

loyalties lead to senseless disputes. More seriously, they usually reflect personal beliefs and have little to do with the needs of the business.

Applications and networks produce even more disputes. Application developers usually work to meet customer expectations, leaving it to the network specialists to come up with the necessary protocols, bandwidth, and other technical accommodations. Meanwhile, the networkers tend to be blind to the customers' needs and think mainly in terms of protocols. The result can be a network that's vastly overengineered for some applications and seriously inadequate for others. From a financial standpoint, too much money goes to places where it does too little good.

Issues to consider

The advent of networks, groupware, and other kinds of collaborative technology raise many issues that must be addressed. They include:

- *Electronic commerce.* The Internet and other on-line services are forcing organizations build electronic links with customers, suppliers, and business partners. Networks must have the capacity to accommodate external as well as internal communication.

- *Security.* Once you let the outside world in, you'll find it hard to keep others out. Security must be built into the network. It might cost, but losing a major contract to a security breach could cost even more.

- *Real-time applications.* Telecommuting, electronic commerce, and global competition mean you may well need to keep the network up and running 24 hours a day.

- *Personal computing.* E-mail and other forms of electronic personal communication put new computing power and influence in the hands of keyboard-punching employees. Management must strike a balance between those who develop innovative solutions to their problems and those whose different drummers are completely out of step with the organization's goals.

- *Ownership of information.* As organizations increasingly rely on external communication and Web servers, they risk losing ownership and control of their own information. They also risk contamination of internal information, and there are legal issues the courts are only beginning to resolve.

- *Any-time access.* Employees who need access to information often need it right now. The challenge is to make this data available without compromising security, and without overloading the network.

- *Hidden costs.* Beyond the costs of maintaining adequate network capacity are the "soft costs" of maintaining help desks, training resources, upgrades, and software distribution. Like network costs, these can easily exceed the costs of the application itself. They also have an unpleasant way of adding up, particularly when you do not adequately anticipate them.

- *Disappearing resellers.* Many existing networks were built by integrators and resellers who are no longer available. Many have gone out of business. Others have moved on to more profitable fields and have little patience with providing follow-up support for old customers.

- *Mergers.* From the newspaper mergers of the '70s, through the corporate raiding of the '80s and the bank and entertainment mergers of the '90s, corporate union has become a way of life. Often this means making a force fit of radically different network structures.

What can we do?

It's important that business managers get a grip on both the costs and the value of their network resources. It's equally important that technical professionals identify best-fit technology and keep management informed about its cost.

The best way to keep from being hit by unanticipated costs is to turn them into anticipated costs. Follow these steps:

- Prepare a detailed inventory of your current network infrastructure, including components, services, and personnel.

- Determine what you are spending now. Include the costs of salaries, support and maintenance contracts, and communication services.

- Identify the old, obsolete, and overloaded—those parts of the system that must soon be replaced.

- List the major business initiatives you plan to take in the coming year.

- Determine what it will take, in terms of implementation, acquisition, and support, to technically accommodate your plans.

Step 1: Take inventory

- What resources do you have now?
- How much do they cost?
- Are they suitable for long-term use?

Step 2: Set your goals

- Where do you want to go?
- What will it take to get there?
  - People
  - Technology

- Identify any training or development needs you might incur.
- Find out which forms of technology will best implement your plans. Don't forget to consider newly developed technology that will be developed during the year.

What a Notes Network Needs

Every product has its shortcomings, and Notes is no exception. Workgroup members using Notes can move a lot of data—or try to. That means a Notes network must be up to speed on and able to handle high-capacity loads. Building this kind of network, or expanding your existing links, may well be more expensive than the Notes software itself. It's necessary, though, if you are to take full advantage of your investment in workgroup software and processes. Planning and careful choices also can help limit the expense.

Step 3: Identify what it takes

- New technology
- Training and development

Organized chaos

A Notes database is a collection of documents made available for group members to read, respond to, and expand upon. A mature Notes database is often a very large collection of material. Notes does two things: it provides e-mail to help members exchange their documents and thoughts, and it provides an organizational scheme for its mass of documents. Instead of having to dig through an electronic stack of papers, Notes patrons can find the documents organized into categories and can search and display the fields contained in each document.

Still, Notes is a free-form kind of database, and that can lead to challenges for network designers and managers. In daily use, Notes exercises a host of client/server connections that can put a serious strain on a network's capacity. This is particularly true when you go beyond Notes's roots in LANs. The typical LAN usually has enough speed and bandwidth to meet the program's appetite for capacity. WANs, on the other hand, tend to be slower, with routers, gateways, and other junction points that constrict traffic like the junctions of urban expressways. Even on a LAN, a poorly designed document can bring response time to a screeching halt.

You can't always solve these problems, but there are several things you can do to reduce their impact:

- Make sure you understand exactly how Notes works and what kinds of network traffic it generates.

- Design documents to minimize document sizes and shorten network transfers.

- Choose the right network protocols for the job.

Making Notes more efficient

- Chart the traffic flow
- Improve document design
- Choose best network protocols
- Replicate local databases

- Make use of Notes's replication feature to maintain local databases and minimize LAN traffic.

How Notes creates traffic

Notes is organized around databases, which it can store on network servers running on a variety of platforms including Windows NT, OS/2, Netware, and Unix. Workgroup members can also create local databases on their own systems. These databases usually are organized by subject. Within a database, you can use categories and subcategories to further organize the contents.

A database view displays individual documents under section headings that represent their assigned categories. These documents can include e-mail messages, free-form text, graphics, multimedia elements, or documents that combine any or all of these forms. A document can also contain doc links, which are references to other documents. For example, a document detailing a sales transaction could contain a doc link to a record that contains information about the customer. Another link could lead to an on-line product brochure.

When someone gains entry to the server, Notes displays a workspace view of the available database. Individuals can customize this display to suit themselves. When the member selects a database, the server sends a view that displays the available documents, arranged by some combination of variables such as the topic, author, subject, or date created. The network administrator will probably designate a main view to be displayed as a default, but here, too, individuals are free to customize their own views.

Notes is a connection-oriented product designed mainly to let individuals make contact with a server. How the network accomplishes that task is left to the using organization. In all but its earliest versions, Notes does not dictate an underlying communication protocol. It is designed instead to work with whatever protocol is already running. That usually—though not always—means Netbios for Windows and OS/2, IPX for Netware, and TCP/IP for Unix. In fact, Notes can support clients that run different protocols.

Designer documents

Like a poorly managed government agency, a poorly run Notes database can easily suffocate people under a load of virtual paperwork. Good document design can help relieve this problem.

When one large organization set up its Notes database, it imposed no controls over how large a document could be, or how many attachments it could attract. The result was a collection of long documents complete with sound, graphics, and video. When a workgroup member tried to open one of these documents, the most efficient method would be:

- From the database view, double-click on the document's title.
- Take a coffee break.

With luck, the document would appear on your screen by the time you returned.

As this company learned, good document design can relieve these problems. It devoted some time and expense to redesigning the documents. The cumbersome graphics and other large-file-size elements were turned into attachments that were no longer automatically downloaded with the parent documents. Readers who open one of these documents do not automatically receive the multimedia elements. Opening them is now an option, and experience has shown that when given a choice, only a few people exercise that option.

Pick a protocol

Another way to reduce traffic and speed response is to make use of Notes's ability to work with multiple protocols. Different protocols generate different amounts of traffic at different times during a session. The right choices can help hold down network volume.

In general, TCP/IP generates less network volume than the others. In an ideal world, that makes it the best choice. Of course, we don't live in an ideal world. If TCP/IP is not already installed at both the server and client levels, installing it can add several hundred dollars per system to the cost of upgrading your network. The good news is that TCP/IP is becoming more widely available on platforms that used to support other protocols exclusively.

Invitations and RSVPs

When Netbios manages a communication session, it engages in long sequence of repeated messages and acknowledgments (Fig. 5.3):

- A *name query* to help the client recognize the server it wants to reach. The query travels over the entire network, past routers and bridges, and over

Heavy traffic

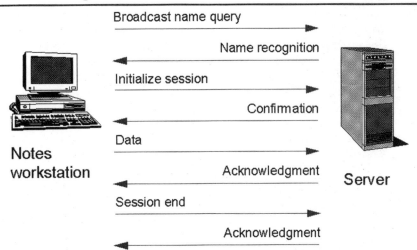

Figure 5.3 A Netbios session involves multiple exchanges, particularly when setting up a session.

hills and dales. It is repeated, usually several times, until the client identifies the intended server.

- When the server receives a name query, it sends a *name recognize* response, enabling the client to identify the server.

- With a satisfactory response to its first query, the client sends a *session initialize* message. As with most messages in this sequence, the server must issue a response, which the client will wait to hear. Also as usual, this can be a multiple exchange of messages. Unless other traffic is in motion between the two systems, they exchange confirmation messages every 30 seconds, to make sure the connection is still alive.

- Once everyone is alive and active, the two systems begin to exchange data. Each, of course, must acknowledge the other's transmissions.

- Finally, the client sends a *session end* signal, which of course must be acknowledged.

If you must use Netbios, there are ways you can limit the traffic volume it generates. If someone is constantly opening and closing a Netbios connection, keep it open all day instead of constantly logging on and off. That way, you can eliminate the two-way exchange of invitations and RSVPs needed to establish a new session.

You also can install data link switches (DLSs) on each of the routers that link Netbios systems. These use intelligent routing to send a message toward its intended destination. This cuts out the messages that go out on fishing expeditions all over the network.

IPX behaves much like Netbios with one significant exception: an IPX broadcast stops at the first router it encounters; it cannot jam traffic across the entire enterprise network. But as a component of Netware, IPX has another traffic generation problem. Netware uses a service advertising protocol (SAP) to keep all routers and servers informed about the applications and services available on the network. SAP sends out a new report every 60 seconds. When a network is large enough, these SAP messages easily can sap a network's carrying capacity, and SAP's advertising becomes a form of network junk mail.

TCP/IP generates much less traffic. It does use broadcasts to set up a session, but these are stopped at the first router. It has nothing comparable to the recurring SAP status reports. The drawback is that every TCP/IP resource must be manually defined in a DNS directory.

Hot-rodding Windows and Netware

If TCP/IP is not a practical alternative, there are ways you can make the other protocols more efficient:

- *Allow larger messages.*   Netware typically is set to use messages of 576 bytes. You can set this as high as 1500 bytes—the practical limit if you are using Ethernet.

- *Send several messages at once.*   Both Netbios and Netware set their window sizes at 1. That means only one message can travel the network at a time. If the network requires that a document be split into five documents, the entire network comes to a standstill until all five can be sent and acknowledged. If the window size is set to 5, all five messages can be sent at once.

Accommodating replication

Replication is one of Notes's most important features. Unlike a traditional database that operates on a single server, Notes is designed to send copies of its databases to individual workstations and remote sites. In fact, replication has become so popular it is being applied to many other client/server databases as well. Replicated databases can reduce network traffic, since their patrons need not constantly be dragging down the data from a single server.

There is one obvious problem. If you try to maintain more than one copy of a database, you must find some way to coordinate the copies. Otherwise, changes made to one database may never find their way to the other. One party—sometimes both—is operating with databases that fail to reflect the current status of things.

Five offices; five replications

Figure 5.4 In this scenario, each branch exchanges replicas.

Say a sales representative in Miami downloads a database of customer information from corporate headquarters in Chicago. That afternoon, a clerk in Chicago enters a change in the database information. The replicated database in Miami is now out of date. If the change represents information the sales rep needs to know, the gap can be serious.

Notes responds to that problem by automatically updating remote databases. When the clerk in Chicago enters the change, it is automatically transmitted to the duplicate database in Miami as well. This ensures that the databases in both locations are reasonably up to date. The only lag is time needed to send the updates.

Creative use of this feature can help limit long-distance network traffic. Perhaps the Miami sales rep is one of five in the Southeast, all replicating the database on the Chicago server. If so, when the clerk enters the change in Chicago, five updates must make their way to the southeastern branch offices (Fig. 5.4).

In this situation, it might be wise to maintain the replicated copy at a regional office in Atlanta. That way, the five southeastern sales reps can share this database; these five people alone are unlikely to put too great a strain on network capacity. And when an update must be made, only a single change must make its way to the Southeast (Fig. 5.5).

As a rule, replication makes sense if a number of people at one site will make use of the replicated database. The right number of people depends on the amount of data they use and how often they need to use it. If there are

Five offices; one replication

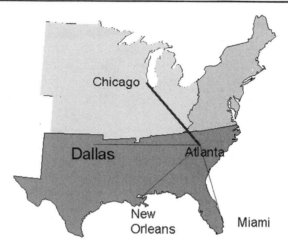

Figure 5.5 In this alternative, several offices share a single replica.

only a few people at one site, it usually makes more sense to maintain a single copy of the database at a central site.

Replicating at the field level

Though well-planned replication can reduce network traffic, the replication process itself still can easily generate enough wide-area volume to cause wheezing and congestion. Until version 4, Notes cut its replication features no more finely than the document. That means if the clerk in Chicago made a single change to a single field, updating the replication sites meant transmitting the entire document. The clerk could generate an oversized burst of traffic between Chicago and Atlanta, just by changing an order's status from back order to delivered. The entire order document would have to go south.

Notes 4 can replicate individual fields, which means that if the order status was the only field that was changed, the order status would be the only new field that was transmitted. This feature saves network traffic just by being there, and you can make it even more valuable. Again, a well-designed document is the key. Set up individual fields for the information items most likely to be changed.

Say, for example, the sales manager in Chicago wants to add a comment to a document already present in the Atlanta database. Furthermore, the document is laden with graphics. Even under Notes 4, if the comment is added to the existing text, everything in the text field—including all those graphics—must travel the wire. If there is a separate field in which to add comments, only the comment will take up network space.

Automatic downloads

Individuals can also use replication to their advantage. This is particularly true of dial-in employees who open the database periodically to look for any changes. You can set up the system so when these people dial in their databases are automatically updated. You can establish a rule for this, such as sending only information that has changed since the last call, or after a particular date. The remote employees will no longer need to browse through the database while the clock runs on their connect time.

Browsing is a particularly effective way to build up traffic on a network. Consider a database of legal documents and case citations, each document ranging from 5000 to 10,000 words. A law clerk looking for court rulings on a particular subject might scroll through the database document by document, reading only the headings that contain the main points. A single clerk could use a significant percentage of your bandwidth. A roomful of clerks could bring the network to a screeching halt.

And legal documents don't usually include graphics or video. Add these features, and one person alone could lay claim to as much as half your network capacity.

There are several ways you can attack this problem:

- Careful document design.

- Making sound, graphics, and multimedia available only to people who request them.

- Educating workgroup members on document design and proper network use.

- Providing financial incentives to reward those who are careful and penalizing those who are not.

Managing remote computing

Remote users also need education. One of the things they should learn is that main-office habits often spell trouble on the road. An action that would travel unnoticed through an office LAN can harden the arteries of a WAN.

Encourage remote employees to do their database replications whenever they visit the main office. Then, they can browse through the contents without consuming valuable network time and capacity. Other steps you can take include:

- Provide docking stations so visiting mobile workers can plug in their laptops to work on the network and replicate databases for use in the field.

- Provide for selective replication. That way, mobile employees can log onto the server and pull down only those documents or fields that are new or have recently been changed.

- Provide the fastest modems possible. State-of-the-art equipment always costs more, of course, but the time saved could be well worth it.

Easing e-mail jet lag

- Make replications in the office.
- Provide docking stations
- Use selective replication
- Provide fast modems
- Monitor file sizes

- Set up a system of warnings that let mobile workers know when a document they are about to replicate is more than a comfortable size for the network connection. Given that information, many will choose less time-consuming alternatives.

Boosting Bandwidth

The typical network is tailor-made for e-mail. A standard Ethernet LAN runs at 10 Mbps, and token ring's standard top speed is only a little faster at 16 Mbps. That's plenty for the occasional bursts of text messages from a basic e-mail system. It's not nearly fast enough for the sound, video, and other multimedia transmissions that make up an increasing portion of network traffic today.

Furthermore, the typical LAN is optimized for just the sort of traffic basic e-mail generates. Both Ethernet and token ring are shared media networks. They allow only one conversation to take place at a time. Every person on the network shares the same allotment of network capacity. Even in a client/server configuration, that is rarely a problem. The server can engage in a brief exchange with one workstation, then move on to handle someone else's traffic. Since the time spent serving an individual workstation usually is short, it hardly matters that the others must wait in line.

It does matter, though, when an organization becomes heavily involved in workgroup computing. Now, instead of a simple exchange of messages, there is a continuous stream of traffic. Often, this traffic is between one workstation and another. The server is only a way station.

Furthermore, workgroup computing tends to extend beyond the boundaries of an individual LAN. A project might require that you collaborate with someone in another department, in another building, or on the other coast. Your

LANs must be connected with each other, and every link increases the bandwidth requirements. If you install a backbone to serve a group of 10 Mbps LANs, the backbone may need to run at 100 Mbps.

The type of material being transmitted creates even greater demands. Graphics transmissions are substantially larger than text files, and video messages are infinitely more demanding of your network resources. And video is a key part of modern collaborative computing. Applications like video conferencing, training, and high-end presentations generate traffic that is not only large but also continuous over a long time span.

Consider this: a single frame of broadcast video takes up about 12 Kb. The transmission rate is 60 frames per second. That's enough to overwhelm a conventional LAN and leave other workgroup members starving for network time.

The good news is that if you increase a network's speed, you increase its capacity. The better news is that faster network technology is available. The bad news is that network performance comes at a cost. Even though the cost premium is diminishing, a faster network still costs substantially more than a slower one.

An enterprise system

A good option for many systems is an enterprise network with these components:

- LANs running at the standard 10–16 Mbps. Normally, you need not run a departmental LAN at higher speeds.

- A backbone at each location, connecting these LANs and running at 100 Mbps.

- Some combination of leased lines and satellite links, public or private, linking the backbones.

The high-speed backbones are the keys to such a system. Options for creating them include:

- Fiber Distributed Data Interface (FDDI)
- Fast Ethernet or token ring
- Asynchronous Transfer Mode (ATM)
- Switching hubs

From copper to fiber

FDDI technology is similar to token ring, but it runs on fiber optics instead of copper wire. FDDI is capable of the 100 Mbps needed for a high-capacity backbone. It is also more secure. It's hard, though not impossible, to intercept a message send over fiber-optic lines.

However, if FDDI runs at 10 times the speed of conventional Ethernet, it also can cost up to 10 times as much. As with many newer forms of technology, the cost differential is becoming smaller as the numbers of vendors and customers increase. It is also a relatively new technology which uses its own protocols. Not all software is compatible with it.

Faster favorites

Speeded-up versions of familiar systems are understandably popular. Fast Ethernet offers 100 Mbps performance, and the hottest versions of token ring now can reach 64 Mbps.

These alternatives are attractive because you can implement them while remaining on familiar ground. You should be able to use existing wiring and software, and these supernetworks are much less expensive than FDDI. Even so, they can cost as much as three times more than their slower brethren.

Hitting the ATM

If 100 Mbps seems like a lot of capacity, remember that 64 Mb of random access memory (RAM) also once seemed like a lot. As transmissions become more complex, today's FDDI and fast Ethernet speeds may become just as inadequate.

If you want nearly unlimited networking capacity, consider ATM. This is a switching technology that borrows much from the telephone system. An ATM connection is much like a phone conversation. Though millions of other phone calls are in progress at the same time, you and the other party have your particular hookup all to yourselves and can take advantage of its full capacity. This connection—a temporary dedicated line—is made with a series of switches. The only real limit on the system's capacity is the number of lines the switches can put together.

ATM is also a switched technology, and as in a telephone call, a data transmission has the full bandwidth of its own private line. Other transmissions can take place at the same time, over other lines. ATM is also designed to provide high capacity on demand. If you need to send a long video now, you can send it now. The recipient need not wait until the system is ready.

In addition, ATM is a packet-switched network that divides its data into small packages, or packets. These packets can move individually around the network and be reassembled at the destination. ATM also lets you use channels of different capacities, from 150 Mbps to 2.4 Gbps, on the same network.

As with other high-speed technologies, the big drawback to ATM is cost. It is also a maturing standard that has yet to win full acceptance.

Switching Ethernet

You need not convert to ATM to get the advantage of switching technology. A switching hub for Ethernet turns that familiar network into a multichannel system with vastly expanded capacity. As with fast Ethernet, you can expand capacity without having to replace existing equipment or familiar techniques.

Naturally, the extra capacity bears a price to match. Nevertheless, fast Ethernet and switching hubs are giving this old standby a nine-lives reputation. Though backbones represent the greatest need for higher bandwidth, the faster versions of Ethernet are also viable choices for LANs that carry so much traffic they need the higher capacity.

Meanwhile, ATM is gaining acceptance as a high-end response. That leaves FDDI positioned—or caught—in the middle.

6

The Directory Dilemma

The first telephone directory was published in New Haven, CT in 1908. It had 50 listings. Today, an organization may have 20 or more e-mail directories serving many thousands of people. Managing those directories and keeping them up to date is a formidable task. When a directory system is spread over multiple networks and e-mail systems, it is a job none of the component systems does well.

Someday, universal directory services based on the X.500 standard may become widely available. Until then, you must contend with directory services that often were not designed for the multiplatform use you now require.

Typically, a directory is maintained as a database, a list of names and e-mail addresses. As people leave or move, the directory must be updated. That can be a time-consuming chore on a simple LAN. As people and systems are interconnected, the number of directories multiplies. Not only must you keep all these directories up to date, but you must keep them in synch with each other. It is a difficult process with plenty of room for Murphy's law to be applied. It's also a slow process. Many organizations schedule only periodic updates, perhaps once a week or month. Even administrators who try to keep their directories current are often unable to do so. Each lag in the process makes communication more difficult and increases security problems.

It's no wonder, then, that e-mail administrators long for automated updating of multiple directories. Unfortunately, automation leads to technical and practical problems of its own.

Dialing Directory Service

However you choose to link your e-mail systems, you must keep directories current and available. An integrated e-mail system must have a way to manage and coordinate internal and external mail categories. Like other kinds of data on an enterprise network, the directory system must operate transparently. Patrons should see what appears to be a single, comprehensive directory, even if it contains listings from diverse and incompatible systems.

Theory vs. Practice

- What we need:
  - Multiple directories that look line one
- What we get:
  - Multiple directories, each looking like the only one

Many LAN e-mail directory systems come with unfortunate built-in assumptions: that theirs is the only directory in town. There may not even be any provision for exchanging directory information beyond the local network. Whenever there is a gap like this, there are third-party utilities to help fill it, but these still do not cover the shortage of enterprisewide directory services.

Three product classes

The directory services in available e-mail products usually fall into one of three classes:

- A proprietary directory that supports only the product in which it appears
- Directories based on the X.500 standard
- Hybrid approaches

The single-vendor directories are by far the most common. They leave you with the tough task of integrating directory systems that never were meant to be integrated.

There are some directory synchronization tools available, but they do only part of the job. These products collect information from different directories, reformat the data, and ship it to other directories. Through this process, information can be collected, updated, and displayed within a local directory service. A cc:Mail user would see information from multiple other sources displayed as though they were all using cc:Mail directories. That's an impressive feat considering the diversity with which these systems work, but they still do only part of the job.

An ideal directory system

- Maps entries between systems
- Records all changes
- Provides easy access
- Allows for control
- Reports status
- Integrates with corporate directories
- Integrates external directories

What you need

An ideal directory system requires much more, including ways to:

- Map names and addresses between e-mail systems.
- Record changes, deletions, and additions
- Provide access to remote directory information through native interfaces
- Allow administrative control over directory sharing, security, and scheduling
- Provide status and reporting information for network management
- Provide integration with non-e-mail directories, such as corporate directories
- Integrate external e-mail directories from suppliers, customers, and business partners

There is a standard

The X.400 standard has become a useful brand of adhesive for enterprise systems. Many organizations have adopted it as a standard, because it is immediately useful and practical. It has helped establish the conditions in which you can establish a stable messaging structure, even over diverse and changing systems.

There is one problem: X.400 does little to help you synchronize your varied directories. "If you have five mail systems feeding an X.400 backbone," says one user, "you have five directories to synchronize. X.400 doesn't do it."

When it comes to directory services, though, X.400 gives way to its younger brother, X.500. This is potentially a directory standard that will solve most of the problems and meet most of the needs. The key word is *potentially*. X.500 has not yet achieved the solid level of acceptance and use that defines a true standard.

X.500 has long been a holy grail of e-mail directory management. The standard describes a tree structure that is intended to support global services that extend across organizational and geographical boundaries. A product that can do this is necessarily complex—one reason X.500 has been slow to win acceptance. In addition, the early (1988) definition of the standard needed more sophisticated access control, administrative and management tools, and replication and knowledge-sharing abilities. All these have been addressed in later versions of the standard.

Pure and impure X.500

At the same time, some X.500 products have entered the market, but some are more X.500 than others. Some offer similar functions but don't actually support the X.500 protocols. When the time comes to make a full implementation of X.500, these products won't provide for exchange of directory information with real X.500 products. One clue: if a product supports the Directory Access Protocol (DAP), it has access to the protocol that handles communication among distributed X.500 servers.

A hybrid approach

Until something like X.500 becomes a realistic solution, you must look for something else. It is not easy. The directory systems of diverse systems are only marginally compatible. What's more, they often require different forms of management. For example, when you are editing directory information, some directories require full updates; others will accept only changes. Some of them use individualistic identification schemes.

One suggested solution is to build a Directory Information Base (DIB). This is a database that can store many kinds of directory entries including individuals, organizations, and message transfer agents. Different views—much like those in Notes—can display the data in different ways: by name, organization, or management scheme. The management grouping is particularly important, since management schemes will correspond to individual systems within the organization. There could be one management domain for Lotus users, another for Exchange, and so on.

You also can store various attributes for each entity: descriptions, organizational information, telephone numbers, and office locations are examples. X.500 also uses these kinds of attributes. The trick is to assign attributes so they match those recommended in X.500. The coming standard lets you store all manner of attributes, including those that describe synchronization gateways and the characteristics of various workgroups.

You can use the DIB to give patrons automatic access across the organization's multiple e-mail systems. A Vines user could contact the DIB to find an address in a cc:Mail system. Meanwhile, synchronizing the DIB with X.500 standards lets you use the DIB on top of X.500 until the day the standard achieves more widespread acceptance. Initially, you'll have a workable substitute. And when X.500 does come to your organization, you'll be ready.

What Modern Directories Must Do

Messaging systems have undergone a rapid evolution, expanding to support attached documents, embedded objects, and rich text formats. In the process, the directory services of those systems also have had to grow. Second- and third-generation messaging systems adopted hierarchical browsing and cascading directories for transparent multidomain addressing. Store and forward messaging systems were improved with directory synchronization tools that allowed mail administrators to maintain consistency across the distributed network of routers throughout an enterprise. Also, directories have been the focus of standards-setting work, primarily with X.500 as a directory standard for interenterprise directory services. As messaging systems expand, their directories assume more functions; at the same time they inherit the rich resources and services of the overall messaging system.

A richer directory model

Directories have followed a path that began with a host-based companywide directory of e-mail users. From there, they evolved to LAN-based directories of workgroup users, and to companywide and personal directories of e-mail users with personal name and address books.

The directory of a current-generation messaging system is a document within the object store. This means the directory can extend its reach beyond traditional role as the "white pages" and "yellow pages" of employee names and locations. The directory becomes a critical service as the hub of the enterprise network that binds all corporate assets: people, places, documents, and applications. By leveraging the flexible document architecture of current messaging systems, the directory system lets users customize and expand their directory entries to reflect the range of attributes or properties they require.

Directory roles

Now, directories can help manage resources like these:

- *Systems.* For some applications, the destination for a message is not a person but a server, a fax machine, a telephone, or other electronic endpoints. The addresses of these resources can be maintained in a directory.

- *Distribution lists.* Electronic mailing lists can be held in the directory, to be expanded for distribution by e-mail or fax.

What we expect of directories

- Communication with multiple systems
- Expandable mailing lists
- Encryption keys
- Multiple roles
- Routing

- *Public key certificates.* The directory is a suitable repository for storing public key certificates. Secured applications based on public key technology require a repository to store public keys for verifying digital signatures and for encrypting message contents among communities of users.

- *Roles.* Directories can associate individuals with organizational roles. These roles can be used in workflow processes, and so workflow-based messaging applications can be directed to roles instead of specific individuals whose roles might change. This makes workflow processes easier to manage when people are on vacation or when they change job responsibilities.

- *Routing lists.* The route a message takes across hubs and routers is often determined by availability and expense. These factors can vary with the time of day, the urgency of the message, and other factors. An entry in a directory can describe the optimum routing logic, so a particular address is always accompanied by routing instructions to ensure timely and efficient transport.

Rich content

A directory can inherit all the attributes of the system's shared object store, making it a richer source of name and address information than traditional directories. These attributes include:

- *Rich text.* As part of the object store itself, directories and their contents enjoy the same rich text support as other documents. A directory document can contain such objects as user images and voice, embedded objects, and tables.

- *User-defined fields.* The directory can contain as much or as little information as the system administrator needs. The contents of the directory

An advanced directory can provide

- Formatted text
- Definable fields
- Document links
- Security

are not limited to conventional directory format. Directory documents can include user-definable fields. By defining individual fields, users can make use of a personal or private view of data that is not necessarily available to other users of the directory.

- *Linked documents.*   Because the directory itself is a document in the object store, it is possible to create links from within the directory that point to other documents in the object store. This lets administrators attach important descriptions and information to an entry in the directory without incurring additional storage overhead. Linked documents help resolve the need for separate directories maintained by multiple owners of directory resources. There are likely to be many groups within any organization that require accurate and timely data regarding all or part of an organization's list of employees, suppliers, and business partners. Examples include human resources, finance, customer support, manufacturing/development, purchasing, and management information systems (MIS). Each of these departments often has records that have counterparts in other departments but with different sets of information. You now can create a universal directory for each of these groups. Users open the directory and find relevant information regarding individuals, groups, resources, and other elements by linking to related documents such as employee history records, telephone number listings, and account histories.

- *Security.*   Although the directory can contain or can link to a rich store of data regarding each entry, security requirements affect directory documents to the same extent as any other document or object in the object store. Sensitive information such as employee salaries and customer credit rating data is secure from unauthorized access. Administrators have the flexibility to allow users to read, edit, or create documents and fields within documents.

Directory replication

As an integral part of the object store, a directory inherits all the replication functionality of the overall system. Robust directory management requires that replication be:

- *Bidirectional.*   Any changes made to the directory on any servers are automatically synchronized during replication, which accounts for changes, deletions, and additions on both sides of the connection. In contrast, directory propagation, which only sends changes in one direction, overwrites any changes that may have already been made on the recipient directory.

- *Granular.*   Directories are often large databases, which means they require significant network resources when they are replicated across an enterprise. The replication process should recognize which documents within the directory have been changed, added, or deleted, and replicate only those changes. Replication of the entire database would needlessly burden system resources.

Client/Server Directories

In many organizations, the goal is to establish a kind of client/server directory system. There would be at least one global directory of all users, plus smaller directories scattered around the network. As information in the global directory is updated, the changes are automatically transmitted to the remote directories.

One issue that arises with this kind of system is exactly how much information should be stored in the remote directories. Store too much, and the remote directories grow heavy and unresponsive. Store too little, and performance suffers because too much traffic must pass through the central directory. Furthermore, you lose the advantage of a distributed directory system. If needed information is available on the remote directories, a remote user can call into any network and have access to the full system's directory listings. If that information is only on the server directory, it is available only if the traveling employee can find a way to connect to the central database.

That is a balancing act that can be performed with some educated good judgment. The more significant issue is directory synchronization. How can you keep the information up to date when there are, say, 20 directories and 15,000 patrons? It's been estimated that in the worst-case analysis, with only limited directory services, you will need one network technician for every 100 users. A good directory system can improve that ratio to one technician for every 500 users.

One size does not fit all

Some e-mail vendors, including Lotus, have developed sophisticated directory systems. Lotus, for example, offers an Automatic Directory Exchange (ADE) that automatically updates all cc:Mail addresses.

Unfortunately, most of these features are proprietary; they will not update other vendors' directories. The main reason is that each vendor's directory is a database with a unique file structure. Companies like Lotus and Microsoft use open APIs with which customers and third-party vendors can design translation programs. This is a major project in itself, though, and few organizations are likely to undertake it.

Third-party tools are available. The Lotus division SoftSwitch provides a directory synchronization protocol (DS/P) that translates directory information among multiple e-mail systems including most of Lotus's leading competitors. Even these products, though, may fall short of the need. For example, two directory systems may support user authentication, but the synchronizing software will translate only the raw directory information. If you want to maintain access control, you will have to add the user authentication material separately.

The Lotus messaging service

To help integrate these third-party legacy and messaging systems into the Lotus Communications Architecture, Lotus is enhancing the Lotus Messaging Switch (LMS), formerly known as Soft Switch External Message Exchange (EMX). The enhanced LMS provides these services:

- High-fidelity message switching among varied messaging environments.

- A high-function "boundary MTA" acting as the nodes to connect internal networks to external networks for X.400 and SMTP. LMS has access controls, rules, and other features necessary for systems providing this boundary function.

- Directory synchronization among all major environments.

- X.500 support, including native support for the X.500 Directory Access Protocol (DAP), the Lightweight Directory Access Protocol (LDAP), and the Directory Systems Protocol.

At an East Coast insurance company headquarters, about 50,000 people work with a diverse network of e-mail systems including Notes, cc:Mail, Microsoft Mail, Office Vision, and All-in-1. In 1993, the company began testing EMX, and it went into service the next year. EMX sends as many as 500 administrative and address changes through the system each day and has greatly simplified mail system management.

E-mail vs. network directories

If that sounds like all the problems have been solved, they haven't. EMX and its successor LMS work only with e-mail directories. Network operating systems have their own directories, and telephone systems use yet another system. All these point to essentially the same places: individual employees' desktops. It would seem natural—and would greatly simplify administration and software development—if these multiple directories could be combined into one.

One such product, Banyan's Universal Street Talk, is available through third-party hardware and software suppliers, but like so many other products it is a proprietary system.

X.500 to the rescue?

The X.500 standard has long been held out as a possible solution, but it's been holding out for a long time now. It remains long on promise and short on commercial application.

Work on the standard began about a decade ago, when the International Standards Organization (ISO) set out to devise a standard that would build directories on distributed databases. The first standard, published in 1988, suffered from some limitations. For example, it did not anticipate the present demand for database replication. It was also a bureaucratic type of standard, requiring that you define your addresses in exactly the right format. This would require that organizations completely reorganize their existing addressing schemes.

In a way, the original X.500 was also proprietary. It was designed to work well with X.400 systems, but with little else.

A more recent version, issued in 1993, provides for replication and lets organizations customize their addresses. It gives vendors much more latitude in designing their products—one criticism is that the later version swings too far in that direction. There are no accepted APIs that describe how to move information from one X.500 system to another. X.500 has also been judged too bulky to run on personal computers.

An X.500 directory system includes a list of mailing addresses, plus the software needed to move it from one location to another. This information is stored in a global Directory Information Tree (DIT). It then can be spread to subordinate directories, called Directory System Agents (DSAs).

On the client end, a directory user agent (DUA) presents directory options to the employee. The DUA then contacts the nearest DSA, which connects the employee to an appropriate directory. The DSAs then can exchange information so the individual can locate and address and send a message.

There is a PC version of the standard; it uses LDAPs as the means of client access.

Lotus looks at X.500

Lotus officials acknowledge that they aren't sure what role products based on the X.500 standard will have in the fast-growing world of interpersonal messaging and multimedia networking. They express a feeling, though, that after several years of keen anticipation, false starts, and expert predictions, there is a strong possibility X.500 is finally coming into its own. They cite three main reasons for their belief:

■ With an increasing requirement for enterprisewide directories, X.500 has a potential role that goes beyond supporting messaging. X.500 could become the central backbone of the enterprise directory, as well as the underlying infrastructure for security-based electronic commerce and that of other network applications. The enterprise directory adds another dimension to both product and services profiles, and it introduces the concept of directory-enabled applications.

■ The latest version of the X.500 standard adds major features like replication and access control. Software vendors now can seriously develop and market directory products that conform to the specification and provide a large enough range of functions to be useful.

■ In corporate service, X.500 has not earned more than a passing interest until very recently. In the past, the main concern has been to sort out problems relating to messaging, such as downsizing from mainframes to LANs, or coping with the surge in SMTP traffic. Many of these issues are now resolved, or strategic directions at least have been set. Now a new problem is getting attention: corporate networks often have tens, if not hundreds, of databases and directories which are creating an increasingly unwieldy management nightmare for administrators. From the network operating system to human resources, from payroll to the raft of mail systems, administrators are confronted with a logjam of incompatible and noninteroperable directory systems.

X.500 is a possible response to all these needs and is being incorporated into both Lotus e-mail products. The company still hedges its bets, though, asking in effect, "even if it works, is it really a good idea?"

X.500 Technology

Directories are databases, and databases have been around in one form or another for a long time. All proprietary mail systems, have their own directories. One of the achievements at SoftSwitch over the last seven years has been to successfully develop and deploy a protocol to synchronize disparate systems so that they seamlessly interchange data. All communications products use a directory of one sort or another.

But why X.500? Sales of Notes, cc:Mail, or other e-mail products have not been noticeably affected by their lack of X.500 functionality. If X.500 is to become a major factor in directory services, vendors must show they can add value right now. So far, it hasn't happened.

Between 1988 and 1993, progress in developing products and services based on X.500 was severely hampered by several factors including:

■ The immaturity of the standard

■ The lack of a market for products or services

■ The complexity of the issues involved with not only the engineering, but the deployment and management of X.500 systems

Why X.500 may finally be here

- Objections to X.500:
  - Immaturity
  - Lack of a market
  - Implementation issues

- Overcoming the objections
  - Increasing maturity
  - Increasing need
  - Resolution of many issues

As standards go, the X.500 directory is considered by many analysts to have a good chance of long-term success. The 1993 version of the standard only became widely available in 1994 and has gone most of the way to completing the directory picture. Although a new edition of the X.500 standard is scheduled for release in 1996, X.500 (93) is generally considered adequate for serious deployment.

X.500 describes a model for a global directory, but it can be used for other purposes. The structure may consist of objects and attributes, both defined by the standard with their own rule sets as well as created by user organizations.

X.500 advantages

Compared with other directory services, X.500 has several distinguishing characteristics:

- It is designed to underpin a distributed global directory service that can maintain a consistent and coherent naming and addressing structure across multiple domains.

- It is intended as a locally managed repository of information not just to network users, but also directly to network applications like e-mail and security services.

- It supports distributed applications with extensive query and searching techniques beyond a simple mapping of network names to addresses.

A key advantage over other directory technologies is scalability, both stand-alone and as an interenterprise communications mechanism. Scalability enables an X.500 DSA to:

- Interrogate and shadow any number of X.500 servers without compromising a user's view of a single, seamless DIT

- Distribute information over different servers without affecting the virtual structure of the DIT

- Exchange information across heterogeneous environments

A single X.500 server can contain information on anything from 100 to 1 million entries depending on the type of database access employed. Potentially, when connected to a global X.500 network, this server would have access to a virtual database containing billions of entries.

Another X.500 advantage is its integration with network applications. From an administrator's point of view, X.500 holds a complex network information matrix together.

Directory synchronization

Most corporate e-mail initiatives reflect a simple need: unify a variety of different messaging infrastructures into a unified system. Behind this requirement is the need to synchronize naming and addressing information across diverse systems.

Directory synchronization products are usually client/server based. They allow directory information to be copied between disparate mail (or database) systems through a central repository on the server. The directory synchronization protocol is often based on e-mail messages and must ensure that the synchronized server information is broadcast to the local directories, sending update information between the server and the various agents. The server may be based on any centralized or distributed database, flat file or relational. It can also be X.500, although service as a messaging switch base is not the best long-term enterprise use of X.500.

Database replication and X.500

Replication is an important feature of distributed database environments such as Notes and X.500 systems. Without some form of replication or updated caching, performance during information retrieval can suffer. X.500 shadowing enables the virtual global directory to function in real time by distributing both data and knowledge references. It also reduces the costs of inquiries.

X.500 (93) describes a form of replication called shadowing. One DSA can establish a shadowing agreement with another, whereby one of the DSAs, the shadow supplier, contracts to provide the other, the shadow consumer, with a copy of some part of the DIB, and to keep the consumer informed of any changes which occur to that information.

Two protocols are used to support shadowing:

- The Directory Operational Binding Management Protocol (DOP) is used to establish a shadowing agreement between the two DSAs.

- The Directory Information Shadowing Protocol (DISP) is used to transfer updates from the supplier to the consumer.

Notes replication

Notes uses database replication to distribute and update copies of the same database, stored on different servers. This replication process allows users on different servers, in different time zones, or even in different countries to share information. The servers connect to each other at scheduled intervals to replicate their databases' documents, access control lists, and design elements.

Replication makes all copies of a database essentially identical, over time. If a user makes changes in one copy of a database, replication ensures that those changes are added to all copies, as long as the replication options are set up to do so. A database manager is responsible for a Notes database and its documents on Server A. Another database manager creates a replica copy of the database on Server B. Through replication, Notes copies the information from the original database to the replica; they now have identical information.

Server A and B replicate according to a schedule set up by their administrators swapping any changes made since the last replication. For example, a user working on the replica on Server B could add a document. After replication, Server A's database would contain the same document. They are again identical. Replication enables users at different locations to update the same database, or even the same document, simultaneously, knowing their changes will be incorporated into other copies of the database during replication. The administrator can also choose to replicate or not replicate portions of another server's replica database perhaps only certain documents to save disk space or to avoid receiving nonpertinent information.

Extending X.500

X.500 arose from 1984 discussions of the directory requirement for X.400. X.400 study groups concluded that there was too much information to be handled and that, on closer examination, the possibilities of the directory go beyond messaging. It is still a common misconception that the only role of X.500 is to store e-mail addresses. This is a key element and is usually the first entry point for most enterprises, but it is not X.500's only function.

E-mail addressing will continue to be a primary function, but X.500 has a variety of other uses related to maintaining a computer network and network applications. These are areas in which other technologies are lacking in comparison with X.500:

- *Distribution lists.* Electronic mailing lists can be held in the directory, to be expanded for distribution by e-mail or fax.

- *Security.* The X.500 directory is a highly suitable repository for storing public key certificates. Secured applications based on public key technology require a repository to store public keys that are used for verifying digital signatures and for encrypting message contents among large communities of users. Scalable public key infrastructures can provide the basis for secure electronic commerce. X.500 with the related standard X.509 pro-

Not just for e-mail

- X.500 can also handle...
    - Distribution lists
    - Security
    - Electronic commerce
    - Workflow applications
    - Message routing
    - Topology mapping
    - Document information

vides an ideal vehicle to achieve this. X.509 assumes a hierarchy of certification authorities (CAs) which can be mapped as a virtual structure onto the X.500 white pages DIT. The hierarchy represents trust chains of CAs, with communities of communicating CAs needing to establish the trust path of every other CA within their community in order to be able to transact securely.

- *Electronic commerce.* X-500 can hold vital information concerning trading partners to which your corporation needs quick access to process electronic commercial transactions.

- *Workflow applications.* Directories are able to associate individuals with organizational roles that can be used in workflow processes. Workflow-based mail can be addressed to roles rather than individuals. Other applications can make use of specific attributes to determine the outcome of workflow processes.

- *Message routing.* Internet Mail system components now store their routes in the Domain Name System (DNS). Similarly, X.400 MTAs are able to publish routing information in X.500 directories.

- *Mapping topologies.* These could be the layout of the corporate network, the distribution of document servers such as the World Wide Web, or a description of the infrastructure of a hospital.

- *Document information.* Work has been carried out in Europe on storing bibliographic information for libraries in X.500; a business application could be storing the contents of a product catalog.

In all these areas, experimental development, deployment, and piloting has been carried out in the research community. There is an opportunity for the corporate world to step in and use that work to good effect.

User interfaces

The one-word distinction between Directory User Agent (DUA) and the more recent Directory User Interface (DUI) emphasizes the difference between directory applications, the directory user interface, and DUA software services, or libraries, that provide access to the directory. Few directory application developers are in a position to build their own DUAs. The actual user interface is built on top of the DAP operations and is more accessible. Several different types of X.500 operations are reflected in the different styles and types of DUAs that are currently available.

One of the more serious problems with X.500 DUAs has been to mask the underlying structure and assumptions of the X.500 directory. Currently one of the more attractive interfaces to the X.500 directory is Mosaic gateway through the World Wide Web. Most of the DUIs available today are not integrated into any other application. To be successful, a directory must be accessible from within an application and should be interactive. Mail users prefer to use directories from within their mail system. Real user benefit is going to be derived from making directory access a seamless background operation. There are several styles of DUA:

- A command line
- A forms-based interface
- A directory browser

A command line DUA often allows users to give instructions similar to raw X.500 commands. This is a flexible tool but it provides an unattractive, nonintuitive interface. Few people would want to use it.

In good form

Forms-based interfaces are used in both UNIX and Windows-based DUAs. They provide a simple and natural way to present a query to the directory. The limitation of the form-based interface is that unless it is configured for a particular DIT configuration, it will have either too many, not enough, or the wrong query lines. The optimum structure recommended for use in directory pilots is simple and flat: country, organization, department, and person. This suits most small and midsized organizations. Many public access X.500 servers all over the world are configured to assume this model as the basis for inquiries.

A strength of X.500, however, is that it lets large organizations create heterogeneous subtrees. In the case of very large corporations, these go as many as six levels deep. In some circumstances, it is appropriate to use a location object class to structure the company's hierarchy; but this might not apply to other organizations that are not geographically distributed. In short, for a forms-based user interface to be truly effective, it must be designed with prior knowledge of what it is going to work against. In a commercial environment, this may be appropriate and even desirable; but it would suggest the need for a lot of different forms depending on where (and for what object) a search is being made.

Browsing X.500

The navigational browser, which lends itself readily to a full graphical interface design, is the most popular form of DUA. It allows users to move up and down the X.500 hierarchical DIT, in a manner similar to Internet surfing or the Windows File Manager. The browser is great for "gee-whizzing." From a practical point of view, and from the perspective of someone who needs to make a search, it can be a slow-moving diversion. The browser presents a potentially confusing maze, particularly to the uninitiated.

Browsing can make the X.500 directory attractive to users, but it requires an appreciation of the directory model. It is also expensive. In addition, not every organization wants to have its organizational chart raked over by its competitor, or to have its employees spend hours surfing an X.500 directory.

Match method to task

No one style of DUA is ideal; each has its merits, depending on the task it's required to perform. Creating a single interface that can find the extension of a colleague in an adjacent department, as well as the e-mail address of a hotel in Tokyo is not practical. The problem lies not so much with the technology, but with the attempt to create a public directory that has the potential to include every residence and working person on the planet. The opportunity to exploit this diversity is there, but not within a single interface.

One limitation of the X.500 directory interface is that it is not really feasible to have type-down addressing. For interactive, wide-area searches, it is conceptually impossible. A search for John Doe, ACME, Inc., WI, USA requires four strategic pieces of information which cannot be entered simultaneously. In practice, telephone users do not refer to their directories more than once or twice before they transfer the information to their personal telephone books. The X.500 directory replaces the big directories, not the personal editions.

Using the World Wide Web

Only a few years ago, the World Wide Web (WWW) was a research community document server with hypertext links that could provide useful tools to establish connections between elements in research documents. It was an interesting and clever piece of technology which seemed unremarkable from a practical perspective. Drawbacks included the overhead required for document conversion and the need to establish a critical mass of servers and material. Now, easy-to-use browsers have made the Web a phenomenon. Even people who have never knowingly made contact with a computer in their lives, know what the Web is. From a user's perspective, the WWW is fun, free, relatively easy to use, colorful, global, and occasionally useful.

The WWW has not succeeded because it meets any obvious need. WWW is not integrated with other applications. It can be very slow and by design is not structured. Searching for an entry can be entertaining, but is often difficult and time-consuming. The Web's success has come about through the combination of factors—the tremendous upsurge of interest in the Internet, partly as a result of the federally sponsored national information infrastructure initiative, and as a concept to stimulate and substantiate some of the popular myths about information highways. This Internet "killer application" is a combination of a useful technology with a simple and attractive interface that hit the streets with perfect timing.

X.500 is not going to happen that way, and it should not be expected to. Nevertheless, in order to enable e-mail, electronic commerce, and other telecommunications services to fulfill their real potential, a global infrastructure is vital. The WWW phenomenon demonstrated how this can happen.

X.500 in the Marketplace

Gillette has won a niche in the marketing hall of fame for its early recognition that it was not in the business of selling razors. It was in the business of selling razor blades. In fact, the modern product is little more than a razor blade with a disposable handle attached.

Where the money is

From a vendor's perspective, the enterprise directory is like the razor. There is money to be made, but not necessarily from the direct sale of an X.500 directory engine. The blades are tools, applications, and services. Customers want unified directories, but no one vendor is going to satisfy all the requirements of a large corporation. Vendors will succeed on their applications' ability to work with those of other vendors.

X.500 alone can't meet every need, either. Its technology will play an important part in the directory picture but will not, by itself, provide solutions to the real-world problems administrators must confront. It is also unlikely that stand-alone directory user agents are going to be much in demand by an increasingly sophisticated user base. For example, a telephone icon that leads to an enterprisewide directory could become a common feature of all desktop applications. The people who click on that button will not care whether it connects with an X.500 directory or some other kind of service. Most won't even want to know.

The number of vendors committed to X.500 products has increased dramatically and continues to grow. At the same time, though, the number of vendors actually developing X.500 technology source code is small—probably less than a dozen worldwide. Their numbers are likely to shrink rather than grow. The technology is complex, and many have learned from their X.400

experience: it is easier and more popular to offer systems integration service ability than to develop applications based on standards. In addition, X.500 is only one of several available tools for creating an enterprise directory.

What X.500 needs to succeed

To claim the enterprise space which unifies all data sources, vendors must extend well beyond messaging. In order to place X.500 at the center of the enterprise data flow, vendors must provide:

- Direct translation services between all data sources and the X.500 directory
- Managed responsibility for objects and attributes as well as the relative authority of data sources

A 1991 forecast predicted that the market for X.500 products would grow from $7.1 million in 1991 to $350 million in the year 2000, and that X.500 application packages would grow from none in 1991 to form nearly 50 percent of the total X.500 product revenues in 2000. These predictions are still on target, according to a more recent report. If anything, they appear to have underestimated the potential market for X.500. Products based on the standard have begun to appear, and there is an increasing demand for the means to create enterprise e-mail directories.

X.500 in the Enterprise

In the corporate world, X.500 and directories are a hot issue. With other messaging issues more or less under control, organizations are looking more closely at the problem of maintaining enterprisewide directories.

X.500 may or may not be the answer; it depends on individual circumstances. Some corporations are primarily interested in integrating mail directories. Others are reaching beyond that to establish integrated enterprise directories that serve multiple applications including e-mail.

In moving from a hodgepodge of proprietary directory systems to a unified, standards-based, enterprisewide system, not all customers want to jump in at the deep end. One of the roles a vendor can play is to help customers judge how quickly and how far they need to go to maximize the benefits of an integrated infrastructure. This requirement will vary from one site to another.

You can index the efficiency of any organization by its ability to send and receive communication. As an accepted part of their working life, people expect to use a range of sophisticated communication media: telephone, fax, telex, postal mail, and now electronic mail. Telephone companies and postal administrations are increasingly aware of the need to accommodate customers clamoring for a whole range of new services unthought of 10 years ago. Meeting this demand requires a global infrastructure.

Every organization that wants to benefit from this revolution must help create that infrastructure. The growth of the WWW demonstrates that this can be achieved when necessary. Four years after Western Union executives concluded that the telephone was an interesting novelty, there were 60,000 telephones in America. Similar stories are told about the spread of fax and even telex. The same will be true of messaging. And while telex and fax have done well without any significant directory support, e-mail is used much differently. It is used much more like the telephone, but it is still grappling with entry-level costs and large-scale infrastructure deployments.

The external directory

Within a large organization, X.500 can play an important role integrating all the disparate databases and sources of information that are scattered across the enterprise. A unified enterprise directory should be visible both internally and to suppliers and customers outside. How this is achieved will vary from one organization to another. An X.500 directory can have an important role as the external face of an organization in much the same way as the Web.

It is increasingly important that corporations better organize and present their data in order to communicate. Within most organizations there may be six or seven administrative departments that maintain records about employees, trading partners, and resources:

- Personnel/human resources
- Finance
- Customer support
- Manufacturing/development (suppliers)
- Telephone operators
- MIS

Each of these departments often has records that are duplicated in other departments but that contain different sets of information. Large organizations are finding it increasingly important to synchronize the management of disparate databases. Many see X.500 as the technology that can hold it all together and facilitate the distributed management of centralized information. In that context, directory synchronization is the enabling technology that can transform X.500 into a useful business tool.

Setting directory priorities

The directories of most large corporations consist of at least one primary source of information, plus some subordinate sources. In a typical enterprise, many of these sources of data will refer to the same subject or person, so it is necessary to establish rules to determine which sources have priority over others.

For example, is Susan Harris still on the payroll? The human resources database would be a more authoritative source than the corporate telephone directory. But if you were simply trying to look up Susan's telephone extension, the telephone database would be the primary authority. It may seem frivolous to formalize this kind of conventional wisdom, but there is a good reason to do so. Ownership and responsibility for information has usually been assigned by institutional habits that far predate computer databases. If you are to present a unified directory, you must rethink these habitual assignments and make sure the directory does a good job of directing. People should be led to the best sources of the information they need.

Many organizations are reappraising all their directory strategies as a result of the messaging infrastructures built up over the last several years. At present, the success of MIS departments to achieve a desired vision of a totally integrated corporate directory will vary considerably. As part of the Lotus strategy, the company assumes that corporate policies pertaining to the integration of all information sources will evolve over time. X.500 may or may not be part of that picture.

Security concerns

As long as an organization is self-contained and protected from the outside world, the problems of security are manageable. If you admit the world through X.500, the privacy and security of personnel and of an organization itself might be violated. Publicity to the contrary, this rarely happens, but it is a serious enough danger that you should minimize. There are at least two situations where a central X.500 directory can have the opposite effect:

- *Firewalls.* Most commercial organizations now connected to the Internet ensure that the integrity of the company's network is maintained by placing the machines with Internet access outside some kind of firewall. The simplest form of secure directory is to have two different systems: one for internal use and one with no sensitive information for use outside the company firewall. This means those outside the firewall should not have access to the full content of a central X.500 directory.

- *Access controls.* A directory can contain sensitive information about people. Some information such as salary details should be protected even inside the organization. Other data, like home telephone numbers, should not be spread outside the organization. Every organization expects to have different types of information about its employees and its business that should be available only to certain privileged individuals or groups of individuals. X.500 has different types of access controls that allow different sets of users different forms of access rights, down to the attribute level. Privacy concerns and national data protection laws discourage making data available through a public X.500 directory.

Adding value to the organization

The principal asset of an institution is knowledge. Knowledge is the sum of information and judgment. Ensuring that the right amount of appropriate information reaches the right number of appropriate people who are able to make qualitative judgments is one of the keys to successful business management.

As a result, more and more companies have appointed chief information officers (CIOs) to regulate the flow of information both within and beyond the enterprise. The CIO is not concerned with any particular product or technology but with communication and workflow among people. An MIS department is generally concerned with computers, computer peripherals, and how people communicate via their computers with other computers, computer applications, and computer peripherals.

Know your audience

In considering where to position X.500 and directories in general, it is important to understand which audience is being addressed: the CIO or the MIS manager. Notes, for example, has developed tremendous appeal to CIOs. The question of the conceptual differences between a database and a directory has not been raised often enough to have made an impact on most enterprise information managers.

The value inherent in adopting X.500 as the corporate directory backbone is hard to justify from the standpoint of short-term benefits, desktop visibility, or revenue gains or savings. To many MIS managers, the adoption of X.500 will seem like an additional overhead creating more work for little overall gain.

There is value to be gained, but X.500 is short on instant gratification. In the enterprise world of the future, business is going to be transacted electronically, integrated voice and e-mail will be the standard forms of interpersonal communication, and directories will hold the whole show together. It requires one network service to rely on the X.500 directory to justify its existence and to transform it from an interesting technology to a mission-critical application.

Future X.500 systems will act as repositories for an array of different information types and sources across the enterprise. This service must provide more than basic X.500 functionality. It must intelligently process inbound and outbound data flows and manage the ownership of and responsibility for individual pieces of information. From the user perspective, the real benefit of any directory service, whether it is X.500 or something else, will be the flexibility and overall usefulness of the interface, particularly when integrated into both desktop and communication applications.

7

E-mail for the
Enterprise—and Beyond

When the Unisys Corporation decided to install a new enterprise-wide e-mail system, it opted for a standard desktop system: Microsoft Mail.

What Unisys soon learned is that Microsoft Mail is exactly as advertised: a desktop e-mail system suitable for LANs. As a company representative put it later, "Microsoft Mail is like most other LAN applications. They are designed for one department in one building on a LAN."

Designed for Close Quarters

Unisys discovered what many other organizations have learned before and since. Most current e-mail products are easily at home in local surroundings. The trouble is, many users want to expand their e-mail horizons. They find that expanding over long distances and diverse systems is much different than exchanging e-mail messages over a purely local network.

In the beginning, Unisys faithfully followed the blueprint Microsoft had laid out for using its e-mail product. The firm connected its outlying post office servers to a central hub server, where they deposited and retrieved messages. Thousands of e-mail patrons send and receive their e-mail messages by way of this single server. By the time their numbers began to approach 20,000, the number of connections being attempted were more than the server could handle. Messages were being delayed, and people were complaining (Fig. 7.1).

The company did find a solution. It scrapped the central server in favor of multiple servers arranged in a tree-shaped configuration. The new layout minimized connections by keeping local traffic local, moving it only within its own branch of the tree. Only traffic destined for other branches would pass through the central server (Fig. 7.2).

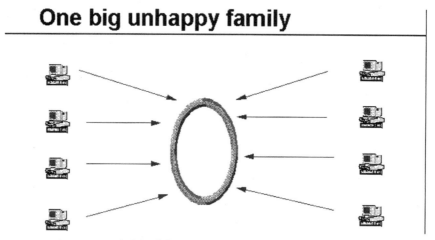

Figure 7.1 As more people joined the network, traffic became congested.

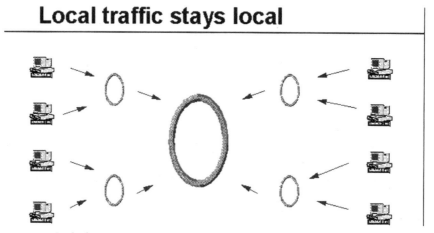

Figure 7.2 Linked nets reduce traffic on the central backbone.

Not unique

This problem is not unique to Microsoft Mail. It is a characteristic of all LAN-based e-mail applications that use shared-file systems. As larger numbers of clients try to connect, the system becomes a bottleneck that keeps the e-mail from getting through.

It's not the only problem you will encounter, either, as you try to expand e-mail from the LAN to the enterprise. You'll also encounter problems like diverse operating systems and the challenge of maintaining large e-mail directories. These are akin to the problems others have encountered trying to extend client/server systems over multiple platforms and to enterprisewide scale. One of the things e-mail has in common with client/server database development is that neither has been fully able to solve these problems.

There are e-mail products designed to span the enterprise and multiple systems. Notes is one. Microsoft Exchange is another. Having settled on Microsoft Mail, Unisys had been hoping its big brother, Exchange, would solve its problems of scale. The Exchange Server is a true client/server messaging system designed to work on server platforms like Windows NT. At the time, though, Exchange Server was still a future product, and Unisys was having problems right then. The company decided to go with what it had—Mail—and work with the features it did have to offer.

A Ride on the MTA

A Mail post office is a local mail server designed to handle local clients. Mail uses its shared file system for the e-mail directory on each post office. Each post office has a mail transfer agent (MTA). An MTA is a gateway that moves messages between the local post office and a remote server. As the Unisys e-mail system grew, the company found itself with 190 MTAs, all trying to contact the same central server.

Unisys decided to capitalize on the system's use of local post offices. It set up a group of local mail hub servers, each connected with a small group of local post offices. A typical local hub serves a building or campus. A message for another post office connected to the same server goes directly from the hub server to the other local post office.

Only messages destined for other parts of the organization travel upward to the next level of the tree—one of five corporate hubs. As with the local hubs, only messages destined for other corporate hubs go beyond this level. In addition, each corporate hub has links to outside services like the Internet.

While the local hubs handle two-way MTA traffic, the corporate hub uses a pair of MTA servers, one for inbound messages, and the other for messages being returned to the local level. Each also has a third post office server handling two-way connections with outside systems and other corporate servers.

The new design has solved the delays, even as the system grows to a planned 27,500 users connected to 400 servers.

Advantages of a big network

Unisys employees found they can do many things with their extended e-mail network. For example, the network makes available a growing number of standard corporate forms, from business card order forms to equipment tags. An employee can retrieve a copy of the master form by e-mail, fill it out, and distribute it by the same e-mail system to the people who must read and act on it. The system has cut overnight delivery charges, mail handling costs, and photocopier use.

You Can Get There from Here

Goals like this—and success at meeting them—are what keep many organizations trying to extend their e-mail systems to their entire enterprises and

Four levels of e-mail service

- Monitor traffic and service
- Control the system
- Automate support
- Provide management access

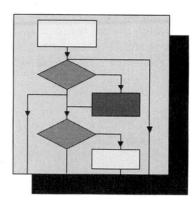

beyond. Not only are they trying to link all their employees in intraenterprise systems, they are trying to connect with business partners through interenterprise systems like electronic document exchange (EDI). Then, there's the third possibility: extraenterprise communication through media like the Internet.

None of this is easy. Enterprisewide e-mail often means sending messages across diverse messaging packages running on an equally diverse variety of operating systems. You might find PCs, Macs, Unix systems, and perhaps others, all needing links to your enterprisewide e-mail system.

Arrested development

Few LAN e-mail products have yet reached the level of sophistication and multivendor interaction needed to stand up in enterprise network service. Lotus Development has identified four levels of e-mail management:

- Level 1: *Monitor* network traffic and service.
- Level 2: Provide *control* to prevent and correct problems.
- Level 3: *Automate* support and maintenance activities.
- Level 4: Provide *access* for management and control.

Few LAN e-mail products have made it past Level 1, Lotus says. Products at this level can:

- Monitor the status of e-mail network components like gateways, directories, servers, and post offices
- Track delivery times
- Chart network use for chargebacks to client departments

At level 2, controls should include:

- Cleaning up obsolete messages
- Adding, changing, and deleting directory entries
- Controlling peak-hour traffic
- Conducting remote restarts

The level 3 support and maintenance features should include:

- Recording directory changes
- Rerouting messages around failed links
- Synchronizing deliveries
- Managing after-hours delivery of large messages and attachments

At level 4, the application should let administrators monitor, control, and automate e-mail management from local or remote workstations.

Since Lotus published this list a few years ago, a few enterprise-level messaging systems—notably Notes, Exchange, and Groupwise—have taken on some of the functions from higher levels.

A management strategy

Establishing enterprisewide e-mail is still a tough goal to meet, but it's getting easier. It's really a two-step process, if you take giant steps:

- Minimize the number of gateways in the system. Or, as Unisys did, minimize the amount of traffic through the gateways.
- Match the products you buy to the organization's business needs.

Gateways and Their Alternatives

The basic question: How do you pass messages among systems that have different formats, different message transport protocols, and different addressing schemes? There are several possibilities, each with the usual mix of advantages and drawbacks. In the past, the most common choice has been to set up point-to-point gateways between each system. It's a measure of this approach, however, that it has a growing number of alternatives. These include:

- Using a public e-mail service.
- Setting up an e-mail backbone that uses existing protocols. These could include a standard like X.400 or a proprietary approach such as SoftSwitch.
- Message switching. In this approach, you maintain in-house message switching, either developing your own or using technology from vendors like Novell.

Two giant steps

- Minimize gateways
- Focus on business needs

- Communication servers, in which multiple processors substitute for multiple gateways.

The gateway approach

Gateways translate messages and addresses from one type of mail system to another. A *point-to-point gateway* is a portal that lets each type of system communicate directly with every other type. E-mail vendors and third parties supply gateways that can connect just about every popular e-mail system to any other. These include LAN-based, host-based, minicomputer, and public e-mail services.

A typical gateway consists of a PC equipped with a LAN adapter and a modem. It logs onto the network like any other client and runs an executable file found on the server. It then serves as an e-mail carrier, polling each local and remote server to deliver and pick up the mail. Gateways also have these functions:

- Forwarding messages between servers on the same e-mail system.

- Translating and sending messages between different e-mail systems.

- Enabling remote users to send and receive mail.

You'll need one gateway for each possible pairing of system types. Each system must have a gateway to connect with every system except itself. That means the number of required gateways can quickly multiply. If you must connect seven types of systems, for example, you'll need 21 gateways.

For smaller, less diverse networks, point-to-point gateways can be economical and (relatively) easy to install and maintain. They're good choices for up to three e-mail systems, which would require only three gateways.

In more complex environments, though, you will experience some serious diseconomies of scale. Say, for example, you have cc:Mail on a PC LAN, IBM Office Vision at corporate headquarters, Notes at a division office, and Groupwise

Problems with gateways

- Possible errors
- Security risks
- Traffic congestion
- And you always seem to need more of them

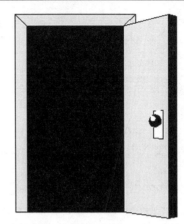

somewhere else. The four mail systems would need six gateways for all to communicate. Integration, equipment, communication, and administration costs will quickly grow as the network grows more complex.

Management, installation, support, and administration staffing add extra costs as well. In a system with six gateways, you will need administrators with experience integrating six different pairs of e-mail environments. Rarely will such a combination of talent be found in a single employee. Someone will also have to be familiar with all the individual e-mail systems themselves.

Gateways have other problems as well. It's easy to overload a gateway. The more gateways in the system, the higher the chances a message will encounter a busy signal. There also is some risk to the integrity and security of the messages that pass through them.

Going public

For many companies, it might be more practical to use a public e-mail service. These include traditional services like MCI Mail and newer offerings that combine Notes and advanced communication techniques.

When you use a commercial service, the provider owns and administers the gateways. You don't have to buy, install, maintain, or administer them yourself. A Notes user can maintain a Notes address book for all correspondents, whatever their systems. The service provider maintains the gateways and makes the necessary translations. You need no gateways of your own, at either the sending or receiving sites.

All this comes at a price, of course. For high-volume use, public services can be very expensive options. On the other side of the balance sheet, the public networks save administration, maintenance, and support costs. The startup costs are low compared with installing your own gateways. The service also is

Alternatives to gateways

- Backbones
- Message switches
- Communication servers

available from nearly anywhere on the planet. They provide a secure, reliable way to talk with trading partners.

Getting some backbone

A *backbone* is a central system that uses a single e-mail protocol to distribute messages between connected networks. The backbone translates an incoming message into its own format, then retranslates it into the format of the receiving station.

A backbone is an attractive choice to maintain e-mail systems that use diverse networks. Adding a new e-mail network is almost as simple as plugging it in. Backbone architectures can be easier to manage and administer, and can save equipment and resource costs. Administrators, mail managers, and support personnel need only learn their local e-mail systems. Then you can provide central management for the backbone. A backbone also simplifies planning and makes it easy to manage setup, growth, and administration. Using a common backbone also simplifies communication with trading partners and with other business units that have diverse systems themselves.

The X.400 messaging standard is emerging as the primary backbone for international and intercompany e-mail. Most public e-mail services provide X.400 services, and many large companies are setting up X.400 backbones. As the market grows, X.400 gateways are becoming increasingly stable and more widely available. Growing volume is also decreasing the cost of setting up an X.400 system.

No technology is without its problems, and X.400 is no exception. Setting up a backbone requires central planning and software development. In turn, these tasks are demanding of staff resources. Unresolved problems include directory integration, management tools, and e-mail APIs for mail-enabled applications.

The message switch

The message switch is a relatively new approach, but one favored by Novell among others. You can build a switch on a single computing platform. This switch accepts incoming messages from a variety of transport protocols. It then delivers them without going through an external gateway. The message switch's primary benefit is that it eliminates the need for gateways.

The communication server

One approach to gateway overload is a communication server. This is a server equipped with disk storage and multiple processors. Each processor serves as a gateway, reducing the need to dedicate individual PCs to this duty. In addition, these systems usually come with management software that automatically tracks server activity. This gives mail administrators a way to manage all the gateways in the server from a single point.

Communication servers now act as front ends for a variety of communication services including X.400, fax, and the Simple Mail Transfer Protocol (SMTP). In addition, they often have advanced directory services and rules-based message handling. These make it easier for remote users to set up and use their systems. One ultimate vision has communication servers acting as the go-betweens to connect internal e-mail systems with employees who use cellular and wireless networks.

X.400 Gets Some Backbone

X.400 has become the technology of frequent choice in organizations that must link diverse e-mail systems. Products that use this protocol are winning reputations for doing the job reliably and well.

It has taken some time for X.400 to win this level of acceptance—this is no Windows 95. There have also been problems to overcome. One has been a shortage of good products incorporating the standard. Once on the market, these products, which are supposed to link diverse e-mail systems, often proved incompatible with each other.

A second major drawback to X.400 is its lack of directory synchronization. A much younger standard, X.500, addresses the problem of getting diverse directories into synch; X.400 is almost completely silent on the issue.

Understanding X.400

X.400 is an MHS whose protocols have been adopted by the ISO. The X.400 protocols define a standard for store-and-forward messaging, including message creation, routing, and delivery services. It runs over an X.25 packet-switched network or asynchronous dial-up lines.

In practice, X.400 lets you build e-mail networks that can span a variety of systems. X.400 is:

- Vendor-independent
- Available for a variety of computer systems, as native applications or as gateways
- Used and accepted around the world

Like nearly any standard, X.400 is less rigid than its proponents would like to believe. It comes in two basic versions, identified by the year each was issued: 1984 and 1988. The older standard still defines the protocol's basic services. The major addition in the later standard is asynchronous transmission, useful for mobile PC users.

Client/server application

X.400 works on client/server principles. The client side is a UA. The server is an MTA.

The UA works like a personal mailbox. It is the main point of connection with the individual. The UA prepares, submits, and receives messages. Other services can include text editing, presentation services, security, message priorities, and delivery notification. The user agent observes no particular standards except the message format. The product developer is responsible for providing a user interface. The message transfer agent routes and relays the messages. Its main responsibilities include establishing the store-and-forward path, maintaining security, and routing the messages.

When it receives a message to be processed, the UA sends the message to the local MTA. The MTA checks the message for errors—technical, not grammatical. If all is well, it sends the message on its way. If the message is intended for a local destination it goes to the appropriate local UA. If the message is not local, it goes to the next MTA en route to the destination. Successive MTAs repeat this process until the transfer is completed.

A connection of MTAs makes up an MTS. Other X.400 components include:

- *Distribution lists* (DLs), which are like electronic routing slips.

- A *message store* service that stores messages until recipients receive them. It complements the UA for PCs and other systems that are not always on line.

- *Access units,* which provide connections to other kinds of communication services like telex and the postal service.

For e-mail system managers, X.400 provides for a *management domain,* a group of MTAs and their associated UAs managed by a single organization. An administrative management domain (ADMD) is run by the telephone company or another external communication service. Its private equivalent, a private management domain (PDMD), can be run by another type of organization.

Delivering the mail

In operation, X.400 mimics the postal service. It handles a message much like a letter, complete with an electronic envelope. The address part of the envelope includes the information necessary to deliver the message. X.400 can deliver messages to other X.400 users via a message transfer service. It also can reach other communication facilities via an interpersonal messaging service.

As with the postal service, you must identify each recipient by a unique address. This can be a name that identifies a unique entity such as an employee number, or one that identifies a particular destination.

Normally, an X.400 service will look up the name in its directory to locate the address within the system. X.400 addresses consist of attributes that describe a user or distribution list, or which locate the distribution list within the mail system. Attributes can be:

- *Personal.*   For example, the recipient's name
- *Geographical,* such as a street address, city, or country
- *Organizational,* such as the recipient's business unit
- *Architectural,* such as a user agent identifier or management domain

In practice, X.400 names are long and complex. Fortunately, you can assign more manageable aliases.

The message transfer system also handles two other kinds of traffic: probes and reports. A probe is like an empty envelope. Use it to find out if you can deliver a message as expected. You might send out a probe to test a path, asking the receiving MTS if it can accept a particular message type. If you test first with a probe, you reduce the chance a recipient's system will reject an important message.

A report does much the same thing, but does it after the message is transmitted. It is a status indicator that relates the progress or outcome of a transmission.

Directories and security

Directory service is not an X.400 strong point; that is where X.500 shines, or will eventually shine. In fact, the 1988 version of X.400 suggests that you use X.500 to record names, store distribution lists, maintain profiles of user agents, and identify authorized users. X.500 lets people create names that make sense to them. They need not contend with names designed to make sense to the system.

In its current version, X.400 also has some security features. These can authenticate the originator of a message, verify the party that originates a delivery or nondelivery notice, check for altered contents, and verify that all recipients received copies. The standard also provides for return receipt and registered mail services.

A complete e-mail security system does not exist. X.400 offers nothing, for example, to find out whether someone is impersonating an authorized user. There is nothing, either, to make sure no one delays, reorders, or improperly duplicates a message.

Pick the Right Products

In the computer trade press, much is often made of a vendor's product strategy; too little is often made of their customers' strategies.

You'll see articles that describe Microsoft's strategic vision, or that of Lotus or Novell. Certainly, these and all other vendors have strategies for their own survival and growth, and these translate into product lines that follow particular philosophies. The really important question, though, is what your orga-

Two approaches

- Cross-platform strategy
- Message handling service

nization is doing to ensure its own survival and growth. A vendor's strategy is important only to the extent that it supports your own.

That is the key to the second giant step in developing an enterprise network system: find a vendor and a product line that fits your own business needs.

At this point, it is possible you could encounter a conflict: the best fit to your needs may involve increasing, not decreasing, the number of gateways you must manage. Try to avoid a system that forces you to add new gateways to support specific applications.

Most e-mail products have similar features and functions. They even look much the same on-screen. There are major differences, though, in how they implement these features. There are two basic approaches:

- A *cross-platform strategy* that uses a common messaging format for different client operating systems

- The *MHS* available in Novell networks

These approaches are not mutually exclusive. Significantly, both IBM/Lotus and Novell use both. Microsoft uses neither.

Crossing platforms

The cross-platform approach adapts to multiple operating systems at the workstation level. Disk Operating Systems (DOSs), Macintoshes, OS/2 systems, Unix workstations, and others can each run their own versions of Notes or Groupwise. A single server acts as a kind of United Nations translator, serving all these diverse systems simultaneously. Larger networks may require more than one server, but not many more.

This approach can eliminate many of the gateways you might otherwise need to translate messages among these systems. You easily might get away with a single gateway, linking the server to third-party services and other parts of the outside world. What's more, this system simplifies administration, since all the messages and directory information are on a few servers at most. There is less equipment to connect and maintain, it's easier to identify and solve problems, traffic flows more efficiently, and there are fewer delays.

The major drawback to this system is that the vendors assume many of these burdens on your behalf. You might not have to make major adaptations to different kinds of platforms, but the vendors do. For example, each platform requires its own file locking and encryption software. Multiplatform fax software is still in its infancy.

If the vendor has not yet provided all the appropriate software for the platforms you want to use, there is no other source. In addition, each vendor uses a proprietary messaging format. If you want to link with another type of e-mail system, you'll need a gateway.

Handling the messages

The second approach relies on MHS to establish a common messaging format for all platforms. E-mail systems that adopt this method use Novell's standard message format (SMF) API as a link to MHS. This means any vendor whose e-mail package conforms to the API can communicate with all other packages that support MHS.

This system needs no gateways to translate messages between different platforms or different flavors of e-mail software. In addition, you can use Netware for such tasks as setting up directory services. You can also use Netware services to monitor server performance, manage disk space, and generate error reports. In addition, there is a constant flow of new services being added via Netware loadable modules (NLMs).

If this approach makes heavy use of Netware services, the drawback is that it relies too heavily on Netware. All other network operating systems are effectively shut out. It's possible to work around this limitation, but it is not easy.

Fitting Notes into the Picture

Lotus has recently found itself with overlapping e-mail products: Notes and cc:Mail. The company's acquisition by IBM has stirred the new parent company's product strategy into the mix.

How the IBM and Lotus strategies are to be merged has been a matter of conjecture, but with version 4 of Notes, Lotus has made a clear distinction between its two e-mail products:

- Notes, a client/server application, is intended to provide enterprise-level computing, regardless of the size of the enterprise.

- cc:Mail, a file-sharing product, provides e-mail services for LANs and other smaller workgroups.

LCA links the systems

Bridging these two systems is the Lotus Communication Architecture (LCA), designed to provide a flexible framework that can extend messaging across nearly every major platform, plus remote access and the Internet.

LCA's central feature is a Notes/cc:Mail Communication Server (CommServer). As implemented in Notes 4.0, CommServer provides four key functions that bridge the file-sharing and client/server systems:

- Router-to-router internetworking between post offices. This service replaces the hub routers in cc:Mail networks.

- A message transport for and X.400 gateways and SMTP gateways to the Internet.

- Messaging and directory interoperability between cc:Mail and Notes. This includes directory replication in both directions, automating directory exchanges, and enabling tight integration of the two systems across the organizational environment.

- Interactive administration across integrated networks.

Better postal service

At the same time, cc:Mail is gaining an improved file-sharing post office. It runs as a back end, in parallel with existing servers, which means you can gradually migrate from the old system to the new. A new cc:Mail client takes advantage of the back end. This client also has an interface to Microsoft's MAPI. This means it can contact any MAPI server, the most significant being Exchange.

The server version of Notes 4.0 also incorporates full MAPI support for cc:Mail clients. This lets e-mail patrons use the cc:Mail front end with the Notes back end and ease the migration from e-mail to full workgroup computing. The system also works in reverse: any MAPI-compliant mail client, including Microsoft Mail, can use Notes as a back-end messaging server.

Another product, the Lotus Messaging Switch (LMS) links Lotus products with interenterprise and extraenterprise gateways. LMS serves as a translator for many external services, including the Internet and legacy systems.

Gateway to MHS

Notes has an MHS gateway that provides for mail exchanges with other MHS-compatible systems. This gateway can communicate with a stand-alone Netware host or with a Netware file server. To do so, it makes use of an NLM that provides for Netware Global Messaging (NGM).

A message from a Notes system to a foreign MHS goes through these steps:

1. A mail router at the Notes server finds the recipient at its foreign domain address.

2. Notes routes the message to the Notes server that operates the MHS gateway.

3. The gateway transfers the message to the file server's incoming gateway directory.

4. MHS software at the host finds the message and scans its own routing table for the recipient's mail directory.

5. The MHS software then routes the message to that directory.

A gateway being a gateway, there are some drawbacks:

- The formatted rich text documents of Notes are converted to American Standard Code for Information Interchange (ASCII) text. Most of the formatting information and all graphics are lost.

- Though Notes can transfer multiple binary attachments to HMS, from that point each MHS message is limited to a single attachment.

- This is strictly an e-mail connection. You cannot replicate databases.

- Signed mail goes through without the signature.

- You must use one of the mail form templates supplied with Notes; home-grown templates may not transfer all their fields.

- The 79-character names permitted in Notes must be translated to a maximum of eight characters for MHS.

- If the recipient is in a different domain, an automatic reply may not reach the sender.

Novell Opens Messaging

Novell's Groupwise seeks keep mail-enabled client applications from dependence on specific underlying services. The vehicle for this quest is known as the Novell Collaborative Computing Environment (NCCE). NCCE includes components of the former WordPerfect Office, SoftSolutions, and InForms. This framework supports a central strategy known as the Open Messaging Environment (OME).

Through NCCE, Novell offers compatibility with any server, adding value through Groupwise application components. These include scheduling, calendar management, an address book, workflow management, electronic forms, and discussion databases. NCCE also connects with many external service providers, including the advanced X.500 directory services.

Document management platform

This system rests on a SoftSolutions document management platform that can track information across all connected networks in the organization. Components include APIs that link to Groupwise services as well as applications from other vendors. With MAPI as a common messaging API, organizations can mix components like Groupwise, Windows 95, Notes, and other clients.

Novell also intends to support any manufacturer's back-end server. Because NCCE is a native MAPI service provider, any MAPI-compliant application can operate with Novell's back end.

Novell has been developing this system in three phases:

- *Interoperability* establishes basic gateway connections between MHS and Groupwise through Netware NLMs. This lets the two services coexist in a single environment.

- *Integration* focuses on administration facilities and directory services. In the initial part of this phase, Groupwise can synchronize directories with Netware 4.1, which handles all administrative chores.

- *Convergence* is the ultimate objective. This phase establishes an improved message transport agent (another MTA) between Groupwise and MHS. This architecture is designed to support collaborative services like work-flow management, scheduling, task management, and forms processing.

To serve long-term customers, Novell is making each change backward-compatible with the old MHS. This lets the customers build new features onto existing technology while moving toward an integrated, open environment.

At the client level

Groupwise provides most of the client components of the NCCE framework. Like NCCE messaging, the client software lets you add third-party applications to replace any of those in the kit. A "universal inbox" includes e-mail, calendar and schedule management, workflow management, an address book, document management, imaging, and voice mail.

Microsoft Goes Its Own Way

Microsoft, as usual, is going its own way with MAPI, hoping to set a standard others will follow. Also as usual, others are following.

The central product is Exchange, both as a server and as a desktop product. The goal is eventually to provide client/server messaging across DOS, Macintosh, and Unix platforms, all versions of Windows, and by dial-up. In addition to e-mail, Exchange supports a forms designer and other packages to build custom front ends.

Position players

Exchange comes as both a back-end server, designed to run on Windows NT Server, and a front-end client distributed as part of Windows 95. The client operates as a universal inbox for messages from sources like mail, rich text documents, X.400 transmissions, images, and others. It also provides remote- and local-access discussion databases available to any location that has access to an Exchange Server.

The server supports fault-tolerant directory synchronization and will interact with Lotus's Vendor Independent Messaging (VIM) by way of a VIM/MAPI converter. The server also supports common protocols like X.400 and SMTP and provides services like e-mail, scheduling, calendar management, documentation libraries, and discussion databases.

The server also takes advantage of NT provisions for hot backups and integrated directory services. You can manage any server on the network from any client location, and you have the advantage of NT's multilayer security features.

Mixed servers

Organizations that want to convert to Exchange can do so gradually. Exchange uses MAPI to provide drop-in compatibility for multiserver mail environments. The Exchange server also includes an X.400 gateway for internetworking.

At your option, you can upgrade either the front or back ends in whatever order best supports your objectives. For example, Microsoft's MTAs are designed to improve carrying capacity as upgraded servers come on line. If higher capacity is your primary goal, you may want to upgrade the server now, taking advantage of MTAs, and adding clients later.

Exchange vs. Notes

In the eyes of their creators, Notes and Exchange are head-on competitors. In the eyes of customers, the two products actually may prove to complement each other. Many organizations use both products, taking advantage of the strongest features of each: Exchange as a message platform and Notes for workgroup cooperation.

This may or may not be a deliberate choice. One part of an organization may be building Notes applications while another uses Exchange for similar purposes. Then, when they try to exchange information across platforms, they run into the same difficulties you encounter when you are trying to do any type of cross-platform messaging. Even in the best-case analysis, administrators will have to support both types of applications while making sure they continue to talk to each other. Even so, the natural division of duties—Exchange for messaging and Notes for collaboration—tends to assert itself.

IBM Thinks Centralized

IBM's acquisition of Lotus probably also means a merger of their e-mail strategies, with much of IBM's workflow technology either scrapped in favor of Notes or integrated with the Lotus platform.

IBM brings to the joint venture a client/server strategy that starts with its traditional host-based interests. In this environment, IBM has its eye on such extended applications as accurate and secure financial transactions. This requires what IBM calls "assured delivery" of messages and data. Furthermore, IBM wants its systems to support workgroups of all sizes, from small departments to hundreds of thousands of people. A third objective is that its messaging systems be compatible with all the standards now in common use, including VIM and MAPI.

Messages and queues

IBM's communication strategy relies on a messaging and queuing package called MQSeries. It is positioned as middleware, designed as a liaison between Office Vision, and newer client/server offerings.

MQSeries also serves as a multiprotocol backbone for scheduling, workflow automation, and other messaging-based applications. The product is designed to integrate a total of 19 disparate mail and other communication protocols— in effect, nearly everything on the market.

IBM is also including hooks to DB2, its client/server database. One reason: DB2 provides much of the reliability and security assured delivery requires. One likely response of the Lotus acquisition is that Notes will also gain access to DB2 databases.

Client systems

On the client side, IBM has been working on a series of client platforms, running on OS/2 , Windows, and the Macintosh, that will incorporate e-mail, workflow management, and scheduling. It can also share the same store of data with other IBM applications.

The server will work with any VIM- or MAPI-compliant front-end product. That means customers who want to use cc:Mail or Microsoft Mail with the IBM server can do so.

Saving workflow software

Since the acquisition, IBM has backed away from many of its own groupware products in favor of Notes. One exception has been the workflow product Flowmark, which runs on OS/2 and AIX operating systems. Flowmark is being integrated with Notes so you could start a Flowmark process from within Notes. Flowmark then could manage the workflow process, feeding data about its progress into a Notes database.

Notes Cuts Across Platforms

In Notes, Lotus's approach to multiplatform messaging is essentially proprietary. Notes and its companion product, cc:Mail, use what Lotus calls a platform-independent messaging system designed to transport messages between Lotus messaging applications running on varied operating systems. In addition, links are available to common standards like X.400 and the SMTP and to competing e-mail products.

As Lotus product literature puts it, Notes was "designed from its inception to support the multiplicity of operating platforms found in and among all organizations." This built-in capacity overcomes the limitations of relying on standards like X.400, or of providing a messaging product only within the context of a particular operating system.

Exceeding standards

X.400 cannot insulate customers from all interoperability problems, Lotus officials say. The protocol provides some interoperability with other vendors' mail systems that run on other platforms. Nevertheless, you must still contend with differences in these platforms' directory implementations and user agent interfaces.

Notes is designed to provide a shield from the complexities of both network and computer operating systems. With a cross-platform messaging system, developers can build an application once on one platform and then deploy it on any other platform. This approach takes advantage of the native tools and services of each platform on which it is deployed.

This approach also maintains flexibility as systems grow and become more diverse. Organizations occasionally replace an existing computer or network operating system in favor of another for a variety of reasons such as performance, scalability, or cost. These decisions are made outside the context of the messaging system. Indeed, when changing an underlying platform, most companies intend to move existing applications from the old platform to the new one. The communication-centered applications built on top of a platform-independent messaging system can be leveraged on the new platform as well. For applications that are directly tied to the underlying operating system, such a change would require that the applications be rewritten.

This is particularly important to companies considering mergers or acquisitions. The ability to seamlessly absorb the operating system and network topology of an acquisition candidate is rarely one of the factors considered when making an acquisition. System administrators can hedge against future acquisitions by investing in a platform-independent messaging system that will easily connect newly acquired units. They need not worry that someday they must abandon their investments in existing platforms and networks.

Out of the operating system

Lotus also claims an advantage over competitors who bundle messaging components into their operating systems (translation: Microsoft). "Inclusion of 'free' software in a bundle is not a measure of altruism on the part of a vendor, but rather an attempt to lock customers into a product strategy," Lotus maintains. Such a packaging technique can work well for both parties if the integration of the products actually adds value that could not be found elsewhere, and if it does not preclude the use of the combined products for other business purposes. Even so, the reduction of messaging to a server or network operating system service does not create value beyond what an enterprise could find by selecting a messaging system that resides on top of the operating system.

Four-tier communication

The Lotus communication architecture is arranged in four tiers. This architecture allows for flexibility, including the use of a variety of Lotus and third-party products; simplified acquisition, installation, and management; and straightforward connectivity to external parties. The four tiers are:

- *Client layer.* This layer, which sits on desktops and laptop computers, includes the user agent, made up of the user interface, a text editor, sorting and categorizing logic, and rules and other programming editors. For groupware, the client layer also includes the full database and development functionality of the server, enabling mobile clients to act as both clients and servers. The client layer supports a variety of client types, including both the file sharing and client/server versions of cc:Mail; Notes and Notes Express clients; and third-party mail clients such as the one bundled with Windows 95.

- *Departmental server layer.* Clients typically connect to a departmental server or, in the case of file-sharing mail systems, to a departmental post office. These servers provide a message store, directory services and transport services for messaging clients, and additional database-oriented services for groupware clients such as Notes. Typically found on robust server platforms (OS/2, UNIX, NLM, Windows NT), this layer can also use a traditional client platform, such as Windows Version 3.

- *Enterprise server layer.* In most large networks, customers implement a layer of servers at the enterprise level. These servers act as hubs for both store-and-forward messaging and for database replication. Quite often, users are not directly attached to enterprise-level servers. Instead, these servers act as concentration points for the departmental layer servers.

- *Interenterprise services layer.* This layer provides services to connect a department or enterprise with external business partners, suppliers and customers. For external organizations or remote offices that also use Notes and cc:Mail, this layer provides connectivity through AT&T Network Notes, the Internet, commercial value-added WANs, SMTP, and X.400 protocol compliance. This layer does not presuppose that an organization has already implemented cc:Mail and/or Notes across the entire enterprise. A single departmental server can take advantage of interenterprise services as well as an enterprise at large.

File sharing and client/server systems

Until recently, there has been an essential division between cc:Mail and Notes:

- cc:Mail is best known as a file-sharing system most suitable for local networks.
- Notes is primarily positioned as a client/server application.

The file-sharing version of cc:Mail adequately satisfies the needs of many companies. Lotus feels many successful users of cc:Mail have no plans to immediately move their systems to client/server architecture, and this constituency has a stake in the continued investment and support of file-sharing cc:Mail. At the same time, the general adoption of client/server technology, and the need of many companies to move their e-mail system to that architecture, makes a client/server version of cc:Mail both necessary and desirable.

Lotus says it is committed to the ongoing enhancement of the file-sharing cc:Mail client and post office, and is investing in post office/router technology and the cc:Mail user agents that access the post office/router infrastructure. The next release of file-sharing cc:Mail, version 3.0, ensures that customers will enjoy improved functionality and administration without having to commit to a new underlying architecture.

At the same time, Lotus is providing two kinds of client/server ability for cc:Mail customers:

- The new cc:Mail client will be able to interoperate with Notes servers for client/server-based messaging.
- cc:Mail users can continue to experience the cc:Mail user interface, even if they decide to take advantage of an integrated client/server, messaging/groupware environment using Notes and Notes Express clients.

Many Lotus customers will operate mixed environments consisting of cc:Mail file-sharing systems and Notes servers hosting either or both Notes clients and cc:Mail clients. In these environments, Lotus provides integration for administration, operation, and management. This integration includes directory integration, as well as integration of the management systems.

Connecting Notes and cc:Mail

Notes users have the option of conducting their electronic mail messaging in a Notes mail environment or in a cc:Mail environment. Notes mail and cc:Mail users can exchange mail with each other via the Lotus Mail Exchange facility.

In fact, the alternatives are not limited to Notes mail. You can choose an alternate mail program that complies with VIM. You can exercise the option when setting up Notes; you can specify your mail program as Notes mail or cc:Mail. If you are working in a Notes environment that uses cc:Mail (or Notes mail) exclusively and you do not intend to send cc:Mail documents to Notes databases, you do not need any additional software. However, if you are working in a mixed environment of Notes mail users and cc:Mail users, or if you intend to send cc:Mail documents to Notes databases, you need the Lotus Mail Exchange.

The Lotus Mail Exchange Facility is a Notes server add-in that provides mail exchange, directory exchange, and mailbox conversion capabilities for Notes Release 3 and cc:Mail for Windows 2.0 mail programs. The mail exchange ability lets Notes mail and cc:Mail users exchange mail, converting messages from the format of the sending mail program into the format required by the receiving mail program. The mail exchange function also lets Notes application database users whose sole mail program is cc:Mail to mail Notes documents to cc:Mail users or cc:Mail messages to Notes databases. The directory exchange capability enables automatic exchange of user address information between Notes mail and cc:Mail, so that users can address recipients in the syntax of their native mail program. The mailbox conversion capability enables users of one mail program to change to the other, automatically transferring the contents from a Notes mail database to a cc:Mail mailbox or vice versa.

Basic functions

The built-in Notes support for cc:Mail:

- Converts Notes-formatted messages to cc:Mail recipient's native format (converts Notes forms, keywords, and tables into cc:Mail text).

- Converts body of Notes mail message into text or file items in cc:Mail.

- Extracts embedded images from Notes mail, converts images to a standard file format, and attaches to cc:Mail message as file items. Extracts other embedded graphics and attaches to cc:Mail messages as file items. cc:Mail does not support import or export of graphic formats, so cc:Mail graphics items, including snapshots, cannot be translated in Notes mail.

- Supports and preserves multiple file attachments in Notes mail and cc:Mail. Preserves Notes Direct Document Exchange (DDE) and object linking and embedding (OLE) objects as attachments.

- Preserves mail receipt report and delivery priority settings and maintains the TO:, CC:, and BCC: fields of the Notes document.

- If the Notes mail message exceeds limit of text, recipients, or header information allowed by cc:Mail, divides message into multiple text items.

- Allows launching of cc:Mail via Notes and sending of Notes documents to cc:Mail users.

- Allows users to use cc:Mail native addressing syntax.

- When cc:Mail users send Notes documents via Mail—Send or Mail— Forward as Attachment, Notes preserves it document integrity, including all forms functionality, by transforming documents into database attachments. cc:Mail recipients can view the document via Notes by double-clicking the attachment.

Added functions

In addition to the basic set, the Mail Exchange facility provides these functions:

- Converts each cc:Mail message item, such as text, fax, or file, to descriptive entry in Notes mail message, followed by contents of item or attached file, as appropriate. Converts body of Notes mail message into text or file items in cc:Mail.

- Lets Notes mail users send mail as encapsulated databases to cc:Mail users, by composing mail message using form that contains MailFormat field set to specify encapsulation.

- Enables Notes users who rely exclusively on cc:Mail for their mail program to send cc:Mail messages to Notes databases.

When recipients of cc:Mail encapsulated databases are Notes mail users, transforms encapsulated databases back into normal Notes mail documents.

Added integration

To further integrate its two products, Lotus is releasing a product called the Notes/cc:Mail Communication Server (CommServer)—it was formerly known as the LCS. CommServer is the Notes version 4 server bundled with full function connectivity to cc:Mail networks. At your option, it can also host native X.400 and SMTP MTAs.

CommServer provides four main functions:

- *cc:Mail Router backbone.* CommServer nodes will often be used to replace hub routers in cc:Mail networks. A CommServer node will communicate with several cc:Mail routers acting as a hub and with other CommServer nodes. In this sense, it performs precisely the same router-to-router function as hub routers do today, but will be available on more scalable platforms (e.g., UNIX).

- *Native X.400 and SMTP connectivity.* For organizations with X.400- and SMTP-based constituencies, CommServer nodes can host X.400 and SMTP MTAs, and thus provide this standards-based connectivity for cc:Mail networks. These MTAs can be used as transport between CommServer nodes for such purposes as to allow CommServer nodes to operate on X.400 or SMTP backbones. The MTAs can also provide access to X.400 and SMTP user communities. Each of the MTAs is optional.

- *Integration of cc:Mail and Notes environments.*   For organizations that operate Notes, CommServer nodes provide full integration of cc:Mail and Notes, including messaging interoperability, directory interoperability, and integrated management. CommServer Conversion Services will provide high-fidelity mapping between cc:Mail objects and Notes objects. CommServer Directory Services will extend the replication of Notes Name and Address Books and the Automatic Directory Exchange function of cc:Mail in order to make cc:Mail directories act like replicas of Notes Name and Address Books. That means changes are automatically propagated in both directions.

- *High-function management.*   This is provided by a pair of companion products: cc:Mail View and Notes View. In an integrated environment, cc:Mail View will act as a proxy agent to Notes View.

CommServer is characterized by its modular architecture. While it includes all the technology and services first articulated in Lotus's announcement of LCS, CommServer presents cc:Mail and Notes customers with a single and flexible enterprise-scale back end. Any Notes server can be deployed as a CommServer enterprise messaging server to connect not just other Notes servers but also cc:Mail subnetworks. A CommServer that is first implemented as a cc:Mail hub server can be extended with no additional technology investment to act as a Notes application hub server. CommServer is a true common back end for cc:Mail and Notes.

Version 4 enhancements

Many features of Notes Version 4 are designed to enhance its usefulness in mixed, enterprisewide service. The server provides a distributed, replicated object store, a security service based on public key cryptography, and programmable agents. Notes clients provide a user interface for interacting with local and remote databases, for messaging and for application development. Lotus is improving the robustness of Notes V4 in several ways:

- *Server support.*   Notes V4 will continue to support the breadth of popular servers, including Hewlett-Packard (HP), IBM, Sun, and SCO UNIX, as well as Windows NT, OS/2, and Novell.

- *Extended client support.*   Notes V4 clients include Windows 3.1, Windows 95, Windows NT, OS/2, Macintosh, and UNIX.

- *cc:Mail User Interface.*   The mail system conforms to the cc:Mail user interface specification. Users see the cc:Mail client user interface and will experience the same look and feel as the stand-alone cc:Mail product.

- *Enterprise scalability.*   Notes V4 features greater scalability and performance. Many organizations choose to implement an enterprise layer of servers to manage large-scale applications. In addition to serving as a departmental server, Notes V lets administrators deploy it as an applications hub server with no additional technology investment.

- *Native X.400 and SMTP support.*   Because X.400 and SMTP are such fundamental transports in enterprise and interenterprise messaging environments, the Lotus X.400 and SMTP MTAs can be installed directly on Notes V4 servers, in addition to installing them on Notes/cc:Mail Communication Servers. This provides departmental-level servers with interenterprise connectivity.

For large enterprises

In large enterprises, Lotus components typically coexist with legacy systems and messaging components from other suppliers. To help integrate these third-party legacy and messaging systems into the Lotus Communications Architecture, Lotus is enhancing the LMS to provide these services:

- High-fidelity message switching among X.400, SMTP, IBM SNADS, IBM Office Vision, DEC All-In-1, and VMSmail, as well as among numerous other messaging environments.

- A high function "boundary MTA" acting as the nodes to connect internal networks to external networks for X.400 and SMTP. LMS has access controls, rules, and other features necessary for systems providing this boundary function.

- Directory synchronization among all major environments.

X.500 support, including native support for the X.500, DAP, the LDAP, and the Directory Systems Protocol (DSP).

Notes on the Web, and Other Add-Ons

Andersen Consulting is one of the largest Notes users in the world. Yet when it came time to implement an interactive training program, Andersen chose the WWW. The stated reason: although about 20,000 Andersen employees are connected by Notes, the consulting firm did not want to impose that choice on clients who would be using the training program. Other large Notes users have also chosen to use the Web for some operations.

Can the Web Replace Notes?

Some Web partisans believe Notes can be replaced by hypertext materials posted on the Web. They feel Notes is too expensive and complex for many organizations, who could use the Web as a more attainable alternative.

For most organizations, though, the two platforms serve different needs. The Web is a quick and easy way to spread information. It is a simple way to get information to a broad population, including people who don't use Notes. It is also a way to reach audiences you might not know about.

Nevertheless, Web audiences tend to be disjointed collections of individuals. Notes works better with identified groups who establish continued working relationships. It has features like document coordination and version control few Web servers can match. Notes is also able to handle larger volumes of information flow. A Web site can bog down once it reaches a certain level of volume and complexity.

Can Notes Replace the Web?

In version 4, Notes includes a Web browser that can deliver documents to a Notes database. There is also an add-on product, InterNotes Publisher, a link between Notes databases and the Web. It lets you export a Notes database and all its documents to the Web. The Publisher can be even more valuable for managing the Web site once you establish it.

An organization that establishes a Web site soon finds it wants nearly all its public information material to be available via the Web. That includes sales

InterNotes Publisher provides...

- Direct conversion to HTML
- Document and view management through Notes
- Workgroup management

and marketing information, customer support information, press releases, and financial statements. Lotus even advertises job openings at its Web site.

The problem is to manage all that material. There was no central management for such a diverse collection of information in pre-Web days. Now you must not only establish a management scheme, but you must do so within the informal, unmanaged atmosphere of the Web. Someone must collect that information, check it for accuracy, and determine what information should and should not be available to the public.

Publishing on the Web

The InterNotes Web Publisher lets you publish notes information on the World Wide Web, providing access to the growing millions of Internet users.

By translating Notes documents and databases into Hypertext Mark-up Language (HTML), the format used by standard Web browsers, the InterNotes Web Publisher gives you the means to create and manage enterprise Web sites. Often, no one person or department can provide all the content appropriate for a Web site. The InterNotes Web Publisher uses Notes's collaborative authoring environment to distribute the process of creating and maintaining Web content.

The InterNotes Web Publisher is a Notes server application that runs in conjunction with a standard Web HTTP server. The InterNotes Web Publisher automatically converts Notes documents and views into HTML documents for a Web server. By converting Notes views, the InterNotes Web Publisher provides a navigable structure for the Web site. In the process:

- Notes doc links become hypertext links.
- Attachments to Notes documents are preserved and can be downloaded from a Web browser.
- Notes tables are converted into HTML tables.

- Bitmaps in Notes documents are converted into in-line GIF files.

At the same time, the Web publisher provides a Notes database that controls translation parameters such as font mapping and selecting views to translate. The product also consolidates logging and report generation, and handles other processes.

Behind the Web publisher

Many companies have looked toward the Web distribute information to customers, business partners, and other public audiences. In addition to providing a rich graphical interface, the Web offers global reach and a growing base of clients.

The challenge for most organizations, however, is to set up and maintain an enterprise Web server. This typically requires major investments of both people and equipment. If several authors or departments contribute the information, managing a Web site becomes even more time-, labor-, and resource-intensive.

All documents intended for the Web server must be translated into HTML and linked to other documents. This often requires a staff of dedicated HTML and Web specialists. Moreover, Web documents typically have links that refer to other documents on the same Web server or on other Web servers. Any time documents are added or deleted from the server, the hypertext links and any references to those links must be updated. The complexity of creating and maintaining documents and links on a Web server inevitably creates a management bottleneck.

Notes as a workflow tool

You can take advantage of Notes to establish an information management workflow process, using forms and view to catalog the diverse documents. Then, using InterNotes Publisher, you can create a hypertext file and place it on the Web.

Notes also helps you manage the connections between hypertext documents. Old documents should be cleaned off the system. When you delete a document, though, you take the risk of leaving unknown numbers of hypertext pointers, which point to a document that is no longer there.

With Notes, you can use a view instead. A view presents a list of documents that is automatically updated whenever you add or subtract. When InterNotes publishes a database on the Internet, it also publishes the views. These views replace hypertext links and give people another way to navigate through the database.

Automatic conversion

The InterNotes Web Publisher automatically converts Notes databases and documents into HTML so that they are accessible to popular Web browsers such as NCSA Mosaic or Netscape. The Publisher takes advantage of Notes's distributed authoring and management environment to create Web sites. Individual authors prepare their own information in Notes. Using Notes's replication and distributed storage structure, authors from geographically decentralized workgroups can contribute documents to the corporate Web server.

The Publisher also creates HTML documents of Notes views to give Web browsers the same navigational structure as the original Notes database. As content changes and as contributors submit new material, the Publisher automatically updates the home pages and all links to the new documents, without any manual intervention.

Getting the News

InterNotes News is a Notes server application that exchanges Usenet news articles between Notes and news servers, using the Network News Transfer Protocol (NNTP). This product gives Notes users a secure and easy way to participate in Usenet newsgroups from the Notes environment. By reading news articles from Notes, users can expand on key Notes functions, including hierarchical views of discussion threads, full text search, and multiple indexed views of the news articles.

InterNotes News offers users:

- Access to Usenet newsgroups without a personal Internet connection

- Use of Notes macros, full-text search and mail forwarding to manage Usenet newsgroup articles

- The ability to participate in newsgroups by writing and posting a response from Notes, or replying directly to the author using Notes mail through an SMTP gateway

Joining newsgroups

Newsgroups are forums where users share information about a topic or brainstorm on an idea. Business users have found Usenet newsgroups useful to develop product ideas, conduct ad hoc marketing research, and to gather competitive information. Research and development professionals find newsgroups one of the best ways to stay current on fast-moving technical issues.

InterNotes News runs on a Notes server with an Internet connection. It exchanges Usenet news articles with NNTP servers. Usenet news articles are brought into Notes discussion databases, preserving discussion threads. Notes users have full access to all Notes's features when interacting with newsgroup articles and can participate in newsgroups by writing and posting a new topic or response.

InterNotes News provides...

- Managed access
- Consistent work environment
- Replication power

Latest news

InterNotes News provides these benefits:

- *Managed access.*   Because InterNotes News is configured for specific newsgroups, it is possible to provide access to only those newsgroups appropriate for business use. Notes Access Control Lists for databases can restrict access to newsgroup databases to those whose jobs require it. In addition, because only one Notes server is required to make news articles available to an entire company, an organization has to manage only a single Internet address instead of one address for every user.

- *Consistent work environment.*   Employees who already conduct their internal business in Notes can use the same techniques to communicate with InterNotes newsgroups. With Notes, users can use full text search and views to search through news articles by a variety of criteria such as date, author, or topic. They also can forward articles to other users or databases.

- *Replication.*   Because Usenet news articles are stored in a Notes database, important documents can be shared among workgroup members or with other employees. All responses made by Notes users anywhere in the enterprise are replicated back to the Notes discussion database and posted to the Usenet newsgroup on the Internet.

Using the Web Navigator

In Version 4, the InterNotes Web Navigator is a standard feature designed to give Notes users easy assess to information on the Web. The Web Navigator

The Notes Web Navigator

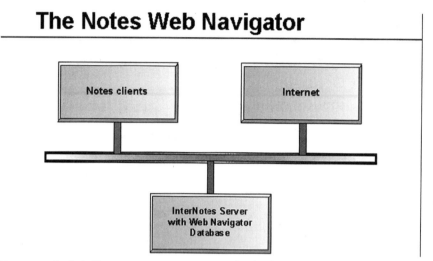

Figure 8.1 An InterNotes server can connect multiple clients with the World Wide Web. (*Lotus Development Corporation*)

consists of a database and an allied task on a Notes server—called, for these purposes, the InterNotes server. This server:

- Stores the Web Navigator database
- Runs the Web Navigator server task
- Operates the TCP/IP protocol
- Maintains an Internet connection, directly or by proxy

Local and remote Notes users can use this database the same way they retrieve information from other Notes databases. Only the server need be connected with the Internet. The server then can use that connection to serve all its client workstations. If you prefer, you can maintain more than one InterNotes server, each with its own database. This way, you can provide several points of access to the Web. Figure 8.1 shows how the server can connect multiple clients to the Web.

Translating Web pages

When a Notes client requests access to a Web page, the Web Navigator retrieves the page from the Internet, translates it into a Notes document, and stores it in the Web Navigator database, where it is available to the client. The page need be retrieved only the first time it is requested. Subsequent readers will find it already available on the server database. Once a Web page is in the database, clients can read it, copy it into a private folder, cut and paste the contents into other Notes documents, mail them to coworkers, or do anything else you normally can do with a Notes document. Figure 8.2 diagrams the process.

Translating HTML to Notes

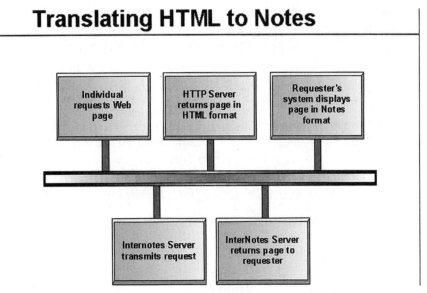

Figure 8.2 Now the Web Navigator retrieves a Web page. (*Lotus Development Corporation*)

The Web Navigator database offers only one-way communication. You can retrieve a page from the Web, but you cannot create one. Web site creation is a job for the InterNotes Web Publisher.

Managing the database

The Web is a fast-changing environment, and some pages change almost constantly. That means the Web pages in a Notes database can quickly become outdated. To help keep its stored pages current, the Web Navigator comes with a *Refresh agent* that has much in common with Notes database replication. The agent regularly compares the date of each Web page in the database with the date of the same page on the Internet. If the Internet page is newer, the Refresh agent retrieves it.

The Refresh agent refreshes only hypertext transfer protocol (HTTP) pages; it does not refresh file transfer protocol (FTP) pages, Gopher pages, or private pages stored in a user's private folder in the database. The Refresh agent updates Web pages using this procedure:

- The agent checks the Refresh documents field in the Document Management section to see if the agent has been enabled.

- If the agent has been enabled, it compares the date on the Web page in the database with the current date.

- If the date on the Web page in the database is the same as the current date, it does not refresh the page.

- If the date is not the same as the current date, the agent retrieves the last modification date located in the HTTP header at the Internet server and compares that date with the date on the Web page in the database.

- If the last modification date retrieved from the Internet is newer than the date of the Web page in the database, or if the agent cannot retrieve the last modification date, the Web page is refreshed in the database.

You can enable the Refresh agent to run automatically at preset times, or you can run it manually. By default, the Refresh agent is set to run nightly at 3 a.m. to update pages within the database. To use this schedule, open an administration document and choose Enabled. To change the time when the Refresh agent runs, edit the Refresh agent, click on the Schedule button, and enter the new starting time. To run the Refresh agent manually, open the administration document and click the Refresh Now button.

Binge and purge

As the Web Navigator database gains new Web pages, the database will naturally grow. With a lot of Web activity in the organization, your database could become extremely large in a short period of time. To manage the size of the database, specify purge criteria in the administration document. Once you have set the criteria, a nightly purge agent will run at 1 a.m. to keep the database at a manageable size.

The purge agent uses criteria you set in the document management section of the administration document to purge the database. You specify the maximum database size and the percentage of maximum size desired when the purge operation is finished. The purge agent runs through the criteria in this order:

- The agent checks the Expired header from each Web page in the database. If the Web page has expired, it deletes that page in the database.

- The agent then checks the document creation date on each Web page in the database and deletes pages older than a date you specify.

- It then checks for pages that are larger than the size you specify.

When the database size you have specified is reached during the purge, the purge agent will stop at that point and queue up to run the next night.

Working with URLs

Each Web page is identified by a Uniform Resource Locator (URL). This is the code columnist Dave Barry once described as the result of a mouse running across the keyboard. Within this seeming gibberish are several pieces of information. Consider this URL:

```
http://www.mypage.com/home/html
```

This URL contains these elements:

- The network protocol, in this case *HTTP*.
- The World Wide Web
- The name of the page
- The type of page, in this case commercial or *com*
- An identification as a home page
- The contents, which were created using hypertext markup language or *HTML*

Web pages almost always contain hypertext links to other Web pages. When you click on one of these links, the target page is displayed. When using the Web Navigator, you can follow any of these types of links:

- *HTTP.*   The hypertext transfer protocol used to display HTML documents
- *FTP.*   The file transfer protocol used on FTP servers
- *Gopher.*   A Web search program or browser
- *Mailto.*   A link to an e-mail system

Notes automatically creates links for any URL text that appears within the rich text fields of Notes documents. For example, if you create a mail message with a URL within the text, it will become a link to that URL. When the recipient opens the document, the link is activated. If the recipient double-clicks on the URL link, the server will be asked to display the linked page.

The Home navigator

The Web Navigator database comes with a graphical Home navigator that represents a collection of starting points to browse the Web. It is made up of icons that link directly to Web pages, display views of Web pages already loaded in the database, display the search form, and open documentation about the Web Navigator.

You can use the Home navigator as is, customize it to suit the needs of your organization, or create one of your own.

Filling out forms

Many Web pages use fill-out forms to gather input from readers. These forms range from the simple, with just a few input text fields, to the complex, with text fields, radio buttons, check boxes, and other elements.

The Web Navigator supports Web fill-out forms so when a Notes user opens a page in the database that contains a form, the Web Navigator immediately creates a Notes form. The user can complete the form and use it to submit information back to the Internet server. If the Internet server sends a response document back to the user, that document will be saved in a private folder for the user within the Web Navigator database.

Authenticating identities

Some Internet sites contain pages that require users to authenticate, or verify, who they are before they can access the pages. The Internet server accomplishes this authentication by requiring the user to provide a user name and password that was chosen in a previous visit to the page. The next time the user attempts to open that page from the Internet server, access will be allowed only after supplying the user name and password. After the user has visited the page once, Notes encrypts that page to protect confidentiality and then saves it in a private folder in the database.

When a user provides a user name and password for an Internet server, Notes caches them at the Notes client until the user exits Notes or clears user settings. The user needs to provide the user name and password for a particular Internet server only once for each Notes session.

Notes Does Images

The Internet accessories are only two of several companion products available for Notes. Other add-ons include Lotus products that extend Notes into areas like these:

- Imaging
- Video and desktop conferencing
- Telephone and pager access
- Network management
- Application development

Most people have figured out by now that the "paperless office" is a contradiction in terms. Most corporate information is still in the form of paper stashed in a file cabinet. Document imaging can help manage that load of paperwork by incorporating paper-based information into electronic form. Documents are imported as graphic images that the computer can display; they can also be converted into searchable text.

Lotus Notes:Document Imaging (LN:DI) is a suite of applications that lets you incorporate paper-based information into network communications. LN:DI products can capture, process, and manage this information in the form of images. The suite includes:

- Lotus Image Viewer
- LN:DI Professional Edition

- LN:DI Mass Storage System
- LN:DI Image Processing Server
- LN:DI Workgroup OCR Option

Image Viewer

One component of the suite is the Lotus Image Viewer for Windows. This product is bundled with Notes and cc:Mail, and strictly speaking it is not an add-on. Lotus considers it a core component of its basic communication structure. With the Image Viewer, you can retrieve scanned images directly from Notes or cc:Mail. This provides a simple way to display images without the advanced knowledge often required with document imaging systems.

Professional Edition

The LN:DI Professional Edition provides increased flexibility and control over the storage of image files. With the Professional Edition, you can create and share compound documents that include:

- Images from a variety of sources
- Scanned paper documents
- Fax transmissions
- Files created in other operations

Mass storage

The LN:DI Mass Storage System (LN:DI MSS) provides advanced storage management for image-enabled Notes applications. LN:DI MSS provides a scalable alternative to storing large image files in Notes databases. The system lets you use hard drives and optical drives for storage.

The system lets administrators create preconfigured storage profiles that specify how image objects will be stored. The administrators then can use MSS to automatically move image documents over time to the most efficient storage medium while still granting easy access to workgroup members.

Processing Server

The LN:DI Image Processing Server provides a single point of administration and setup for workgroup image processing. It receives requests from LN:DI clients, Notes mail, and third-party gateways. It then delivers the requests to the appropriate imaging option. When the requested work is complete, the processing server updates the appropriate Notes databases.

The processing server also serves as a foundation for optional imaging components.

OCR option

The LN:DI Workgroup Optical Character Recognition (OCR) Option lets Notes users send TIFF and PCX image files through an OCR process. This process converts the image to editable text. It can return that text to the user as a Notes mail message, or it can insert the text into a Notes document.

OCR reduces the time, expense, and error of retyping important documents. In addition, when the scanning ability is combined with the Notes full-test search ability, you can readily retrieve the information stored in image documents.

Fax server

The Lotus Fax Server lets Notes and cc:Mail users send and receive faxes by way of their desktop mail services. This server handles both incoming and outgoing faxes and responds to more than 40 commonly used fax devices.

Videoconferencing

VideoNotes gives Notes users quick access to digital video data. At the same time, it stores video objects on servers optimized for that type of storage.

Since video objects often are huge, storing them within Notes documents could quickly use up all available disk space. Using OLE, VideoNotes embeds identifiers for stored video objects within Notes documents. The objects themselves are stored elsewhere. The product includes a Site Manager that runs on a Notes server and manages the storage, tracking, and delivery of these objects.

In real time

RealTime Notes is a group of software and Notes databases that add desktop conferencing to the Notes package. Working with the Intel ProShare conferencing software, RealTime gives Notes users quick access to the ProShare conferencing abilities from within Notes.

RealTime also provides SmartIcons you can use to establish a real-time desktop conference connection directly from the Notes desktop. Using the features of ProShare, members can simultaneously share and edit files, images, and other Notes applications. RealTime Notes also takes advantage of Notes information access, management, and security features.

Telephone Access

Lotus offers a Phone Notes Application Kit that provides an API for developing a telephone interface that provides access to Notes databases and documents.

The kit uses Notes forms that connect with Notes and voice processing software. A developer can complete a Phone Notes application by completing the forms and storing them in a Notes database.

The API uses Notes programming commands that perform such tasks as:

- Interacting with an individual through menus and prompts
- Interacting with Notes to create, copy, delete, and forward Notes documents and to execute Notes macros
- Controlling application execution by evaluating conditions and capturing events

Pager gateway

The Notes Pager Gateway lets Notes users compose and send messages to a pager in much the same way as e-mail messages. The gateway uses a standard protocol to deliver messages to a commercial paging service.

With this gateway, notes users can:

- Send or forward messages directly to a pager
- Send messages to both an e-mail account and a pager
- Use Notes macros to selectively send information to a pager

Network Management

NotesView lets you graphically monitor and control an enterprisewide Notes server network.

This product provides a maplike view of servers and connections, including mail routing and server replication. From a single management station, you can monitor and optimize Notes servers across the network, or work with a single server. NotesView provides maps, alarms, statistical charts, and other status information for effective network management.

Application Development

Lotus Forms helps speed application development by making it easy to create electronic forms and to automate workflow across LANs and WANs. This product has two components:

- *Designer,* a Windows-based environment for developing and implementing form-based applications It uses the LotusScript programming language to develop custom applications.
- *Filer,* a tool workgroup members can use to complete and sign electronic forms.

Law, Ethics, and Security

The world of e-mail was changed forever the day Alana Shoars found her supervisor sifting through a stack of printouts, representing messages sent by employees. Shoars was the e-mail administrator in Epson America's California offices, and she was upset at what she saw. She had set up the system herself, with the understanding that it would be a private medium of communication for Epson employees.

The supervisor claimed that since the company maintained the system, it also had the right to read and police the messages that traveled over it. Shoars continued to object, and when she was discharged for protesting too much, she filed suit against the company.

Thus did e-mail enter the burgeoning field of employee litigation. The company won its case, as have most other employers in similar situations. It has since become a well-accepted principle that employers have the right to monitor their employees' internal e-mail. Nevertheless, that welcome clarification has only led to other, more difficult issues such as these:

- You may have the right to monitor e-mail, but exercising that right may not be a good idea.

- If you have access to internal e-mail messages, there is the problem of protecting them from people who don't have legitimate access.

- And there is yet another problem of people who do have legitimate access—granted by authority of court orders and other legal processes.

Monitoring the Messages

The Shoars case was one of the first to bring e-mail into the courtroom, but it has only led a long parade. Marching along behind, at least potentially, are the nation's growing millions of e-mail users. They send electronic reams of material to one another, seldom thinking about the consequences.

Yes, there are consequences. They include:

- The real chance someone else will read their most intemperate comments.
- The danger that old e-mail messages can become courtroom evidence in a product liability or antitrust case.
- The chance that when you set out to protect your e-mail from outside snooping, the government may insist on getting its nose in.

E-mail as evidence

A commission investigating the Rodney King incident found more than 700 offensive e-mail messages sent between Los Angeles police officers. Some of the government's strongest evidence in the trial of Oliver North was a collection of e-mail messages North thought he had successfully erased.

E-mail messages were the basis of charges that a Borland International executive had passed sensitive information to the rival Symantec Corporation. When the executive left Borland for a position with Symantec, Borland management checked the former employee's e-mail messages. What they found there resulted in charges not only against the departed employee but against the president of the company that hired him.

More recently, Atlantic Richfield (Arco) found itself in court, facing an accusation of fraud in the sale of a solar energy subsidiary to the Siemens Corporation. Siemens filed suit, contending that Arco was aware the solar technology was not commercially viable, yet hid that information from Siemens.

In support of its complaint, Siemens produced several e-mail messages exchanged by Arco employees. One called the solar technology a "pipe dream."

Lawyers tell us to expect an increasing number and variety of legal actions based on e-mail. A simple motion for discovery can send legions of lawyers poring through your e-mail messages, looking for evidence to bolster a case against you.

What you say...

- May reach an unintended audience
- May be vulnerable to snooping
- And, yes, can be held against you in court.

Employees have...

- No right to e-mail privacy.
- Every right to fairness, trust, and adequate notice.

A simple policy

At the outset, dealing with e-mail and employee privacy rights is fairly simple. The employees have no privacy rights where company e-mail is concerned. Employers have the right to oversee the use of the system. In return, employers are entitled to reasonable notice that their messages are not as private as they might think.

Those principles are becoming well-established as a foundation for employer policies on use and monitoring of their e-mail systems. Once you venture beyond these basics and into specific cases, though, the question is less clear.

Dangers of monitoring

Though employers have the right to monitor their e-mail systems, there are a couple of reasons active use of this right might not be a good idea:

- Overzealous supervisors
- Possible legal liability

The first is an internal danger. The working world is unfortunately full of insecure supervisors and managers who have come to believe that all employees are out to take every advantage they can get. These are the "leaders" likely to be found late at night with reams of downloaded messages, on fishing expeditions for employee wrongdoing.

This is not only an act of bad faith, but the loss of employee trust and loyalty would be greater than any possible gains. You could tell this supervisor that of the millions of people who use e-mail, there have been only a few isolated incidents of improper practices by individuals. It probably wouldn't do any good.

A better approach would be to require the approval of at least one other person before a supervisor mounts a monitoring expedition. Establish a policy that surveillance should be authorized only under specified conditions. This will not prevent suspicious supervisors from undermining their own departments, but it can help.

Exercise your rights with care

- Suspicious supervisors can abuse their privileges.
- Your knowledge could become a legal matter

Courtroom scenario

Now, consider a not-very-hypothetical courtroom scene. A large corporation has been accused of improper activity. The government has issued subpoenas for the firm's past e-mail messages. Furthermore, prosecutors have found the proverbial smoking gun in an exchange of messages between two second-level executives.

Now, the company president is on the witness stand. "Were you aware of these messages?" the prosecutor asks.

"No, I was not."

"Doesn't your company have a policy that allows you to monitor employees' electronic mail traffic?"

"Yes, it does."

"Then, if you had access to these messages, how can you say you didn't know about them?"

If a scene like this hasn't happened yet, it cannot be far in the future.

Laws light on guidance

Whatever policy you choose, the most important thing is that you have one. You'll get little help from the law in this area; a policy is a necessary substitute.

The law on internal corporate communication ranges downward from uncertain. Even in areas where it was once thought legal questions have been settling, there have been unsettling new legal issues.

For example, not long ago it was thought that the law clearly governed the degree to which commercial on-line providers like Compuserve and America On Line could monitor e-mail messages. Then came the question of pornography via Internet and the question—still unresolved—of whether these services should be held responsible for their customers' messages and bulletin board postings. Issues like that can arise even in a well-regulated environment.

By contrast, an organization's internal e-mail is relatively unregulated and even more open to confusion. Many of the employee privacy cases to reach court have originated in California, whose state constitution grants a specific right of privacy. Even in those cases, though, it has been hard to tell where employers' rights end and employees' rights begin.

"Accidental" discovery

In a case that is not entirely hypothetical, a network administrator regularly checks e-mail messages for the valid purpose of making sure the system is not overloaded. In the course of this work, the administrator finds some questionable transmissions. This discovery leads to disciplinary action against the employees who sent the messages. The employees take the company to court.

The decision will often depend on circumstances. If the e-mail offense was serious—plotting a crime or using company e-mail as a smut exchange—the employer would probably prevail. If the employees did nothing more than criticize their superiors, the company still might win, but it would be on less solid ground. Even a winning case can be expensive, though, grinding through the courts for years while the lawyers bill by the hour.

What happens if...

- You start out to monitor the system...
- Then find you should be monitoring the messages?

Theories of e-mail monitoring

- It belongs to the company
  - The company has a right to prevent misuse.
- Don't ask, don't tell
  - The company has the right, but will rarely exercise it.
- Unlimited use benefits us all
  - Employees will communicate better if they aren't policed.

Provide policy guidance

As recently as 1993, it was estimated that fewer than 10 percent of U.S. companies had e-mail policies in place. In fact, employers who maintain e-mail systems can take any of three well-recognized approaches:

- *Personal use of electronic mail is an improper use of company resources.* On this basis, the employer can state the right to monitor e-mail messages in order to enforce the policy. This is a common approach, made more popular because it emulates similar well-established policies for other company resources like telephones and company cars.

- *Personal use of electronic mail is contrary to policy, but the company will not monitor the system to enforce it.* This seems almost self-contradictory, but many firms have taken this approach. They feel it is more important to maintain employees' confidence than to enforce rigid compliance. Employees who worry about monitoring might hesitate to send valuable messages.

- *Open use of electronic mail encourages productivity and improves morale.* Some companies allow almost unlimited use of their e-mail systems. This includes posting notices on an electronic bulletin board. The company feels this policy provides for a degree of information exchange and cohesiveness that offsets any drawbacks. The company imposes limits only when it feels personal messages are interfering with an employee's work.

Any of these approaches is valid, but there are compelling reasons to take the middle ground. You avoid the extremes of building mistrust one hand and of totally losing control on the other.

Policies to avoid

There also are some kinds of policies to be avoided. They may seem to make sense at first, but they can be the source of many problems:

Policies to avoid

- It's our e-mail, and you can't play with it.
- E-mail is OK, as long as you follow all the rules.

- *All electronic mail messages are property of the organization, and employees have no right of privacy in any circumstances.*   This policy is deceptively close to one which would maintain the company's rights to oversee all e-mail traffic. But a proper e-mail policy is firmly stated, then lightly used. A statement that employees have no rights at all is tantamount to a declaration of war. It is a demonstration that management has little faith in its employees. But if the employees are so bad, why did you hire them in the first place?

- *Private use of electronic mail is subject to restrictions.*   The message must be "appropriate," must have a certain format, or must appear only in designated forums and bulletin boards. With this policy, an organization gives lip service to employee privacy, but cripples that right with bureaucratic restrictions. This is a sure sign that an organization is more interested in protecting itself from lawsuits than it is in respecting the valid interests of its employees.

Enforcement without monitoring

It is possible—and not even difficult—to enforce e-mail discipline without monitoring employee messages. The most effective way is simply to keep an eye on the employees' behavior. If someone is spending excessive amounts of time sending or reading e-mail, it is likely the employee's work is suffering. An alert supervisor should notice a drop in performance and do something about it. After all, it's the lagging performance, not the use of e-mail, that should be the greatest concern.

If you do adopt a no-private-use policy, it is vital that you publicize it. Let employees know exactly where they stand. Don't leave room for unrealistic expectations that their messages will be private. Some employers go so far as to post a policy notice on their e-mail log-on screens.

What makes a good policy?

- Easy communication
- Protection for sensitive information
- Excess monitoring discouraged
- Consistent application

Policy principles

The Electronic Mail Association, an industry group based in Arlington, VA, recommends this foundation for an e-mail policy:

- It should encourage fast, free sharing of information.
- It should protect the company's rights to its proprietary information.
- It should prevent electronic snooping by overzealous supervisors.
- It should be consistent across all media used for employee communication. In other words, the e-mail policy should be essentially the same as the policy on using the telephone.

There are a few instances in which an employer is justified in examining an employee's messages:

- Routine, expected sharing of information during the normal course of business
- Reasonable suspicion of computer crime or the theft of trade secrets
- Investigations of other criminal activity, such as fraud and drug dealing

Avoid extremes

Other authorities advise that you avoid the extremes of either restriction or permissiveness. A policy that all messages are automatically open to scrutiny sends a message of mistrust and suspicion. Employees will return the sentiment. Such a policy also could provide room for doubt whether an employer knew of illegal activities discovered through employee e-mail messages.

On the other hand, a policy of never screening messages has its own danger. Consider the company which a few years ago lost several key executives in an airplane crash. Then consider how such a loss would be compounded if the company was left with no access to the contents of their e-mail files.

Accordingly, many authorities suggest a middle-ground policy that:

- Fits the company's culture
- Allows for incidental use of e-mail for personal communication
- Allows for access when necessary for valid business reasons, but otherwise prohibits employees from reading e-mail messages not addressed to them
- Whenever practical, requires the consent of the person who originated the message
- Is communicated to employees early and often

Controlling the Volume

Often, the problem is not controlling the types of messages employees exchange by e-mail but simply the sheer volume. The number of messages pumped through a busy system can overwhelm individual recipients and the system itself. It's not unusual to make a daily e-mail check and find hundreds of messages waiting. No employee can cope with such a deluge day after day. Ultimately, neither can the system or the people who try to run it.

Unfortunately, there will always be a few managers who grouse that employees are wasting too much time sending e-mail messages to each other. It is these managers who are most likely to suggest that you attack the problem by monitoring messages for "improper" content.

In most companies, people don't routinely waste time sending e-mail. They waste most of their time receiving it. The deluge that reaches their electronic mailboxes every day is a significant waste of time and energy. Even ignoring

How e-mail wastes people's time

- Minor waste
  - Composing and sending messages
- Major waste
  - Reading huge numbers of messages

most messages takes time. You still must figure out which messages you can safely ignore.

E-mail education can help. Teach employees to keep their messages relevant to the recipients' needs and interests. If you try to overwhelm a superior with your bright ideas, the superior will be overwhelmed, all right, but not in the way you hope.

Another approach is to set up a bulletin board where employees are encouraged to exchange ideas and comments among themselves. Let employees who want to spread their ideas use this forum instead of e-mailing everyone in sight. You do run the risk of the type of flaming that has given the Internet such a reputation for rudeness. Education can discourage that tendency; censorship is rarely the answer. More important, participation is voluntary. People who don't want to participate in the exchange need not cope with excessive numbers of e-mail messages insisting that they do.

There's another thought to consider, too: the employees who spend time circulating messages about their work situations are also quite likely the employees who care most about how well the company is doing.

Self-policing is another option. Employees themselves can be frustrated at the amount of inappropriate e-mail they receive. Let these employees help set the standard for electronic communication within the workgroup. They share their thoughts and standards via an electronic bulletin board.

Educate employees

Whatever your e-mail privacy policy, you must make it clear to employees. Don't expect they will simply "understand," or that they will comply with a policy that you have not clearly published and communicated. Communicate with actions, too: don't undermine the policy with lax enforcement.

That's why educating users is also an important element of an e-mail privacy program. Many people think their e-mail messages are private simply because no one has told them otherwise. It's up to the e-mail system's management to ensure that employees know exactly what they can or cannot expect.

There is more at stake here than simply protecting employees' privacy or protecting management's interest in an effective e-mail system. The more that people understand about exactly how their e-mail system works, the more likely they will take care to protect both personal and organizational information. All e-mail patrons should understand these key points:

- *An e-mail message doesn't disappear when it is received.*   It's easy to think of an e-mail message something like a telephone message: Once the recipient receives the message, it disappears from the system. That's not the case. E-mail messages are stored on the system, usually on the post office server, until someone specifically erases them. Often, this takes the form of a periodic purge by the e-mail system manager. Until then, all messages

E-mail training topics

- Messages don't disappear
- Others may read them
- Messages may be altered
- E-mail is not private
- Security is lacking, too

sent since the last purge are still around, sometimes to haunt their senders.

- *Someone other than the intended recipient may read the message.*   Often, there could be many other readers. A recipient has the option of forwarding copies of an incoming message to anyone and everyone on the system. Even if you expect the recipient to treat a message in confidence, it may not always happen.

- *A copy of a message may not be a duplicate of the original.*   A recipient sometimes may add, alter, or remove the contents of a message before forwarding it to other parties. You can decide whether you want to trust another party, of course, but there's nothing in the e-mail system itself to tell you whether that trust is warranted.

- *There is nothing inherently private about an e-mail system.*   Just as there is nothing to tell you whether a message has been altered, there is nothing to guarantee that your private communication will remain private. Many people can read e-mail messages, for many reasons. Management certainly has the right to audit use of the e-mail system and to investigate possible criminal activity. E-mail system managers also enjoy access for such purposes as making backups.

- *E-mail security is far from perfect.*   Hackers, disgruntled employees, corporate spies, and all manner of other people can infiltrate an e-mail system. In fact, security is one of the major weak points of many e-mail systems today.

- *You don't always know who is receiving a message.*   For example, if you use a Reply button to automatically send a response to a message, that response may also go to everyone who received copies of the original. That could include those unknown persons who received blind carbon copies.

Enforcing E-mail Etiquette

Self-policing is also a way to combat another leading problem: a lack of e-mail etiquette. The Internet may be the leading example of electronic rudeness, but office e-mail systems are not always far behind. People will often say by e-mail what they never would say face-to-face.

For example, when an internally developed application crashed, the victimized department manager sent a blistering e-mail memo to the programmer. The manager also sent copies to at least two other managers. The programmer said he felt so devastated he didn't go to work for the next 2 days.

If the manager's aim was to insult the programmer, the message certainly did the job. If the aim was to reach a constructive solution, the message was an abject failure. Public humiliation by e-mail does not win friends or allies. There are many people in many organizations who have yet to get that message.

False sense of privacy

The etiquette problem has one thing in common with the issue of monitoring employees' e-mail. In both cases, the employees have an unrealistic expectation of privacy. The telephone on the desktop is a reasonably private means of communication, usually linking only two people. The computer that occupies the same desktop may seem equally private. After all, most of the work you do on a PC really is personal.

Once you project your work and ideas into the realm of e-mail, however, privacy disappears. Even if you address your message to a single party, that person can relay copies to anyone on the system. Sometimes they go to everyone on the system. The things you intended to say privately you now have

E-mail no-nos

- Don't expect privacy
- Don't avoid
  face-to-face
  communication
- Don't be too picky

said very publicly. By the way, the increasing use and growing sophistication of voice mail are making telephone calls less private, too.

For example, there's the case of several people who signed up by e-mail for a company-sponsored weight control program. Someone thoughtfully—or thoughtlessly—sent an e-mail message to everyone on the network, proudly listing the names of everyone who had registered.

Expressionless communication

Another serious fault is to use e-mail in situations that demand face-to-face communication. There are some things you should not do by e-mail. Criticizing someone else tops the list. If you must complain, do it in person, or at least by telephone.

This is a visual age where written communication skills have suffered. Many people don't know how to express themselves in writing, as e-mail demands that they do. In a more personal kind of contact, communication includes the tone of voice, body language, and facial expressions. A text e-mail message has smiley faces at best. The tempered criticism you could deliver in person becomes a tirade when committed to e-mail.

Recipients have their problems, too. Someone who is flamed by an intemperate e-mail message is more likely to have an intemperate reaction.

Correcting grammar

If many e-mail correspondents are unskilled in written communication, there is a surplus of people who are willing to "help" them. These are the self-appointed English teachers who take it upon themselves to correct others' usage—doing so, of course, with e-mail messages that publicize the mistake.

It's important that our messages not offend, but e-mail does not demand strict compliance with all the rules of grammar. It's more important that people are encouraged to use the system. Messages from unseen critics work against that goal.

Securing the E-mail System

A lawsuit now often means that a discovery motion will make your entire stock of e-mail messages open to opposition lawyers. There's actually some good news in that: at least you know who it is and what they're doing.

This isn't always the case when hackers, industrial spies, or other outside parties invade your system without bothering with legal niceties. You don't have to be involved in top secret information to be vulnerable to such unwarranted access. And e-mail systems are among the most vulnerable of all. Many e-mail packages have large gaps in their security systems. There are plenty of pranksters and unsavory competitors who would value any information they can steal from this source.

Security gains importance

While many organizations worry about hacker invasions via the telephone or the Internet, fewer have demonstrated as much concern about e-mail security. Yet as e-mail use grows, and links expand outside departments and organizations, security is becoming a more vital concern. E-mail security suffers from a lack of management support, possibly because those who control finances don't realize how much vital information now travels over their e-mail networks.

The oversight is understandable. Many nontechnical people are still getting used to e-mail as a way to exchange internal memos. In that kind of message exchange, there is little that needs protection.

Today's reality, though, is that sensitive information is transmitted between business partners. This data travels through multiple servers and gateways, and every one of them is a vulnerable spot. Encryption is probably a minimum standard of protection for this kind of messaging. Also consider tactics like time stamps, which serve as a kind of postmark for electronic mail.

The X.500 messaging standard includes the X.509 security standard. The directory system which is at the heart of X.500 can handle public keys which let recipients decrypt messages encrypted with public keys. But these standards are merely instruction sheets. Someone still has to put these techniques to use. In particular, there is a need for some overall agency, perhaps the U.S. Postal Service, to manage the distribution of public keys.

Meanwhile, an organization can help protect itself by encrypting sensitive e-mail messages and attachments that travel through vulnerable gateways.

Principles of security

In a secure e-mail system, like a secure system of any type, you must make sure that the right people have access to the right information, and that the wrong people do not. Furthermore, you must make sure that the information is correct, and the system is available to those who need it.

The information in e-mail messages often must be kept confidential, at least within the workgroups or organizations where it exists. A secure system does not give anyone access to confidential information unless they can prove they are authorized to receive it. This means proving their identities, usually by one of these methods:

- By something they *know,* typically a password
- By something they *have,* such as a magnetic key card

Access control not enough

It is not enough just to control access to information. The system should also include safeguards to make sure the information is accurate. This is not as important a consideration in ordinary e-mail traffic as it is in database environments. Remember, though, that applications like Notes combine e-mail

A good security system...

- Gives the right people the right information
- Keeps the wrong people out
- Makes sure the information is right

and databases. If people are going to rely on the information in a Notes database, you must make sure that information is reliable.

Human error is the greatest risk here. Many database systems use validation formulas to guard against data entry errors, such as posting a $35,000 salary as $35 million. Notes lets application developers include fields that accept entries only from a list of acceptable values.

Information must be available

Even while a system keeps out the unauthorized, it must not unduly get in the way of those people who must use it for valid reasons. In most circumstances, an e-mail system should be widely available. The more users, the better.

This means the security system should not be so intrusive that authorized users cannot readily use it. It also means the system should be available when people need it. E-mail is a network application, which means it depends on a reliable network.

Assessing human risk

E-mail systems operate over networks, and that means you face security risks from two sources: human error, and network failure. Either could keep the system from fulfilling any of the three main security needs.

Human errors are both simple and frustratingly common. The person who uses a sticky note to post a password on a monitor is a security-breach stereotype. Not far behind is the one who tapes a password to the bottom of a keyboard.

On a much higher level are people who deliberately invade your system, or those who use electronic scanners to pick up messages as they pass through cables and telephone lines.

E-mail has two types of risk

- Human failure
- Network failure

Types of human risk

- Accidents and carelessness
- Deliberate invasion

The first threat is much more serious

Despite the publicity they have gained, hackers make up a relatively small group. The chances one of them will successfully attack your network are actually quite low. Your greater threat, by far, is from the authorized user who, by accident or design, manages to mess things up.

Networks Increase the Risk

The use of a network magnifies these human risks—while it introduces new risks of its own. An e-mail system probably has several points at which it is vulnerable to attack. You must find these vulnerable spots. Then, identify the particular type of threat to which the system is vulnerable.

The vulnerabilities of an e-mail system are essentially the vulnerabilities of the network system over which it operates. In addition, the design of many e-mail systems creates additional weak spots.

The vulnerable spots in a network include:

The perils of networking

- Physical attack
- Natural disaster
- Mechanical failure
- Electromagnetic radiation
- Internetwork connections
- Poor access control

- *Physical vulnerability.* The network is open to physical attack from intruders who break into a building or server room.

- *Natural disasters.* Earthquakes, fires, floods, lightning, and power failures can wipe out your system in a flash.

- *Mechanical failure.* Network components can fail, taking valuable information with them.

- *Electromagnetic radiation.* A network radiates magnetic signals a sophisticated raider can intercept.

- *Internetwork connections.* Whenever one network connects with another, the connection point is a vulnerable spot. In addition, you open yourself to all the vulnerabilities of the other network.

- *Excess access.* Conventional wisdom says supervisors and network administrators should have access to all the information on their networks. In this case, conventional wisdom is wrong.

Physical protection

There are many ways a thief can physically break into an e-mail network. It may be as easy as walking up to your network server and copying or erasing critical information.

One particular physical danger: when you delete a file from a disk or tape, you often only delete the directory reference to it. The data may remain in place for some time, until by chance something else is written into that sector. It doesn't take a lot of expertise to retrieve these "erased" messages.

Sometimes, it takes even less expertise than that. Many sensitive messages have been compromised when people leave printouts where the wrong parties can see them.

Physical protection

- Wipe sensitive information clean
- Limit printouts
- Shred them when finished
- *And most of all, lock the door*

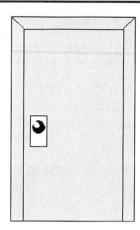

Your best defense against physical attack is the common locked door. Place servers, hubs, bridges, and other key network components in locked rooms, and issue keys only to those who legitimately need access. If you delete sensitive information from a disk, use a method that wipes it clean and destroys the data itself. Limit the printouts made of sensitive messages, and shred them when you are finished.

Coping with disaster

There's not much you can do to prevent a natural disaster. You can only try to be prepared. Where mission-critical information is concerned, that means not only backups but off-site backups. That way, the disaster that strikes in one place probably will not also strike the second.

Fortunately, few organizations must maintain large databases of mission-critical e-mail. It's more important simply that the mail get through. Use uninterruptible power supplies to make sure servers and other critical components remain in service during a power failure. In an enterprisewide system, you can set up multiple servers to back up each other. If one goes down, the others can pick up the load.

Maintaining the network

Key parts of the network can fail for other reasons, too. All electronic and mechanical parts are subject to failure. Disks crash, servers go down, and power supplies suddenly fail to supply power. Gradual wear and tear is less dramatic but can be just as critical.

Make sure you have a ready, reliable source of spare parts, and the ability to install them. Monitor mechanical equipment—particularly hard disks—for

Coping with natural disaster

- Be prepared
- Have a backup mail server ready
- Install an uninterruptible power supply

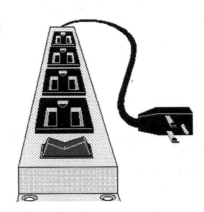

Preventing breakdowns

- Know where to find parts and service -- quickly
- Use preventive maintenance

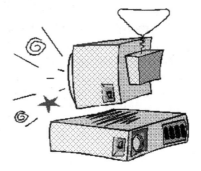

wear. If you have a large enough network, consider a program of preventive maintenance. You can track the useful life of a hard disk or some other critical component. Plan to make replacements just before that lifetime is due to expire. Leaving the equipment in place may give you a few more months, or a few more minutes, but the gains in reliability can be worth the expense.

Stop radiating

If you find yourself vulnerable to electronic spying, there are several things you can do to reduce the stray signals your network sends out. Use shielded cable instead of the more popular unshielded twisted pair.

Better yet, go to fiber optics which use light instead of electromagnetic signals. Fiber optic cables can be tapped, but there is a telltale loss of signal power.

Controlling outside contact

- Use a callback system
- Encrypt messages

Contact from the outside

Almost by definition, an e-mail network must have contact with the outside world. Wherever there is an external contact—with another network, with another organization, or with any outside party, there is a risk of interception. These same contacts are also likely routes of virus infections.

The usual prescription is to limit these contacts—exactly what e-mail is not all about. Even so, you can reduce the risk of outside invasion via your e-mail system.

One method is a callback system for dial-in patrons. The caller is not immediately connected to the network. Instead, the caller must verify his or her identity, such as with a system name and password. If the system identifies an authorized caller, it looks up this individual's telephone number and calls back.

There are some obvious drawbacks. The system can be cumbersome to use, and you cannot readily use it to identify traveling employees.

Encryption is another possibility. When you transmit an e-mail message from Notes, you have the option of encrypting it. Encryption scrambles the message so even if someone intercepts it, the message will be very hard to read. It will not be impossible, however, and encryption does require extra time and overhead.

The boss can be a risk, too

Supervisors and network administrators present risks that you might not expect. It might seem logical that a network administrator should have access to all the material that passes through the administrator's zone of responsibility.

That can be a dangerous assumption. A proper administrator oversees the network, not its contents. For example, if you are exchanging sensitive information about new product plans, there's no reason the network administrator should have access to that information. It can be equally dangerous to assume that department heads should have complete access to the network and its information just because they are in charge.

E-mail has special problems

- Outbound message queues
- Audit trails
- Message size limits
- Management flexibility
- Diagnosis and trouble-shooting

The special needs of e-mail

In addition to general security needs of networks, e-mail presents some management and security problems of its own. These include:

- *Secure outbound queues.* Often, low-priority messages are held in queues for transmission when telephone rates are lowest. Even when the messages are initially encrypted, they often appear as readable text while they wait in line.

- *Audit trails.* System managers should be able to identify excess users of external messages and other costly services.

- *Variable message size limits.* Some users must send longer messages than others; many e-mail systems, however, set the same maximum message size for all users. This doesn't mean, as someone actually has proposed, that senior executives should be allowed the longest messages. Base the limits on need, not on rank.

- *Management flexibility.* Managers should be able to shunt long and low-priority messages to low phone rate periods.

- *Diagnostic help.* When something goes wrong, a manager needs plenty of help to identify and correct the problem.

The open gateway

One of the most vulnerable points in an e-mail system is the gateway through which messages pass to Internet addresses and other external destinations, including other networks within the organization.

When a private e-mail system links with the outside world, it faces an entirely new class of demands for security, not only including protection but management issues such as diagnostics and systems management. Organizations are becoming more dependent on wider and wider versions of e-mail—not just as an intraenterprise tool but as an interenterprise tool.

As soon as an organization adopts e-mail as a standard means of communication, the system begins to carry sensitive information. For that reason, many e-mail products, including Notes, encrypt the messages that flow across the network and are stored in patrons' mailboxes. The encryption system would not be good enough to deter a determined, expert invader, but for most people it can turn sensitive information into unreadable gibberish.

Laying in wait

Troubles arise when the information is transmitted outside the organization, such as through a gateway to the Internet. Usually, these messages are stored in an outbox until a predetermined time for Internet transmission. A message might sit in this outbox for several hours.

A test of the Internet gateway for Notes's companion e-mail product, cc:Mail, showed that when the program prepares e-mail for transmission, it converts it to plain text. As it waits for transmission, it waits in easy-to-read form.

Both cc:Mail and Microsoft Mail share another related weakness. Though senders can encrypt their messages, an e-mail administrator can break the code simply by changing a client's password.

Notes is more sophisticated

Notes uses a more elaborate and sophisticated encryption scheme. The person who sends a message can choose to apply an encryption key before transmitting a message. In fact, you can encrypt any Notes document in the same way. You also can choose other options like encrypting certain fields or encrypting all the documents created with a particular form.

The Notes encryption system uses a matched system of public and private keys. Notes creates a unique public and private key for each user. If someone sends you encrypted mail, Notes uses your public key to encrypt the message. When you receive the encrypted message, you can use your private key to decrypt it.

You must make your public key available to anyone who wants to send you encrypted mail. Notes lets you transmit the key by e-mail. When you register as a Notes user, the system administrator also enters your public key in a public name and address book. Meanwhile, your private key is stored along with your user ID, where only you can reach it.

That means anyone who has access to your public key can send you encrypted mail, but only you can decrypt it. There is one danger: if your private key is lost or corrupted in the name and address book, you must send a new copy to the Notes administrator.

In addition, the ability to encrypt individual fields makes it possible to transmit a document in which some sensitive fields are hidden from unauthorized users, but the rest is open to any recipient.

No security system is perfect, but since only the recipient can decrypt an encrypted message, there is much less risk it will be intercepted en route.

Groupwise, the Word Perfect groupware package, has many of the same features. In addition, it lets you assign a password to a document or attached file. Even if someone successfully used the recipient's password to retrieve the file, they still would need a second password to read the contents.

The government listens in

E-mail encryption has also managed to become politically involved. This happened a few years ago, when the National Institute of Standards and Technology (NIST) proposed a new standard for federal purchases of communication equipment. Under the proposal, the standard means of encrypting messages would be a device called the Clipper Chip.

The chip is an encryption processor that uses the familiar dual key system. One of the keys, however, would be handed to the federal government. Law enforcement authorities would be able to decrypt any message encrypted using the Clipper Chip.

This proposal came to light just as mistrust of the government—and specifically mistrust of federal law enforcement agencies—was heating up as a political issue. The Clipper Chip was never more than a proposed federal purchasing specification, and the law enforcement agencies would need warrants and other legal niceties, and they were mainly interested in tapping the e-mail messages of drug dealers, child pornographers, and similarly delightful people. NIST people hardly qualify as presidential confidants.

Nevertheless, the Clipper Chip was soon being denounced as a White House plot to invade everyone's privacy. This shrill overreaction hardly contributed to enlightened debate of the issue.

The government was particularly ham-handed in its handling of this proposal. In its zeal to go after the bad guys, it gave too little respect to the valid security and privacy interests of the good guys. And despite their overstated conspiracy theory, the protesters did have some valid points to make. In recent months, the government has slowly backed away from the Clipper Chip proposal. The episode still teaches something well worth learning:

If you think your e-mail is private and secure, think again.

The Notes Security System

The advent of groupware has created security issues that extend throughout the enterprise and outward to customers and suppliers. Information can no longer be guarded as the "property" of an individual, department, or company. Today's competitive business environment demands that organizations break down traditional barriers and share information when it is needed to complete a process and to foster innovation and creativity.

Even in this open atmosphere, though, much of the information shared in a groupware application still must remain confidential, protected from accidental or malicious misuse. A groupware platform requires security that is both rigorous enough to protect business information from sabotage and flexible enough so authorized end users can assign varying levels of access to individual documents.

There are four aspects to security in a groupware environment:

- A security facility must prevent unrecognized users from entering the groupware system at large. By denying unauthorized entry, all system resources are protected.

- Of course, even authorized system users do not enjoy unlimited access: administrators must be able to define levels of access to databases and documents.

- Users must be able to rely on the confidentiality and the integrity of information and messages.

- Security also requires techniques flexible enough to be invoked by users themselves.

Notes uses multiple security services to meet these conflicting needs. Notes employs two tiers of security:

- Authentication, which controls access to the system

- Access control, digital signatures, and field-level encryption, which are applied at a more granular level

Authentication

The ability to establish the identities of users as well as servers is the cornerstone of a trustworthy system. The functionality of other security services rests on the reliability of the authentication service. Authentication based on a system using certificates and encryption is recognized as the state of the art: the de facto industry standard for access to X.500 directories is the X.509 certificate, which is based on RSA public key encryption technology.

In the Notes security scheme, a user holds a certificate (or ID file) that identifies the user by name, password, license number, and a private encryption key. The private key has a counterpart public key which is stored in a publicly accessible directory. When a user attempts to gain access to a server, the server checks the public directory for the public key, which it matches against the user's private key. Therefore, even if an impostor masquerades as the user by providing name, license number, and password, the lack of an encrypted private key would prevent the impostor from gaining unauthorized access.

Public/private key encryption is much more rigorous than other authentication systems. Authentication based on passwords does not provide adequate protection against impostors or sophisticated intruders who use network sniffers to tap the wire. In addition, systems that employ proprietary, nonstandard encryption algorithms are easier to compromise. Finally, systems that use private key encryption in which the entire encryption key is stored in a central security server are vulnerable to anyone who gains access to that server.

Access control

Some people should be allowed to see certain pieces of information or entire databases, but should be excluded from other, more sensitive items. The system should be able to control access at many levels to provide flexibility. Because groupware applications manage heterogeneous, unstructured information contained in everyday business documents, access to them must be restricted on a flexible basis.

A system administrator should be able to assign to various groups and individuals different access levels, including access to servers, databases, documents, and fields within documents. Access to each resource should be further refined to include the ability to enter, read, write, and delete information, to make changes to an application or database structure, and to make changes to the access control list itself.

For example, in an account management system, account profile documents might have a default access level that lets only sales representatives compose them but lets all sales and marketing staff read them. Document-level access control provides an even more powerful option. Individual account updates, each of which might contain sensitive information, might restrict reader access only to the account team and sales management. The system should also have the flexibility to allow authorized users to modify the document-level restrictions interactively, while the application is in operation.

Access control should also be flexible enough to accommodate the different modes that a user might assume. For example, when using a client workstation that is connected to the network, an employee might have manager access to a database, but when connecting to a database from a telephone client, when authentication is not possible, he may be granted only reader access.

Field-level and document-level encryption

At times a user may need to share field-level information in a document with another user while ensuring that no other users can view it. Access control can restrict field-level access to categories of users (readers, managers, etc.), but not to individuals. Therefore, for information that should be read only by specific individuals, the database designer can encrypt the sensitive information in the field and then attach the public key of those users to that sensitive field. In this way, only users with the corresponding private keys will be able to read the encrypted field. This encryption can also be used between servers so that only authorized servers can read particular documents or fields.

Digital signatures

Users frequently have to verify that the information they receive actually was sent to them by the sender listed on the document. They also must be sure that none of the information in the document was tampered with. Verification is managed by using digital signatures. This service is the digital equivalent of a trusted courier with a wax seal. When an employee composes a message, he or she creates a digital signature by attaching a private key to the document. When the recipient gets the document along with the encrypted private key, she can decrypt it by using the sender's public key, which is available to her on a public directory. In this way, the recipient can be sure that the document was indeed sent by the proper party, and that no one has intercepted the document en route.

Implementing Notes Security

Notes incorporates these security features with specific features like these:

- Workgroup members are granted or denied access to Notes servers through certificates stored as part of their user IDs. These certificates are electronic stamps attached to their ID files by administrators and other authorities who grant access to particular Notes servers.

- Members can protect their user IDs by applying passwords.

- Each Notes database contains an *access control list.* This list specifies who can open the database, and what each member can do with its information. The database manager creates and maintains this list.

- Remote users can encrypt the material that passes through their modems.

Identifying individuals

Each workgroup member who has access to a Notes server has a user ID. Even a server has its own ID.

The ID contains these elements, established when the ID is created:

Notes security features

- Encryption
- User IDs
- Passwords
- Access control lists
- Remote access encryption

- The ID owner's user name.
- The Notes license number.
- A certificate that governs access to server databases. This access is granted by one or more *certifiers,* usually database administrators, who hold the authority to certify IDs.
- Public and private encryption keys.

After the ID is created, you can:

- Change your user ID
- Add a password to your ID

In addition, a database manager can add certificates that grant access to other servers or databases.

When you try to open a database on a server, the server first checks the certificate in your ID. The certificate contains certifier information; Notes checks to see whether there is matching information in the database. If so, you are granted access.

Electronic signature

Notes also uses the ID to sign your mail messages, verifying that they did come from you. When you sign and send a mail memo, all the certificates in your ID are sent along with it. The recipient's system checks these against its own list of certificates to see if you have a certifier in common. If so, the system can assure the recipient that the message came from you. Otherwise, the recipient will receive a message that the memo's authenticity cannot be assured. If you are the recipient, and you know you and the sender have a certifier in common, the memo may have been changed en route.

Managing Your ID

You can check your ID at any time. From the menu bar, select **[Tools] [User ID] [Information].** The User ID Information dialog box opens (Fig. 9.1).

- The name and location of the ID file
- The number and type of your Notes license
- Your user name

You can use buttons in this dialog box to:

- Change your user name
- Copy a public key to the clipboard
- Identify the certifier who created your ID

User ID is the key to security

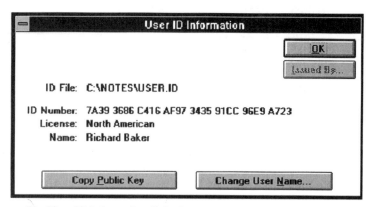

Figure 9.1 The User ID Information dialog box.

Caution: If you use this dialog box to change your user name, you will cancel all certificates issued under the old name. That means you must manually have them recreated. There is a better way, as you'll see in a moment.

Changing your user name

There are several reasons you might want to change your user name. One of the most common is a workgroup member who marries and changes her last name. Or, you might find you are one of several people in the organization with similar or identical user IDs.

Since this process involves changing the certificate information on other people's systems, it may take several hours or even days. You can continue to use your old name until the new one takes full effect.

The name change process works best if you do it by way of Notes mail. This allows you to merge the certificates issued under your former ID into your new ID file. It also means that you can use the new name and read any signed or encrypted mail that was created under the old name. If you do not use Notes mail—if either you or the certifier are not on the mail system—you must manually obtain new certificates for all the shared databases you want to use.

To change your name using Notes mail, select **[Mail] [Send User ID] [Request New Name].** If Notes asks you for a password, enter it. The Change User Name dialog box opens (Fig. 9.2). Type the new name, then click on **OK.** A New Name Request dialog box lets you send your name change request to the certifier.

When the certifying authority receives your request, your ID file is attached to the e-mail message. If the certifier is satisfied the message originated with

You can change your name

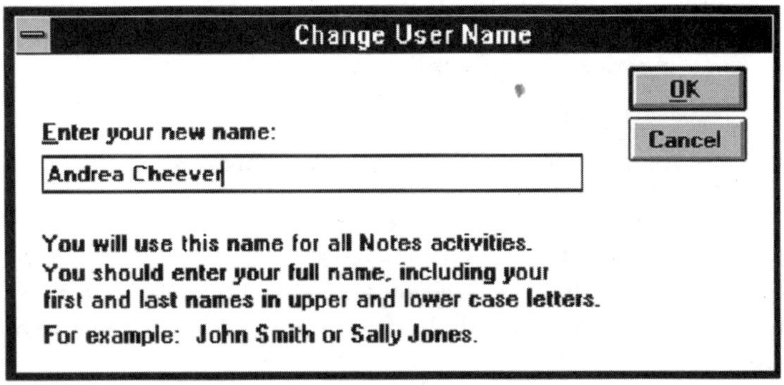

Figure 9.2   Change User Name dialog box.

Merging one ID into another

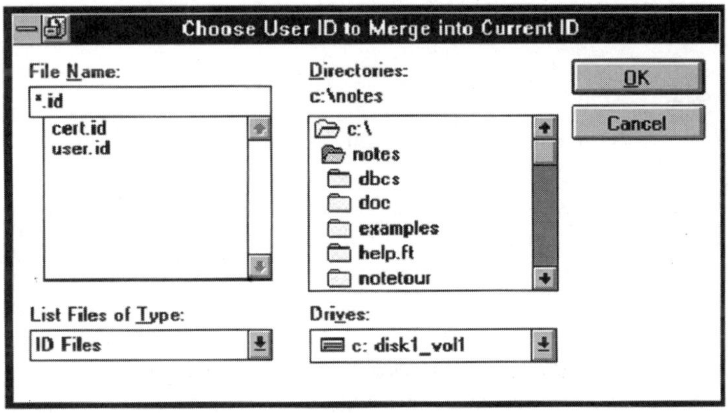

Figure 9.3   Use this dialog box to merge old and new ID files.

you, he or she returns a notice that your name change has been confirmed. Meanwhile, the certifier or database administrators enter your new name in the public name and address book, and on the access control lists for mail and server databases.

You then can merge the certificates issued under the old user name into your new ID. Select **[Tools] [User ID] [Merge Copy].** In the dialog box that opens (Fig. 9.3), select the file that represents your old user name and whose certificates you want to merge into the new name.

Securing your ID

As a workgroup member, you are responsible for protecting your ID and keeping others from misusing it. This is even more vital if you are an administrator with extra authority attached to your ID. Protecting your ID means:

- Keeping your ID physically secure
- Protecting your ID with a password
- Logging off servers when you leave your system unattended

Your ID is stored in a file you can keep on your system, on a floppy disk, or on a file server. In many cases, the most secure method might be to keep the ID on a floppy disk, which you then can store on a secure location. When you use Notes, you will need the floppy disk to gain access to any network databases.

When you first install Notes on your workstation, you are asked to specify the location of your ID file. If you later change your mind, move the file to the new location. For example, if you place the ID file on your hard disk and later decide to use a floppy, copy the file to the floppy disk and delete it from its original location. Next time you use a server database, the system will report that it cannot find the ID file. Enter its new location, such as the drive that holds the floppy disk, and proceed.

Setting a password

The password is a common means of access control. In Notes, if you add a password to your user ID, you can control access from your system to databases on Notes servers. Just as important, though, is what a Notes password *doesn't* do. It does not protect any local databases stored on your hard disk, and it governs access only from your system.

A Notes password can be any length up to 31 characters. Lotus recommends a minimum length of 8 characters. Your organization may have further requirements for password length and wording.

A good password is both hard to guess and easy to remember. Avoid birthdays, nicknames, and other terms that can easily be associated with you. At the same time, avoid passwords you must write down. There is too much temptation to post these passwords near the computer, where unauthorized people can find them. Don't assume you can safely write down your password and hide it at your workstation. Dedicated raiders know all the usual hiding places, and most of the unusual ones as well.

To set a password, select **[Tools] [User ID] [Password] [Set]**. If you already have a password, you will be asked to enter it before you go further. The Set Password dialog box (Fig. 9.4) lets you enter the new password. You will be asked to enter it twice to guard against mistakes; the system will not accept the new password unless both versions are identical.

Setting a password

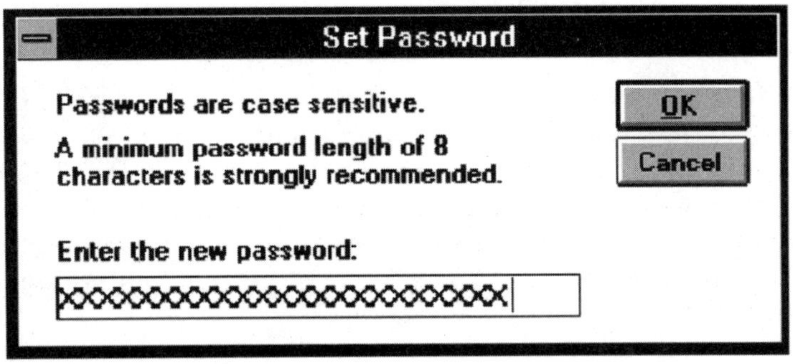

Passwords are case sensitive.

A minimum password length of 8 characters is strongly recommended.

Enter the new password:

Figure 9.4 The Set Password dialog box.

Leaving and logging off

Whenever you leave your workstation, it is important that you log off any server databases that may be in use. The easiest way is to press **F5.** You then must use your password to reestablish contact. If you fail to log off, anyone who passes by your workstation would have access to the databases in use.

You must have a password to make this work. Otherwise, should anyone try to use a shared database from your workstation, the system will happily oblige without asking for a password.

Managing certificates

When you were registered as a Notes user, your ID should have included any certificates you need to gain access to the servers you need on the job. These access needs are always subject to change. As you make wider use of Notes, as your job changes, or as your organization expands its network, you may need access to other servers. To gain this access, you will have to obtain the proper certificates.

You can review your existing certificates by selecting **[Tools] [User ID] [Certificates].** If your ID is password protected, you must enter the password. The Currently Held Certificates dialog box will list your current certificates. Highlight each certificate name, and you will see:

- The name of each certificate
- When each was created and will expire
- The ID number and name of the certifier

Using Encryption

You can use the Notes encryption scheme to encrypt your mail memos. You can also encrypt the fields in a Notes document.

Encrypting a document

When you encrypt a document, you apply an encryption key to one or more fields, then send the key to workgroup members of your choice. Only those who receive the key can read the encrypted fields. The database designer determines which fields can be encrypted; the field brackets for these encryptable fields appear in a unique color on your monitor. You can encrypt these using an existing key, or you can create a new key for the occasion.

To apply an encryption key to a document, open the document and select **[Tools] [User ID] [Encryption Keys].** The Encryption Keys dialog box (Fig. 9.5) shows a list of available keys. Select one, and click on **OK.** The selected key appears in the list of encryption keys selected for that document. This key is applied to all the encryptable fields in the document; you cannot apply different keys to different fields.

If you want to create a new encryption key, select **[Tools] [User ID] [Encryption Keys].** When the User ID Encryption Keys dialog box (Fig. 9.5) opens, click on **New.** The Add Encryption Key dialog box (Fig. 9.6) provides space to enter a key name and any additional information you might want to note.

Adding a new key

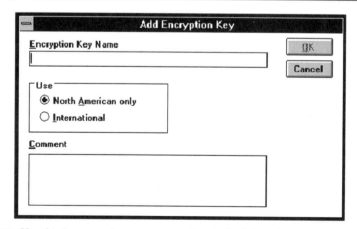

Figure 9.5   Use this box to apply an encryption key to fields in a document.

Keys to encryption

Figure 9.6   Enter a key name, plus any additional comments you want to record.

Sending a key

After you encrypt a document, only someone who has the assigned key can read the encrypted fields. That means you must send the key to anyone you want to read the document.

To send an encryption key, select **[Mail] [Send User ID] [Encryption Key]**. Select one or more keys from the list that opens, then select **Mail.** This opens the Mail Encryption Key dialog box, in which you can enter the names of workgroup members to whom you want to send the key.

Notes will ask you whether to let the recipients forward the key to other workgroup members. If you select **Yes,** the recipient can distribute the key; otherwise, only those you choose can use it. In making that decision, consider the nature of the documents and your relationship with the recipient. Also keep this in mind: anyone who receives any key to an encrypted document can read the whole thing. Though the encryption scheme works with document fields, you cannot open some fields and close others.

Encrypting mail

You must make a public key available to anyone to whom you send encrypted mail, or who sends encrypted mail to you. To make the public key available to senders, the administrator posts it in a public name and address book when you register as a Notes user. A separate private key is stored in your user ID, where only you can gain access to it. That means anyone who has access to your public key can send encrypted mail, but only you can decrypt it.

You have several options for encrypting your mail. You can encrypt:

- *Incoming mail.*   This prevents unauthorized access to your mail while it is in the mail server.

- *Outgoing mail.*   This ensures that no one except key-holding recipients can read your mail while it is in transit, stored in intermediate mailboxes, or on arrival at the recipient's mail file.

- *Saved mail.*   This protects a memo whether or not you send it to others in encrypted form. Other recipients, including administrators, are effectively prevented from reading your mail.

The Technology of Notes

"It's a floor wax. It's a dessert topping." That old *Saturday Night Live* comedy sketch could also describe Notes. It's a messaging system. It's a database.

Notes departs from traditional product design because it is both—and neither. It combines the two to provide a structure in which people can collect and understand information, and share their knowledge. As such, Notes is unlike either of the two types of products it integrates.

Traditional DBMSs are designed to manage information that fits neatly into table form. These are data-centered operations like order processing, inventory control, and payroll management. They are designed to organize information by breaking it down into basic elements. You make use of this information by sorting these elements and executing queries based on the contents of particular data elements.

These database systems are also transaction-oriented. They are built to reflect the most current state of the data. A crucial requirement of an inventory management database, for example, is that it maintain to-the-minute records of goods on hand. It does not impress customers when a sales representative promises delivery of an item that has already been shipped to someone else. But while a well-designed database can track changes in its individual database elements, it is not so good at presenting the proverbial big picture, or at displaying changes in that picture as they occur. They also do not readily handle intermittent access by remote users.

Traditional e-mail and messaging systems are designed to move information. The information can be complex, and it can be addressed to highly selective mailing lists of individuals or functions. These systems cannot readily store or monitor the messages they transmit. Like the telephone, they get their information from point A to good old point B. Without additional help like voice mail or message storage systems, that's about all they do.

How Notes Is Put Together

The objective of Notes is to help people work together. The technical support of that objective includes:

Client/server system

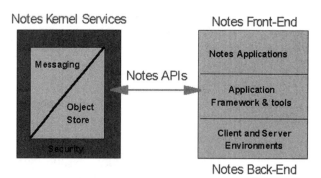

Figure A.1 Notes is a true client/server system.

- Client/server architecture
- A compound object store
- Application development tools

Client and server

Notes qualifies as a legitimate client/server system (Fig. A.1). Its server component is not limited to taking queries from database users and returning tabular results. It maintains indexes, stores and forwards e-mail, replicates databases, and acts as an agent. A Notes server can also accommodate agents and add-ins created by users or commercial third parties. The server can also govern access to information, down to small levels of detail: individual fields in the case of Notes 4.

The client end can do most of the same tasks as the server. This lets individuals replicate databases from the server; write e-mail messages; create, edit, and index documents; and synchronize replica databases over LAN or WAN connections. This power extends to mobile workers. These shared functions give using organizations and their members a great deal of flexibility and choice.

Providing security

Notes security is based on technology from RSA Data Security. This is a system of public and private keys that provides for user authentication, certification, and message signatures. The key system lets you encrypt a document with a public key and decode it with a secret key, providing a high degree of security in network communication.

Notes provides four classes of security:

- *Authentication,* which uses X.500 naming syntax to identify users. Authentication in Notes works both ways. Servers can authenticate the identity of users, and users can authenticate the identity of servers. Authentication is used whenever a user and a server or two servers are communicating with each other.

- *Digital signatures,* which ensure that a given message is from whom it says it's from. This is essentially a user-to-user form of authentication. In addition, this technology can guarantee to its recipient that the message has not been forged nor altered in transit.

- *Access control,* which provides the ability to grant or deny access to shared databases, documents, views, forms, and fields. This function can also control access by individuals to specific Notes servers. For example, an organizational blacklist could be set up to screen out all address lists that include terminated employees or contractors. Or, specific access lists could be set up for high-security servers such as a legal department.

- *Encryption,* which involves ciphering or scrambling information so that even if the wrong individuals gained access, they couldn't understand what they found. Encryption is available at three levels in the system. At the message level, individual messages can be encrypted for one or more intended recipients. At the network level, encryption discourages people from tapping into traffic on a LAN or dial-in line, because they won't see anything intelligible. At the field level, databases can encrypt document fields so only specified users can read them.

These security functions operate across vendor platforms, so you can manage and use it the same way no matter which operating system is in use. The security features also work with any available topology.

Furthermore, Notes has no back doors. These are openings often provided in mainframe and server software to allow access for software maintenance. They are notorious points of entry for unauthorized invaders as well.

Electronic messaging

Messaging comes in three forms (Fig. A.2):

- *One to one,* primarily e-mail between individuals

- *One to many,* which includes activities like publishing on the World Wide Web

- *Database replication* in which databases themselves are distributed among groups

Notes has an e-mail system that uses its native objects—documents—and provides store-and-forward messaging. A Notes server has analysis and management tools that provide best-path routing and fault tolerance. A kernel and an MTA implement features such as blind copies, delivery confirmation, return receipts, encrypted messaging, and sender authentication.

Three kinds of communication

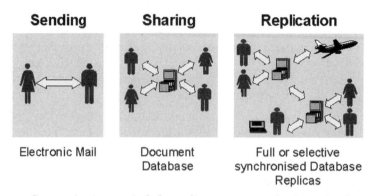

Sending	Sharing	Replication
Electronic Mail	Document Database	Full or selective synchronised Database Replicas

Figure A.2 Communication can include sending a message, sharing a database, or distributing replicated databases throughout the world.

In Notes 4, a communication server adds MTAs for X.400 and SMTP/MIME MTAs in addition to the Notes and cc:Mail transport protocols that were previously available. It also integrates the similar functions of the Notes name and address book and the cc:Mail directory and provides shadowing of X.500, Street Talk, and Novell Netware Directory Service (NDS) directories, reducing the administrative workload in organizations with mixed systems.

Replicating databases

In many applications, store-and-forward messaging is necessary but not sufficient. You need this facility, but you also need more. For example, when trying to synchronize directories, a one-way messaging system is less than ideal. For top efficiency, you need a bidirectional method of document sharing.

Notes provides this function through replication. Databases on different servers can be automatically synchronized, and there is a process for resolving conflicts when different people have made changes to the same items. When copies of a database are replicated, each exchanges the latest modifications with the other; when the process is finished, both are identical. Even if you lose the network link during this process, replication will continue when the link is reestablished. There is no need for the commit and rollback procedures of most client/server databases.

There are limits. Replication is not the answer in a transaction processing system that requires to-the-minute accuracy. In most Notes installations, replication is a periodic or occasional process. Though the replicated databases are brought into synch, there is a period when their contents will vary.

Replication works in conjunction with the Notes object store, where documents and application design elements are self-contained objects.

Peer communication

You can configure a Notes server to communicate in any of several ways:

- A *peer-to-peer* connection
- A *hub-and-spoke* layout
- An ad hoc topology designed to meet the specific needs of the workgroup

Notes is most at home in a peer-to-peer layout in which all servers on a network share equal status and can freely exchange information freely. Among other things, this makes it easier for mobile and remote users to connect with the network.

Notes is also designed for management without a large support staff. Some of the most important improvements in version 4 are in the management area. These include a management workstation application you can use to manage all aspects of the messaging system. Version 4 messaging management also supports standard protocols such as the SNMP. This protocol lets you manage the Lotus Communications Server through other vendors' management systems.

Kernel and Shells

Because client and server modules share so many functions, they also share many core program modules. These modules make up the kernel represented by the Notes API.

One function of the kernel is to insulate its clients from the underlying hardware and operating system. The purpose is to create an architecture that can span existing and future operating systems. Insulating the application developer from the platform's quirks helps create a truly open system, where the choice of software is not dictated by a particular vendor. Application developers at the API level or at the Notes user interface gain three isolation layers:

- From the operating system
- From the network transport
- From physical location of the object store via a transparent form of remote procedure call

Other kernel functions include security, database access and document structures, indexes, and full-text searching.

All these core modules are available to higher layers of Notes, including API programs, in the client and in the server environments, on all the platforms supported by Notes. For example, Notes API code can be written to be completely portable between Windows, OS/2, various flavors of Unix, and the Netware NLM. Table A.1 lists the important modules of the Notes kernel.

Server modules

The Notes server is based on a core program that manages the server's other processes. It also manages the workstations' connections with the server. Most additional server functions are implemented by add-in modules. Some of these modules are necessary parts of the server system; others are available as options or from third-party sources. These add-ins include:

- The *Replicator,* which schedules and connects with other servers and work-stations to replicate databases
- The *Indexer,* which keeps indexes up to date for immediate access by work-stations
- The *mail router,* which directs mail between mailboxes and between servers
- *Chronos,* a module that schedules agents to perform background tasks

Server tasks like MTAs and gateways have three options for scheduling their work:

- *Poll for change.*   This add-in task is the most common in gateway products. It polls the mailbox and other databases for new documents. It can run continuously, or is activated according to a preset schedule. One function of this module is to optimize polling by providing efficient ways to open databases.
- *Event-driven* tasks.   These take place as tasks communicate with the system and each other, generating server activity.
- *Transaction hooks.*   These intercept the server's transactions and can refuse read or write requests. They also can modify a transaction in progress, and can create events that affect other server tasks.

Client/server communication

Drivers in a common network layer implement the transport between client and server. Individuals can select the appropriate drivers for their named ports. If the system runs multiple network protocols, individuals can also make network port selections. A connection in the name and address books selects the appropriate serial port for a WAN connection.

When a connection is established, the first step is to verify the client system's identity. The server creates a random number and encrypts it using the client system's public key. Then it asks the client to decrypt the number; this is possible only with the legitimate client's private key. If the client correctly decrypts the number, it is authenticated. Then, a private key can be created for a secure channel of communication between client and server. The server starts a thread to process the client's requests.

TABLE A.1.   The Important Modules of the Notes Kernel

Module	Description
OS	The operating system isolation layer. This provides platform-independent access to memory, shared resources, semaphores, and environment information. Beneath the isolation layer are optimized implements of these services for each operating system.
SEC	The security module. This provides access to user information, certificates, and encryption keys.
NSF	The Notes storage facility. This subsystem manages the Notes database, allowing its users to create, open, and delete databases and documents, and to store and retrieve information. This function includes on-disk structure management (ODS) which ensures the portability of .NSF database files across platforms and on the network. All the published NSF interfaces are independent of the database location. Remote procedure calls redirect requests to the local disk or to the appropriate server. This RPC layer is also used by other kernel modules.
NET	The network transport layer. This element provides a single interface to drivers for many networking protocols and has the capacity to initiate and receive telephone calls or create LAN protocol sessions. These enable communication over ports defined by connection documents in the name and address book.
COMPUTE	The module that performs calculations. Programs that use the Notes API can ask the compute function to create and evaluate formulas and to implement custom functions.
NIF	The Notes index facility. It manages the indexes of Notes documents as they appear in views. Views define the selection of particular documents, and of columns that display information and calculated values based on these documents. Columns can be sorted or placed in categories and can include a structure of main and response documents. These collections of documents are indexed in a B-tree structure for presentation as a Notes view. NIF is responsible for maintaining and using the indexes, adding and removing information as documents are modified.
FT	The full text index feature. This element provides content-based retrieval and weighting of documents with Boolean logic searches through the full text of any document.
NAME	The user directory service. Strictly speaking, this is not part of the kernel code, but it includes some direct APIs that provide address to the Notes name and address book. The address book is a special Notes database that contains user names and e-mail addresses. The user identification scheme uses a naming model based on the X.500 standard and conforms to X.509 certificate and authentication standards.
MAIL	A direct programming interface to the Notes mail transport.

In addition, the Notes workstation software includes these modules:

Module	Description
DESK	The program responsible for displaying the desktop and the icon layout. It also manages storage, user preferences, and general coordination of the user interface.
EDIT	The Notes document and forms editor. It includes all the support needed to create and use compound documents.
VIEW	The Notes view manager. This module manages the user's interaction with the indexes of a database.
NEM	A graphic environment manager. It provides high level abstractions of the graphic user interfaces displayed on various platforms.

The client/server request protocol lets the client ask the server to perform bulk actions like creating a full text index or searching a collection of documents. This is the first level at which the client delegates processing to the server.

At a second level of delegation, a remote procedure call is exercised inside the kernel modules. For example, if the workstation calls NIFOpenCollection to open an index, the internal RPC layer transfers this request to the server. The server, in turn, checks to see if the index is current and updates the index if it is out of date. If the client requests only a partial view of the database, only the requested portions are transmitted for display on the screen. Due to the RPC layer, these processes are entirely independent of whether the database is on the local system or the server, and of whether the connection is by network or telephone.

These two delegations work to optimize client and server resources and to minimize network traffic.

Inside the Notes Database

A workgroup member has two main tools for working with a Notes database. Forms give structure to documents and provide platforms for editing. Views organize and display various sets of documents. There are also some supplementary tools like macros and full text retrieval.

From an external point of view, you can describe all this in object-oriented terms: The employee interacts with objects in the Notes system. The data of these object instances is held in Notes documents, in fields of various data types. The methods with which they manipulate that data are defined in forms. Views are browsable collections of summary information from many object instances, allowing the user to search, sort, and relate the information in a database.

That is a valid description of what you see from the outside, but internally Notes is much different. Notes makes few distinctions between documents, form designs, view definitions, and other design elements. They are all just different classes of *notes*—the feature from which the product gets its name. Replicated databases not only distribute the object data but also the object methods, using a consistent infrastructure. This form of application distribution is one of Notes's key strengths.

The structure of a note

Whatever its form, a note has a consistent and flexible structure. No matter what its purpose, a note contains these elements (Fig. A.3):

- A *NOTEID,* which identifies this note in this particular database.
- An *ORIGINATORID,* which identifies this note in a globally unique way so that the same document can be identified in any replica of the database.

The structure of a note

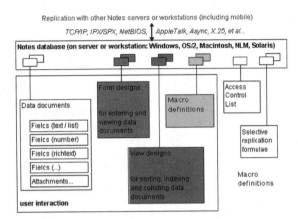

Figure A.3   Internal structure of a note.

This element also identifies the last modification, so replication conflicts due to simultaneous edits can be resolved.

- One or more *ITEMS*. These are the fields that contain data. In terms of the Notes API, the fields in a document are called items; the term Field is reserved to describe field definitions on a Notes form.

The ORIGINATORID is the structure that identifies all replicas of the same note. It has several parts:

- The *file* member contains a unique random number, generated at the time the note is created

- The *note* member contains the date and time when the first copy of the note was stored into the first NSF

- The *sequence* member is a sequence number used to keep track of the most recent version of the note for replication purposes

- The *sequencetime* member is a sequence number qualifier that allows the Replicator to determine which note is newer if the sequence numbers are the same

Both sequencing codes are required. The sequence number is needed to prevent someone from locking out future edits by setting the time or date to the future. The sequence time qualifies the sequence number to prevent two updates from looking like no update at all, and to force all systems to reach the same decision as to which update is the latest. These are the key decisions on which replication is based.

Every note in the database can have a different number of items, of different data types. This document format contrasts with traditional relational database systems, in which the structure of a table is defined for all records. Relationships between documents are provided by some internal structures such as the relationship between main documents and responses, and by any application-defined structures such as lookups into Notes views or external databases to give referential integrity.

The NOTEID is an identifier for a note. It provides a record relocation vector (RRV), essentially a file position pointer to the note as it appears in a database. In the case where it is necessary to store lists of document IDs, to identify collections of documents or lists of unread documents, there is a structure called IDTABLE which is a compressed list of NOTEIDs.

The ORIGINATORID and its subset the UNID are not file pointers, but unique identifiers constructed from random numbers and time stamps. To give fast access to a document knowing its UNID (for example, so that the Replicator can identify documents in common between database replicas), there is an internal index in the database. In relational database terms, the UNID is the primary key. To the user, the views provide the important document indexes, each having application-defined keys.

Classifying items

Some data items contain simple data types and contain summary information about documents. These include the author name, the creation date, the title, and e-mail recipients. Other data items contain compound information like rich text, embedded objects, and graphics. This distinction is important in any object management system, which has to index and sort documents for user accessibility.

In Notes, this distinction is made by flagging items as *summary* or *nonsummary*. Summary items are available for computation in Notes, for lookup into or from external data sources, and for indexing and presentation in views. Nonsummary items cannot be used in computations or collation. They provide the storage for compound objects.

Note classes

Notes can appear in any of several classes:

- *Document* structures are usually identified by the forms with which they are edited.

- *Mail* notes are documents that include reserved items and flags that indicate the documents are ready for mailing. To send a mail document, the document is transferred into a MAIL.BOX database on the server. From there, the mail router agent picks up the document, determines its routing, and forwards the document to another server or to the recipient's mail database.

- *Form definition* notes define the layout of a form on screen, including fields, formulas for default values, input translation, validation, and form security.

- *View definition* notes define the selection of documents and columns, including specifications for displays and calculated columns in views. The view definition note does not contain an index of document in the database; that index appears as a separate object. When view definitions are replicated to other servers, the index is not replicated but is rebuilt locally. This reduces connect time and allows for selective replication and for planned differences between replicas.

- *Design* notes are internal indexes of information about the forms, views, and other design elements of a database.

There also are several less-used note classes. These include single-instance classes that appear once in a database. Often, these are flags that identify particular items so the Replicator can readily recognize them. These classes include:

- *Selective replication definition,* which defines a formula to be used in replications, such as when a mobile user makes a selective replication to a laptop.

- *Shared field,* which holds the definition of a field that can be inherited by more than one form.

- *Icon,* which holds the database icon.

- *Help-About,* a special document that provides information on the database's purpose. This is also called a policy document.

- *Help-Using,* a special document that provides information on database use.

- *ACL,* which holds access control information for the database.

Item data structures

Notes items use two basic structures

- Summary items are stored in a compact structure to expedite their use in calculation, sorting, and classification.

- Nonsummary items use a compound document (CD) data structure that is designed to incorporate the variety of objects that might appear in a rich text field.

The CD structure also includes nesting of paired structured, such as *graphic begin* and *graphic end*. This structure can store duplicate information if needed. For example, a single image can be stored in several graphic formats for quick retrieval on any workstation and operating system. The CD structure also can be extended to support the objects that might appear in future Notes documents. Figure A.4 shows the internal striker of Notes data types; Table A.2 describes the details of these types.

Internal data item structure

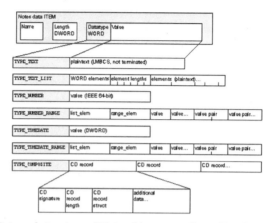

Figure A.4 The internal structure of Notes data types. (*Lotus Development Corporation.*)

TABLE A.2. Common Notes Data Types

Data type	Description
TYPE_TEXT	Plain text, stored in LMBCS (Lotus Multibyte Character Set, a variable-length-character encoding
TYPE_TEXT_LIST	A multivalue item where each value is plain LMBCS text. In the Notes user interface, no great distinction is made between single-value and multivalue items. A single-element text list is transparently converted to a plaintext item. In a Notes API program, you must treat these as two distinct datatypes. This also applies to multivalue number and time/date items.
TYPE_NUMBER	A 64-bit IEEE floating-point number
TYPE_NUMBER_RANGE	A compound multivalue structure: a list of numbers, and/or a list of number pairs
TYPE_TIMEDATE	A comprehensive time-stamp structure, containing:
	▪ The number of days since Julian Day 0 (January 1, 4713 BC) or the constant ANYDAY
	▪ The number of ticks (hundredths of a second) since midnight or the constant ALLDAY
	▪ The time zone (with quarter-hour granularity), and the daylight-saving flag
TYPE_TIMEDATE_RANGE	A list of TIMEDATEs, and/or a list of TIMEDATE pairs
TYPE_COMPOSITE	The rich text (compound document) field structure

Abbreviation: IEEE, Institute of Electrical and Electronics Engineers.

Programming implications

Summary and nonsummary information types have much different access requirements. Summary information is designed for quick retrieval and computation; nonsummary information is designed to handle complex data. Notes accommodates this difference by physically separating summary items into a buffer that is stored for high-speed access. Other information is stored as objects that can be retrieved at lower speed.

Summary data can be manipulated efficiently by the Compute engine and the indexer. The Notes formula language, executed through the Compute module, lets application designers build intelligence into:

- Forms for computation at the workstation
- Views for selection and collation
- Macros, for agent or rule-based functions

The formula language is optimized and tailored for building group collaboration and workflow applications. This formula language is now supplemented with LotusScript in Notes 4. LotusScript is an object-oriented, BASIC-compatible language designed for use in Lotus's entire suite of desktop and communication products. It interacts with each host product with the hosts publishing objects of various classes. These objects can be created and manipulated with LotusScript code. In Notes, developers can write LotusScript programs, executed on forms in buttons and other form elements or as server-based agents. These programs can manipulate Notes documents and data items at a high level.

Searching and indexing

An application designer can create multiple views of the data in a Notes database, and individual patrons can create their own private views. The documents displayed in a view are those which match a formula or which fit into a structure of main and response documents. Other columns in a view can display the results of a formula that can involve one or more fields. The view can group related documents into categories and sort them by date, alphabetically, or by the results of a formula. Numeric information can also be totaled.

The internal representation of a view is a *view definition note* and by an index. This note replicates with the database. The index uses B-tree indexing to sort and summarize the information according to instructions in the view definition note.

If a column is sorted, it must be collated in the index. There are three ways to do this:

- *Key* sorting, collating by the value of a column based on a summary item's value.
- *Tumbler* collation of list item data types. Each value of the list corresponds

to a level in a hierarchical or outline index. As collation is performed, only the ith list value is collated if we are collating the ith level of the hierarchical index. This causes the new index entry to be placed as many levels deep as there are list values. For example, a number list value of "1:2:3" places the index entry three levels down in the hierarchy. If the new index entry requires a subtree which does not yet exist, a ghost entry is created to act as a parent for the new entry at intermediate levels. The result is a hierarchical outline where index entries are created at a variety of different levels in the index depending on the number of values in their list data type.

- *Category* collation of any data types, list or nonlist, to create a hierarchical index. For each category in the collating specification, ghost entries are created for each unique value of the specified, and all duplicate values are placed at the next lower level.

Unlike tumbler collation, the category system collates list data types in exactly the same way as the key method. Each list value is compared, and if the two are equal, the next one is compared to break ties, and so on until the list is exhausted. For example, if a collating specification consists of the categories Folder and Author, and the key Date, the top level of the index will only contain as many ghost entries as there are unique folder names. Below it, the next level will contain all unique author names within that folder, and below each author, the next level will contain all the index entries for each author sorted by date. The result is a three-level outline where all index entries are always at the nth level, and all intermediate category levels always contain only ghost entries.

Database structure

A Notes database is the container for notes of all kinds. The Notes's flexible structures and features are tailored to the need to transport and identify them. Structural features include unique identifiers, last-modified time stamps, and summary information. The container database also reflects its functions: retrieving appropriate information, providing reliability, and supporting replication.

A Notes database is a disk file with the extension .NSF. It begins with header information and an allocation map. Parts of the header include:

- A *database ID* that uniquely identifies the file.

- A *replica ID* that uniquely identifies all replicas of this database.

- A *creation time stamp.*

- A *last modification time stamp.*   This stamp records the time and date of the latest changes to the database contents.

- A *title* and a category assignment.

- A *design class,* which indicates that the design elements should be inherited from a particular template and, unless the designer has decided otherwise, should reflect any changes in the template.

The Replicator task and others use this information to decide whether a database should be replicated, and which database replicas exist on any particular server. The database contents can be scanned for any notes that have been added or modified since a certain time.

The rest of the database contains:

- Notes and other objects
- Summary buffers stored for rapid access
- Nonsummary items in another area of the file

Internally, Notes themselves are a specialized class of object. Other object classes include file attachments, OLE packages, and packed lists of documents such as lists of unread documents. Every object is identified by a Record Relocation Vector (RRV) which is a file position pointer; a NOTEID is simply the Notes's RRV.

Some objects, such as the collections which constitute an index of the database, are never replicated, since they must be built appropriately to each local copy of the database.

System databases

Some Notes databases are used by the system for specific tasks. These are much like any other databases, but the system has given them special assignments. The major system databases are:

- The name and address book
- The mail router mailbox
- The database catalog
- The Notes log

The name and address book, usually called NAMES.NSF, holds a directory modeled on X.500 standards. It contains several classes of documents, identified by their forms:

- The *Person* class contains information about individual users including their names, e-mail addresses, forwarding addresses, and public keys.
- The *group* class contains a named list of people. It is used by access control lists and for electronic mail.
- The *connection* type contains information about ports and other connection details like the server's network address or a telephone number for remote access. It also includes schedules for connections between servers.

The mail router, usually MAIL.BOX, is the database that provides the forwarding store for Notes mail on a server. The router, or mail transfer agent, is responsible for polling this database and forwarding the documents to individuals' mail files or to other servers. In Notes version 4, this task consists of MTAs for X.400 and SMTP/MIME connections.

Gateway add-in tasks usually have their own mailboxes where the Notes router deposits mail according to definitions in the name and address book. A gateway task polls its mailbox and transfers mail accordingly.

The database catalog, CATALOG.NSF, is a catalog of all the databases on the server. It contains a policy document for each database. If replicated, it becomes the organization's catalog of Notes databases. It is maintained by a server task called Catalog, which usually runs once a day.

LOG.NSF is the Notes log, a database that records server activity. Server tasks report their activities to this database, where they can be summarized and reported in views to the administrator. Other administration utilities can include events and alerts defined by the administrator, and systemwide network management tools

Relating documents

An object container is useful only when you can index and relate its contents. One way to do this is with summary fields that collate documents in views. Another technique is to create structured ways to relate documents to each other.

One important relationship is that between main documents, responses, and responses to responses. This outline can relate such documents as discussion topics, documents in a correspondence database, and subjects in an on-line training class.

Other Notes applications can define their own document relationships. To avoid duplication, forms can perform lookups into other views to retrieve a column's contents, and into other documents to retrieve values from key fields.

Notes provides version control through its ability to store prior and current versions of a document as responses to other versions.

Doc links, hypertext links between documents, provide some ad hoc ability to knit related documents together where there is no formal relationship.

The structure of an application may require referential integrity or normalized data structures—ideas normally associated with relational databases. For example, an application might be your central database for customer contact, or it might need to use key values to look up information in a relational database system. You often encounter such situations in applications like workflow management and EDI. Though Notes databases are less structured than most other types, it is possible to give them the structure necessary to function like more formal database structures.

External contacts

External links are essential to integration with transactional or legacy databases and other data sources. Notes provides several methods for making outside contact. It also has open interfaces for third-party providers.

The highest level of integration is found at the platform-specific compound document format. In this situation, Notes can be a container for OLE embedded objects, allowing live application objects to be embedded seamlessly in documents for sharing with other users.

A second level of data integration is available through Notes's import/export filters. By using these filters, you can copy information from application files directly into Notes databases or documents, keeping much of the original application's formatting information. You also can copy information in the other direction, from Notes documents to application formats, again preserving the original look.

The field formulas, buttons, and other elements of Notes forms allow lookups into Notes databases. SmartIcons, macros, and the @DbLookup and @DbColumn functions do the same. They also support the Datalens driver technology, which allows retrieval from external databases including Oracle, Sybase and Microsoft SQL Server, Informix, IBM Database Manager, Paradox, and dBase. The @DbCommand function allows database queries in the SQL and proprietary command languages. It also provides access to stored queries on the database server.

Datalens also supports open database connections (ODBC). These functions can be run from the workstation or, in background macros, on the server for agent-type integration. The Notes Structured Query Language (SQL) driver provides an ODBC interface to Notes data. This gives, third-party applications access to Notes databases without special APIs.

Using the Notes API, many developers have created specific integration tools for their customers. Available tools include Trinzic's InfoPump, a scripted database integration utility which can migrate and synchronize data from a wide variety of sources, on an event-driven or scheduled basis.

Front-end development tools which can access data from Notes and integrate with other data sources in a seamless environment include: Lotus Notes ViP, Powersoft PowerBuilder, Gupta SQLWindows, Revelation OpenInsight, and many others. Lotus Development also sells a range of companion products, including the image-capable Lotus Notes:Document Imaging product, incoming and outgoing fax gateways, PhoneNotes for developing interactive voice response applications integrated with the Notes environment, and an OCR server for scanning faxes or images into Notes documents.

Creating Notes Applications

People from workgroup members to application development professionals can use Notes to create workgroup applications. Form and view design tools allow development of new applications in a fraction of the time required by many other methods. Updates are simple, too: make the changes, they use replication to distribute them.

The database templates provided with Notes provide platforms for many applications. Available templates form the foundations of applications like group to-do tracking, correspondence, customer service, document libraries, discussion forums, status reporting, and team issue tracking. These workgroup applications can be used directly from given templates or modified to suit particular needs. Design inheritance from standard templates and shared field definitions within a database provide data dictionary capabilities, enabling:

- Leverage and reuse of design elements
- Maintainability of the database design including propagating changes
- The ability to set corporate design standards

In-house and third-party developers are creating applications for individual clients. These systems handle functions like sales automation, credit management, to editing, proofreading, project management, document workflow, and resource tracking. There also are vertical applications for doctors, lawyers, pharmaceutical research and development, shipping, transportation, insurance, and banking. The common thread shared by these solutions is that they enable groups of people to better coordinate and share their experience in ways which help them get the job done better faster. This quality of empowerment reflects on their Seville to their customers.

The open connectivity of Notes encourages companies to seek new ways to communicate externally as well as internally. Those who use Notes to communicate with their resellers, customers, suppliers, and other partners find that the enterprise responsiveness is brought to a new level.

Bibliography

Adhikari, Richard. "All Together Now," *Computerworld Client/Server Journal,* June 1995, p. 19.

Barney, Doug. "Notes 4 Improved for Users, Developers," *Infoworld,* Feb. 6, 1995, p. 45.

———. "Notes 4.0 Promises To Be Better at Being Bigger," *Network World,* Oct. 2, 1995, p. 10.

Blum, Daniel, and Gary Rowe. "More Messaging Options Deliver Selection Headaches," *Network World,* March 15, 1995, p. 53.

Brandel, Mary. "Texas Commerce Reinvents Itself," *Computerworld,* Jan. 30, 1995, p. 47.

Brenner, Aaron. "The Low Down on Lotus Notes: Document Imaging 2.5, Part 1," *Imaging Magazine,* January 1995, p. 88.

Burnette, David, and Cedric Higgins. "The Agony and the Ecstasy," *Advanced Systems,* November 1994, p. 24.

Burns, Nina, and Creative Networks. "The True Cost of E-mail Ownership," *LAN Magazine,* November 1993, p. 150.

Cafasso, Rosemary. "Workflow Next Rising Star?" *Computerworld,* March 1, 1993, p. 41.

Cafasso, Rosemary, and Tim Ouellette. "Client/Server Workflow Rolls Slowly Forward," *Computerworld,* May 1, 1995, p. 24.

Clarkson, Mark A. "Hitting Warp Speed for LANs," *Byte,* March 1993, p. 123.

Clegg, Peter. "Lotus Offers Sneak Peek at Notes 4," *LAN Times,* Feb. 13, 1995, p. 116.

Cole, Barb, and Annmarie Timmins. "Lotus Airs Notes-to-Database Integration Tool," *Network World,* Oct. 2, 1995, p. 10.

Connolly, James M. "E-mail Gone Awry," *Computerworld,* May 24, 1993, p. 57.

Cooney, Michael, and Annmarie Timmins. "Lotus Wins Over IBM," *Network World,* July 24, 1995, p. 1.

Dix, John. "The Web: Notes Friend or Foe?" *Network World Collaboration,* September/October 1995, p. 22.

Dorshkind, Brent. "Cheaper Notes Client Answers Lotus' Critics," *LAN Times,* Feb. 13, 1995, p. 1.

———. "Lotus Expands Web Offering," *LAN Times,* Oct. 23, 1995, p. 43.

Eckerson, Wayne. "Three Types of Workflow," *Network World,* July 5, 1995, p. 27.

Eglowstein, Howard, and Ben Smith. "Mixed Messaging," *Byte,* March 1993, p. 136.

Evans, Ron. "New Strategies in Electronic Messaging," *Stacks,* November 1994, p. 35.

Frye, Colleen. "Groupware Strikes Collaborative Chord," *Software Magazine Client/Server Applications,* October 1995, p. 94.

Gasparro, Daniel M. "Moving LAN E-mail Onto the Enterprise," *Data Communications,* December 1993, p. 103.

Gerber, Barry. "Are You Prepared for the Super Apps of Tomorrow?" *Network Computing,* Oct. 1, 1995, p. 75.

Gibbs, Mark. "Private Webs: The Inside Story," Network World Collaboration, September/October 1995, p. 22.

Goff, Leslie. "Notes 4.0 May Send You Back to Class," *Computerworld,* Oct. 30, 1995, p. 103.

Gow, Kathleen. "A True Team Effort," *Client/Server Computing,* September 1994, p. 63.

Harris, Alison. "Notes Next Big Hook for Help Desk Apps," *Service News,* October 1995, p. 23.

Henry, James S. "The Impact of Notes on Productivity: Evidence from Customers," *Lotus Information Library,* Dec. 30, 1994.

Hsu, Jeffrey, and Tony Lockwood. "Collaborative Computing," *Byte,* March 1993, p. 113.

"Industrial Security Group Opposes Workplace Monitoring Bill," *BNA Employee Relations Weekly,* Feb. 24, 1992, p. 211.

International Data Corporation. "Electronic Mail: The New Corporate Backbone." White Paper, 1992.

——. "Workgroup Technology: Tying Technology to Business Objectives." White Paper, 1992.

Kay, Emily. "Know Thy Customer," *LAN Times / Selling Networks,* June 19, 1995, p. 20.

Kidder, Tracy. *Among Schoolchildren,* New York: Avon Books, 1989.

Korzeniowski, Paul. "Needle Hunting," *Byte,* November 1995, p. 51.

——. "Workflow: Easing the Paper Crunch," *Infoworld,* Oct. 10, 1994, p. 62.

Koulopoulos, Thomas M. "Picking the Best Workflow Solution," *Imaging Magazine,* July 1995, p. 82.

Layland, Robin. "Is Your Network Ready for Notes?" *Data Communications,* April 1995, p. 83.

Lotus Development Corporation. "cc:Mail and Notes, Release 3, Integration." *Lotus Information Library, Lotus Notes Knowledge Base,* June 27, 1995.

——. "Empowering the Mobile Worker," *Lotus cc:Mail Knowledge Base,* May 2, 1995.

——. "Forms Automation," *Lotus Information Library, Lotus Notes Knowledge Base,* Third Quarter 1995.

——. "Fourth Generation Messaging Systems," *Lotus Information Library,* May 9, 1995.

——. "Fourth Generation Messaging: Support for Mobile and Remote Users," *Lotus Information Library, Notes Docs Database,* May 1995.

——. "Fourth Generation Messaging Systems: Directory Services," *Lotus Information Library, Notes Docs Database,* May 1995.

——. "Fourth Generation Messaging Systems: Security Requirements," *Lotus Information Library,* Notes Docs Database, Oct. 27, 1995.

——. "Fourth Generation Messaging: The Object Store," *Lotus Information Library,* Oct. 27, 1995.

——. "Lotus Communications Products: Workgroup Computing Defined," *Lotus Information Library,* Third Quarter 1995.

——. "Lotus InterNotes: Expanding Notes to New Extra-Enterprise Applications," *Lotus Notes Knowledge Base,* June 7, 1995.

——. "Lotus Notes: Agent of Change. The Financial Impact of Lotus Notes on Business," *Lotus Information Library, Lotus Notes Knowledge Base,* Third Quarter 1995.

——. "Lotus Notes–Enabled Suite Strategy," *Lotus Information Library,* May 1994.

——. "Lotus Notes: Pager Gateway Relapse 1.1," *Lotus Information Library, Notes Docs Database,* May 16, 1995.

——. "Lotus Notes: A System for Managing Organizational Knowledge," *Lotus Information Library, Lotus Notes Knowledge Base,* Third Quarter 1995.

——. "MHS Gateway," *Lotus Information Library, Notes Docs Database,* Oct. 27, 1995.

——. "MHS Gateway: A Technical Brief," *Lotus Information Library, Lotus Notes Knowledge Base,* Third Quarter, 1995.

——. "Migration Strategies for Client/Server Messaging," *Lotus Information Library, Notes Docs Database,* Sept. 27, 1995.

——. "Phone Notes Overview," *Lotus Notes Knowledge Base,* Third Quarter 1995.

——. "SMTP Gateway Datasheet," *Lotus Information Library, Lotus Notes Knowledge Base,* Third Quarter, 1995.

——. "The Architecture of Lotus Notes," *Lotus Information Library, Lotus Notes Knowledge Base,* July 6, 1995.

——. "The Benefits of a Platform-Independent Messaging System," *Lotus Information Library,* July 12, 1995.

——. "The Lotus Communications Architecture: A Strategy for Customer-Controlled Migration," *Lotus Information Library, Notes Docs Database,* April 4, 1995.

——. "The Notes Database Architecture," *Lotus Information Library, Lotus Notes Knowledge Base,* May 31, 1995.

——. "The Power of a Groupware Application Development Environment," *Lotus Information Library, Lotus Docs Database,* July 10, 1995.

——. "The Value of an Integrated Messaging and Groupware Architecture," *Lotus Information Library, Notes Docs Database,* Nov. 8, 1995.

——. "The Tide and the Glacier: Computing in the 90s," *Lotus Information Library, Notes Docs Database,* Dec. 1, 1993.

——. "Why Groupware Will Change the Way You Work," *Lotus Information Library, Notes Docs Database,* Nov. 8, 1995.

Lotus Information Library, Third Quarter 1995 CD-ROM. Cambridge, MA: Lotus Development Corporation.

Mantelman, Lee. "Attach Things to Your Workflow Pipes One (or More) Ways," *Imaging Magazine,* January 1995, p. 54.

Marshak, David S. "Decision 95: Notes vs. Exchange," *Network World* Collaboration supplement, March/April 1995, p. 24.

Mayer, John. "Message-based Workflow Tools Find Eager Audience," *Client/Server Computing,* October 1994, p. 47.

Mohan, Suruchi. "E-mail Security Ignored," *Computerworld,* Sept. 25, 1995, p. 53.

Mohan, Suruchi. "Lotus Goes Both Ways," *Computerworld,* Oct. 9, 1995, p. 60.

Mohan, Suruchi. "Lotus Will Offer X.500 Synchronization," *Computerworld,* July 3, 1995, p. 12.

Mohan, Suruchi. "LotusScript 3.0 Embedded in Notes 4.0," *Computerworld,* July 3, 1995, p. 20.

Mohan, Suruchi. "Notes Packages Unite Voice Mail with E-mail," *Computerworld,* Jan. 30, 1995, p. 47.

Mohan, Suruchi. "Users Ponder Switch from cc:Mail to Notes," *Computerworld,* Feb. 6, 1995, p. 3.

Mohan, Suruchi. "Users Welcome Exchange as Mail 3.2 Upgrade," *Computerworld,* June 26, 1995, p. 8.

Ouellette, Tim. "Confusion Slows Down Workflow Software," *Computerworld,* May 29, 1995, p. 48.

———. "Workflow Capabilities a Hit with Users," *Computerworld,* July 3, 1995, p. 64.

Radosevich, Lynda. "Replication Mania," *Computerworld Client/Server Journal,* October 1995, p. 53.

Reinhardt, Andy. "Smarter E-mail Is Coming," *Byte,* March 1993, p. 90.

Richardson, Robert. "A Lull in the Conversation," *LAN Magazine,* November 1995, p. 115.

Richardson, Robert. "More Flow, Less Work?" *LAN Magazine,* May 1995, p. 103.

Rothman, Mike. "Groupware and Messaging: Attached at the Hip," *Computerworld,* May 29, 1995, p. 43.

Schlesinger, Lee. "Beta Notes Apps Show Real Promise," *Network World,* Oct. 9, 1995, p. 1.

Schnaidt, Patricia. "X.400 Messaging," *LAN Magazine,* June 1992, p. 19.

Schrage, Michael. "Don't Forget Incentives in Groupware Strategy," *Computerworld,* June 5, 1995, p. 37.

Schwartz, Jeffrey. "EPA: Getting Used to Notes Can Be a Challenge," *Communications Week,* March 29, 1993, p. 11.

Schwartz, Jeffrey. "Some Managers Fear Deploying Lotus Notes," *Communications Week,* March 22, 1993, p. 1.

Shimmin, Bradley F. "Growing Groupware Aware, *LAN Times,* Oct. 23, 1995, p. 43.

Snell, Monica. "Lotus Notes Gains Real-Time Conferencing," *LAN Times,* Oct. 9, 1995, p. 16.

Sobkowiak, Roger T., and Ronald E. LeBleu. "E-mail: Not Just for Gossip Anymore," *Computerworld,* May 1, 1995, p. 37.

Steinke, Steve. "Priority E-mail," *LAN Magazine,* July 1995, p. 46.

Timmins, Annmarie. "AT&T, Lotus Hit Gold with Network Notes," *Network World,* Aug. 14, 1995, p. 15.

Timmins, Annmarie. "Beta Report: Notes 4 Proves to be Enterprise-Savvy," *Network World,* July 31, 1995, p. 1.

Tolly, Kevin. "E-mail Gateways: What's Missing from the Link," *Data Communications,* July 1995, p. 35.

Tolly, Kevin, and David Newman. "Grow Up!" *Data Communications,* November 1994, p. 70.

Udell, John. "Global Groupware," *Byte,* November 1995, p. 203.

Wilson, Carol. "Telecommuting: Interactive Access is Booming," *Inter@ctive Week,* March 27, 1995.

Yager, Tom. "Better than Being There," *Byte,* March 1993, p. 129.

Young, Mark. "Chemical Company Uses Workflow to Meet New Government Regulations," *Imaging Magazine,* July 1995, p. 88.

———. "Workflow Evolution: From Transaction Processor to Process Manager," *Imaging Magazine,* July 1995, p. 77.

Young, Mark, and Lee Mantelman. "Shedding Light on the Mysteries of Workflow," *Imaging Magazine,* January 1995, p. 40.

Index

ABOUT THE AUTHOR

RICHARD H. BAKER is the Editorial Director of
Courseware Development Group in Houston, Texas. He is
the author of numerous books dealing with the application
of technology to business problems. His latest books include
Network Security: How to Plan for It and Achieve It and
*Networking the Enterprise: How to Build Client/Server
Systems that Work*, both available from McGraw-Hill.